BORN IN PASSING

To my father who bequeathed me his travelling shoes.

From the Author

My father's memoir, *The Wanderings of a Wondering Jew*, was rescued from obscurity and published in 2021 by my sister Zu and myself. In it he chronicles his life as an Orthodox Jewish child, born in 1905, growing up in a small Polish town; the murder of his gentle, saintly father; the looming sense of doom and his eventually leaving Poland forever just in time in 1930 to come to England. There he meets and falls in love with the flame-haired Pat. They lived a Bohemian life in London and Paris – he writing and translating, she nursing. After eight years together with no children, they thought they couldn't have any. Then on a trip to Australia in 1940, I was born in passing…

It was an unconventional, globetrotting childhood which gave me an unquenchable love of travel, of far-off places, of different cultures. This is the story of some of those adventures.

ILLUSTRATIONS

Front cover: Allegra and Camille, U.K., 1942.
Back cover: Allegra and first great grandchild Freddie.
About the author, page vii,& viii, Allegra with latest great grandchild Willow.

ABOUT THE AUTHOR

llegra Taylor is the author of several books including the best
selling *I Fly Out With Bright Feathers – The Quest of a Novice
Healer; Acquainted With The Night – A Year on the Frontiers of
Death; Healing Hands; Prostitution: What's Love Got To Do With It?;
Older Than Time – A Grandmother's Search for Wisdom; Ladder To The
Moon – A Woman's Search for Spirituality* and, for children, *Tal Niv's
Kibbutz*. For many years she ran her own music school from home

as her children were growing up; worked as a free-lance journalist
for a variety of magazines including *She; Woman's Own, Annabel,
The Illustrated London News, Choice* and *The Traveller*; and facilitated

creative writing courses in Turkey, Greece, Sri Lanka, Ireland, United States, England and Tobago. For the last ten years from ages seventy to eighty she became an independent celebrant conducting imaginative weddings, funerals and other ceremonies. With her late husband, Documentary Film Maker Richard Taylor she had six children including three adopted in Africa, thirteen grandchildren and (at the last count) four great-grandchildren. She lives on an island in the Thames with her dog Ozzie.

CHAPTER ONE

O vente norte que sedez minha razão
Assorbia e me banha de emoção
O amor errante
Paixao distante
Azul sempre cor de navegante

O North Wind, that seduces my reason,
Assaults and bathes me in emotions
The wandering love,
Distant passion,
Always Navy blue'

Grafitti on a wall in Manaus

I was thirteen the last time I travelled to Brazil. We were fleeing, as usual, from my darling father's bad debts. He had left us in Los Angeles, gone on ahead and found a job writing for a Yiddish newspaper first in Buenos Aires and then São Paulo. He always managed to find prosperous old Jewish immigrants who would give him the benefit of the doubt. He wasn't really a con man. He genuinely believed in his dreams and schemes. He was a gentle otherworldly dreamer – brilliant, kind, innocent, funny and completely unable to understand the world of commerce, useless at earning a conventional living. Couldn't stand the mundane, the commonplace. His enthusiasms were always larger than life. His ideas wildly original but he lacked the organisational ability or the patience to follow anything through. He did not have the temperament to cooperate with others. His early childhood had accustomed him to feeling gifted and that if money were needed it would somehow become available. He'd borrow money from the wealthy jews, be unable to meet the repayments, get impatient with the petty mortals who failed to recognise the outstanding originality of his schemes, quarrel with everyone and we'd be required to move on again. This was an old story. The story of my childhood.

Our mother who loved and adored him was the only person convinced of his genius. She refused to be left behind when he went off looking for greener pastures. She had a scrupulous sense of honour and obligation and worked at any old job – in California she'd been a receptionist to a fashionable surgeon, a barmaid, a chicken farmer selling eggs door to door to movie stars' homes in Beverly Hills, a shop assistant – anything to pay off some of Dad's debts and get enough money together for our airline tickets, take us out of school and pursue him to the ends of the earth. This time, she'd moved us out of our home in Santa Monica, sold our belongings, given away our beloved dog and after a few months kicking our heels in a cheap motel where she mooned around singing the old Frank Sinatra song 'Brazil':

"Brazil"

Brazil…We stood beneath an amber moon
And softly murmured "someday soon"
We kissed and clung together

Then, tomorrow was another day
The morning found me miles away
With still a million things to say
Now, when twilight dims the sky above
Recalling thrills of our love
There's one thing I'm certain of
Return I will to old brazil
That old brazil
Brazil, brazil

we were finally on our way. Dad had sent regular letters asking her to wire him more money and Mum had hassled him constantly to find us somewhere to live because like it or not we were coming. We arrived in Rio de Janeiro – spectacular view as the pilot of our Pan Am Stratocruiser circled round in the air so that we could look down and see the famous Corcovado. Dad had rented a cheap 5th floor apartment for us in the sleazy red light district. 1953. It seemed like a normal childhood to me then.

And now I'm going back to Brazil aged 80. Dad called himself a 'wandering, wondering Jew'. Perhaps it is in the DNA of the Jewish race – constantly exiled, banished and required to leave everything behind and move on with a few coins sewn into the hem of our garments. And I have inherited his wanderlust. Living an unfolding story. I've had a lifetime of it.

This time I'm travelling on my own with my thoughts and memories while I still can. Hip replacement, knee replacement, cancer, cataracts, hearing aids … but the adventure beckons me on. I'm not done yet. I want to collect the bits of me scattered around the globe, revisit some of those places. Travel has always been about trying to find out where I belong, looking for home, longing for some kind of connectedness and understanding, seizing the unknown. I am willing to be surprised, open to the unexpected and to the price of travelling alone which is always a trade-off between solitude and loneliness. I'm alone now for the first time ever – after fifty-seven years of a good marriage, six children grown and gone, thirteen grandchildren all in their twenties and thirties, and even the last beloved dog dead – it has all passed into the final phase. Learning to make my peace with the world and draw the threads together. Whatever happens is the story.

What made Dad the way he was? I frequently find myself reflecting on the drama of his life – the precious only child of older parents who, after fourteen years of marriage, had given up all hope. A miracle baby born in a little Polish shtetl. Little Rachmil, they named him. Rachmil Isaac Honig. Such was the rejoicing that, in thanks to God, his father Elia and his mother Sura commissioned at enormous expense a Torah to be written. The great velvet covered, handwritten

3

scroll was to grace their synagogue in the small town of Tomaschov Mazowietski near Lodz in Poland. The year was 1905.

Little Rachmil was clever and studious at the cheder – the Jewish School – where he impressed his teacher. The boy would obviously grow up to become a rabbi and a learned man. The matchmaker would find a wealthy bride who would enable him to continue the life of a scholar – a great honour and blessing to the community. Things would be as they had always been.

Then one Friday night in 1913 as little Rachmil and his father had just returned from the synagogue and the family gathered for their shabbat meal, there was a ruckus outside and loud banging at the door. A little cousin was sent to answer it. Two men pushed past her and shot his gentle father point blank in the head. In front of his only son. On the Sabbath eve. The reason never established. The perpetrators never caught. Robbers? (nothing was stolen); a grudge?, anti-semitic thugs? (a whole family of neighbours had recently been murdered). Whatever the reason, his childhood ended that night along with all thoughts of the quiet life of a Talmudic scholar. A little boy was left traumatised and cursed with shouting nightmares all his life. All through my childhood for as far back as I could remember I could hear my mother's voice in the night soothing and comforting him as we lay awake in our beds. "Terrible things happened to him when he was a child," she'd tell us. Eventually we heard the whole story. His beloved father's blood pooling on the floor by his dead body, his mother's screams.

Was this the beginning of the end for the Jews of Poland? Dad remembered that the two communities – the goyim and the Jews – had existed side by side in relative peace. The Jews afraid only of the terrifying pogroms by the Russians. Cossaks who would occasionally gallop through the streets on huge snorting horses trampling everything, even children, in their path. There was also the issue of the ongoing trial at that time of one Mendel Beilis accused of murdering a Christian child and using his blood to make the Passover matzos. This horrible 'blood libel' calumny has followed the Jews in every country since Roman times. Beilis was eventually exonerated but the story lingered on. Any excuse to blame the Jews. Hatred was always simmering.

Now, after some months in Argentina writing for a Yiddish newspaper and then in Brazil Dad had come up with some sure-fire, money-making scheme involving promoting an artist. The guy would become world famous, Dad would be his agent, we'd all make lots of money… . In order to pay the bills for hiring the gallery space, the publicity, the taxis, the schmoozing he borrowed some money. Later when it was time for some repayments and things weren't going well Mum got out her sewing machine and made stylish coats out of felt that I had to try to sell to a department store because by then my Portuguese was better than hers. I also managed to talk myself into a job singing in the Gato Preto nightclub. I was rubbish but at thirteen I looked older than I was and managed to belt out

Just one of those things.
Just one of those crazy things.
A trip to the moon on gossamer wings.
Just one of those things.

I lasted one night. 'Just as well,' said Mum. 'It was not a very nice environment.' My next job was as a nursery school assistant in exchange for my seven-year-old brother Yehudi and eleven-year-old sister Zuleika to be able to attend the school. The English Headmaster was a pervy old paedo with dandruff in his nicotine stained beard and Mum rescued us as soon as she twigged.

'Oh God, I ought to be doing something about your education,' she wailed to me. 'The most important thing is that you must be able to support yourself without relying on a man. Earn your own living. Be a piano teacher.' She'd always managed to ensure that I had piano lessons and Zu had ballet lessons wherever we were and now got me a place at the 'Scuola Libre de Musica'. We found a house to move to in the better suburb of Jardim Paulista, São Paolo. I made friends with local kids and fell in love with a Brazilian boy which certainly speeded up my language learning. "I wish I were the wind so I could blow about you forever,' he whispered in my ear.

Zu and I learned all the carnival songs and followed the samba bands as they practised in the streets throughout the year. We cheerfully belted out the lewd lyrics about a 'sacarolha' (corkscrew), and 'resaca, resaca, resaca' (terrible hangover) and 'Maria Escandalosa' without any ideas of what the double entendres meant. But the melancholy rootless place in the depths of my adolescent spirit was touched by that great Brazilian speciality – the really mournful 'saudade' songs – an untranslatable Portuguese word which conveys a mixture of sadness, longing, homesickness, regret, disappointment ... Songs of the favelas and the poverty of the North East sertao, the cangaceiros and the fishermen. 'E Doce Mourir no Mar' (It's Sweet to die in the Sea). Those tragic songs spoke to the deepest feelings in me. I loved the music then and I love it now. And I will dance again in Bahia if it's the last thing I do.

★

After his father's murder, everything changed. Dad wrote me a batch of letters once when he was away in India. I was about ten and still living in L.A. I loved getting his letters – the exotic stamps, his unique handwriting:

My beloved Lalushka, they began. Or sometimes, My own Annaliviapurabella,

'I will bring you a white elephant from India and a tiger to guard you' ...Always the fantasist but so sweet and loving with it. (When I was little he promised me a black horse with a silver saddle for my 10th birthday and Zu would have a white horse with a golden saddle.)

This time he was writing to answer questions I'd asked him before he left and he hadn't been able to find the words. His English was good but eccentric. He spoke like the foreigner he was. I wanted to know about his father – my grandfather – and what happened after his murder.

'Ahh Lali, he wrote, that Friday evening changed my whole life and was the most tragic event that formed my character. That trauma which struck me so suddenly was to last for a lifetime and I naturally grew up as a neurotic boy inclined to depressions and anxieties.'

He described how the whole town of Jews and even gentiles came to follow the bier which was covered in black cloth and carried by four people. He was taken by his uncle's big hand and carried on the waves of the black sea of mourners. After the men came the women with covered heads holding his mother. Their screams and wringing of their hands were heard down the streets and all the shops were closed. Some women, especially the poor who had received alms from his father, tore their hair and cried and wailed in penetrating mourning voices. They praised his father's goodness of heart, his generosity, his piety. They screamed to God. 'How could He allow such a crime on a saintly man? And which Jew will be the next to be murdered?

'I'll write again, my Lalushka. I must try to sleep now. Kiss Zulu and Yehudi for me.

Your own Diddad'

Sometimes he signed his letters Daedalus.

A few days later, another:

'At the grave, I repeated after my uncle the Kaddish prayer which is said in Aramaic by the son in mourning for his parent and I looked down into the grave where father was laid in his white linen garments. Two pieces of broken shards on his closed eyes. I don't remember crying. I felt only an unspeakable terror. '

Coming back from the graveyard, he wrote, was a living nightmare. The rows of people intoning the traditional words – 'May God comfort you amongst other mourners of Zion and Jerusalem'; his mother with a black silk lace shawl thrown over her head covering her grey, tear- blotched face and red eyes. Even stronger than all the fear and pain he recalled feeling overcome with shame. *'I was ashamed of all my uncles and aunts and cousins and the black mass of strangers and neighbours who pitied us; ashamed of their sad looks and shaking of heads and wringing of hands over the poor orphan. I was ashamed of the clear, blue, cold sky, ashamed of the trees, ashamed of Heaven. I was ashamed of God.' ...*

And finally, in a third letter he remembered the coming home from the funeral and finding the house full of people. They had to sit on tiny stools, the beginning of Shiva, the seven days of mourning when everyone comes with loud extravagant praise for the dead – their good deeds, their piety, generosity and saintliness. Old women lamenting and tearing their hair retelling stories of his father – how he had run one night in a snowstorm to bring a doctor to her sick child; had paid the doctor himself, given her money for medicines, brought a chicken and oranges for the child ...

'People talked in low voices about the innocent blood that was shed; the persecution and pogroms in Russia and Poland, old Reb Shmuel chewing the end of his long grey beard contemplating 'the end of days'; how long the Redeemer will be in coming to save his people?

But I no longer believed in the Messiah. I had loved the Messiah as I loved my father and all of a sudden I lost both. I was just an abandoned, betrayed child of a Jew who had been killed in front of my eyes.

I'll be home soon my Lalushka. Take care of yourself.

Kiss your Mummy, Zulu and Yehudi for me.'

Diddad

There was always an underlying haunted quality about him even though he could be very funny and was a wonderful story teller. The time I saw him actually fall off his chair laughing was when he was with a couple of old cronies speaking Yiddish. It's such a humorous language with completely different nuances and cadences from his adopted English. He would cry with mirth, mopping his eyes. I wish he'd taught me.

Well, inevitably the Brazilian venture ended in disarray. Dad's expenditure had got out of hand, he owed a lot of money which couldn't be found. He was arrested, his passport taken away and Mum had to barter the only things of value we'd ever had – two paintings by Jankel Adler and a couple of beautiful silk Persian carpets – to secure his release. A hasty departure was arranged on HMV *The Highland Princess,* a tearful goodbye with my boyfriend at the port, and we set sail for England. I was just sixteen. For my birthday Dad had given me an anthology of Latin American Poetry which he inscribed;

'To my beloved Allegra on her 16th birthday – the only good thing of memory from Brazil – a few snatches of Latin American Poetry and a glimpse of the land and some of the good people. Daddy 1956'

Here is a translation from the Portuguese of an evocative poem by the Brazilian poet Ronaldo de Carvalho:

I hear the vast song of Brasil.
I hear the solemn melody.
Amazon.
The melody of lazy flood, heavy as oil
That swells greater and ever greater
Licking the mud of the banks
Gnawing roots, dragging along islands…

Caimans asleep in the mud
In this hour of pure sunlight
I hear all Brasil singing, humming, calling, breathing …

In my mind I imagined the solemn melody of that huge river – that tropical land in all its humid, secret vastness. It made my heart beat faster. One day I would go there.

★

The first of my life's journeys began at Easter 1940 with my surprise conception in Italy on route to Australia. After eight years of childlessness my parents thought they couldn't have any children. Dad was being sent by a Jewish Charity on a fund-raising mission for the *Kinder Transport* child refugees pouring out of Eastern Europe without their families. Many Jews had emigrated in the late 1800s to Australia and there was a large Jewish community in Sydney. Dad's idea had been to ask Yehudi Menuhin the great violinist who was living there at the time married to his first wife Nola – an Australian – to give a concert for the charity.

The Italian ship was to sail from Naples. On the journey down, as it was Easter Sunday my parents joined the crowds outside St Peter's in Rome for a blessing by the Pope. 'Why not?' said my dad. 'Jews could always do with a blessing.' Then a passionate night in the Hotel Diana in Rome followed by a visit to Pompeii where Mum bought a tiny winged silver penis fertility charm from a souvenir seller outside the ruins. She brazenly wore it on a chain round her neck to the somewhat shocked astonishment of the other passengers on the ocean liner. On the six-week sea voyage to the other side of the world Mum discovered she was pregnant. So whether it was the Pope's benediction, the hotel named after Diana – goddess of women and childbirth or the Pompeii prick that did the trick I was born two days before Christmas in Australia. Sadly, during the voyage Italy had come into the war on the wrong side. The ship was impounded on arrival and scuttled in Sydney harbour, the lovely Italian crew taken prisoner much to the dismay of the passengers who had come to love them.

The concert was a success and lots of money raised for the charity. The Menuhins became friends and years later my brother would be named after Yehudi. My baby album has the tiny black and white scalloped edged photos of that first six months of my life; my pram under a eucalyptus tree; a picnic in Rushcutter's Bay Park; the Charlemount hospital; our address at 200 Macleay Regis, Pott's Point; feeding Kangaroos in Koala Park; me sucking the ear of my stuffed Koala; Dad showing me an edition of Stefan Zweig translated by him into Yiddish – he never knew quite what to do with babies ...

In June 1941 we sailed on the SS *Mariposa* to America stopping at Fiji on the way. In a lovely tradition, departing visitors have a beautiful fresh flower lei made of orchids placed around their neck. When they were a little way out of the port Mum threw her flower lei into the sea. The legend states that if it floats back to land you would return someday to the South Sea Islands. It did. They never returned but I did.

My parents managed to leave me on a train travelling across the country to the East coast of America. During a refuelling stop in El Paso, Texas they got off to stretch their legs and the train chugged off without them while I slept on in the carriage. Horrors! Panic! The stationmaster telegraphed ahead for the train to wait for them at the next town and they hurtled off in a chartered Model T Ford like Bonnie and Clyde.

After a brief stay with Mum's sister Bettie whom she had not seen for several years there ensued a frustrating wait throughout a long hot summer in the Hotel Great Northern, West 57th Street, New York while Mum pined and badgered the authorities to find her a passage on a ship to England. Dad, wanting somehow to serve the country he loved in her time of need had already travelled in a large convoy of ships across the Atlantic to do his bit lecturing to the troops at Aldershot (he was excused active military service on account of his flat feet). I'm never quite sure how his lectures helped the war effort or what the enlisted men made of his thoughts on Spinoza but he became a sort of mascot. The chaps loved him and protected him from the coursenesses of military life – even polishing his boots for him as he was totally useless at such tasks.

There are photos of Mum at the time holding me and staring mournfully out to sea captioned, 'waiting to join my Camille in England' (Camille was the name he chose for himself 'after Saint-Saens'. Henceforth known as C R Honig – Camille Rachmil.)

'It's too dangerous, Madam,' she was told by the exasperated consul. 'There are no passenger ships.' Undeterred she sat outside his office everyday until he finally relented and allowed her a berth aboard one of a convoy of three troop ships sailing in November 1941. She had one of the sailors make her a little canvas sling in which she carried me around day and night in case we were torpedoed. Her horror was of the ship being split in half while I was in the cabin and she was matching the sailors drink for drink in the bar. 'We'll go together,' she said gaily.

Only two of the three ships made it across the Atlantic. Mum was reunited with the love of her life and eight months later Zu was born dramatically placenta previa in the middle of an air raid in London. My earliest memory at eighteen months old is of sitting on the hospital bed eating cherries from a paper bag, unimpressed with the new baby. I've been told it's not possible to have such an early memory but I'm sure of it.

Throughout the war we lived in a flat in North London at Hillcrest Court, Shoot Up Hill. Air raids were a regular feature. I had a Mickey Mouse gas mask and baby Zu had a gas cot. When the sirens went off, all the residents gathered in the entrance hall away from potential flying glass. Mum, of course, refused to go to the Underground shelters, 'To die like a rat in a hole? No thank you.' So we took our chances. She would stand me, bundled up in my dressing gown, on a heavy table in the lobby and get me to sing, "You are My Sunshine" in my piping three-year-old voice 'to cheer people up'. I was a natural show-off and proud to be the centre of attention. For years after the war ended I had a recurring nightmare of London on fire and me holding Zu by the hand – the only survivors – trying to find a way between the burning buildings.

My mother: Eileen Coleen Frieda Patricia (Pat) Hamilton Moore was born in Lewisham in 1912. The fourth of five daughters born to Ethel and John Moore. Her father John, a defrocked vicar, had run off to India with Ethel her mother, the disgraced former wife of Sir Gordon Guggisberg, Governor of the Gold Coast. Their first two daughters Sheila and Judy were born in Simla where John (known as Daddy Jack) got a job teaching in a school. Bettie, Pat and Dickie were born later when the family returned to London. Ethel had already given birth to two daughters, Ena and Nancy, when married to Gugg. She was banned from ever seeing them again after her indiscretion with the vicar who was only trying to comfort her after the death of a stillborn baby boy.

Ethel died of breast cancer when my mum was 8 years old. Daddy Jack married again, the sisters were split up and sent to live with different relatives – Sheila and Judy to a castle in Scotland, poor Dickie to family of religious fanatics who beat her and locked her in a dark cupboard under the stairs. I don't know where Bettie went and Mum was eventually shipped off to a cousin in South Africa to live on a farm where she learned to ride and shoot and take care of herself. When she was 14 she shot a rinkhals – a venomous spitting cobra – through the head.

So both essentially orphans, my parents Pat and Camille, miraculously found each other and clung together like survivors on a raft. After his father's murder and his mother's death not long after, Dad had been forced to live with an uncle who was horrified by the free-thinking, curious little boy's love of books and tried to burn them. Dad hated the narrow-minded orthodoxy of this small fishpond and determined to escape as soon as he could. Germany was where he wanted to go at first – the home of Goethe, Beethoven, Bach – the cultural mecca of Europe. Fortunately he chose England instead or this story would have ended there. The deciding factor was the opportunity to visit Kensal Rise cemetery and pay homage to Karl Marx's grave. He arrived in London and found digs in Bethnal Green.

One day he bumped into a Jew he'd known before – now married to an English woman – who said: *'You don't know anybody in London? Come to my house in St John's Wood. We are having a little gathering for my daughter's 6th birthday.'* Dad arrives at the appointed hour and the wife answers the door. *'My God!'* says Dad doffing his hat and kissing her hand with quaint old-fashioned courtesy *'If you had a sister as beautiful as you I would marry her.'* *'Come in and meet my sister'*, says the wife. And there she was – the glorious auburn-haired Pat aged twenty-one. They arranged to meet at the British Museum next day and Mum, not taking any chances, stuffed her nightie and a toothbrush in her handbag. She told me years later that she was totally smitten and determined to hang on to this one. Untroubled by the scandal they lived a bohemian life in London and Paris, drinking chartreuse in street cafes, loving the songs of Edith Piaf. I always imagined them living like Modigliani and Jean Hebuterne in a garret or like Rodolfo and Mimi in *La Boheme*. Intoxicated by love and art. To hell with conventions – he swearing that marriage was bourgeois and not for him – until she finally dragged him to the Marylebone Register Office.

Dad worked translating books from Yiddish into German and vice versa (Stefan Zweig, Josephus), Mum nursing at St Mary's Paddington. My favourite photo of them at this time was taken in 1937 in Port Said. They are sitting at a cafe table with a waiter in a fez standing by. They are wearing white linen suits and panama hats looking like Hepburn and Tracey or Bogart and Bergman. Looking at that photo when I was a child I thought they were grown ups but in that moment of frozen time I can see now that they are younger than my grandchildren are now. So glamorous and elegant. Innocent and unaware that they are on the edge of a precipice about to fall into the abyss of the Second World War which will engulf everything they have ever known. Their flat in Regents Park Crescent will be bombed, their friends killed.

On September 1st 1939 they were on a train travelling from Paris to Warsaw. Dad so wanted to show her his town and introduce her to real Polish sausage. The news came through that Germany had invaded Poland that very day so they got off the train at the next station and came back to England. The black clouds closed around Poland, the fate of the Jews was sealed and Dad never saw any of his family again. With the exception of one cousin – the one who had opened the door to the murderers on that fatal night and never forgave herself – who somehow got to America and one who ended up in Israel, they all perished in Auschwitz. Once again, what could have been a very short story was granted extra time.

This was when they went on the fund-raising mission to Australia and I was born in passing.

I remember when I was very small – maybe three or four – I said to my mum *'Why don't they send me to go and speak to Hitler in person.'* I was convinced that surely a sensible child could make him see reason. I was still at that age of invincibility and logic. *'He'd just throw you in a gas oven,'* she said. I didn't believe her. All through our childhood she thought it was important for us to know the reality of what had happened to the Jews in Europe. But every time she tried to tell me about concentration camps I'd put my fingers in my ears and run out of the room shouting, *'Don't tell me!'* I couldn't bear her tears and distress speaking such terrible words. In my own time I wanted to know but alone with a book. I read *If This is a Man* by Primo Levi and Anne Frank's diary. And I understood that all this terrible grief was added to the weight of sorrow and horror from his childhood that stoked Dad's nightmares.

Once, when I was about fourteen and footling about trying to play the guitar, I learned a Yiddish folk song for Dad from an album by Theodor Bikel. I thought it would make him happy. But his eyes welled up and then he just sobbed and sobbed. The extraordinary thing about Dad was that he wasn't a miserable person. He was funny and light hearted much of the time. A wonderful storyteller with a fund of Jewish jokes. The ghosts came in his dreams or surprised him in music.

It wasn't him who talked about the Holocaust to us. It was Mum who was not Jewish but took Judaism on with a fierce passion quoting from Ruth in the Bible: *"Entreat me not to leave thee, or to return from following after thee: for whither thou goest, I will go; and where thou lodgest, I will lodge: thy people shall be my people, and thy God my God: Where thou diest, will I die, and there will I be buried."* She became vehemently anti all things German and couldn't stand to hear Wagner on the radio or hear the German language spoken. Dad was much more equable and temperate.

What carried him along was a sense since early childhood of his own uniqueness and cleverness. He always thought that other people with great minds would be delighted to meet him – that he would be an interesting person for them to get to know. He sought them out: He travelled to Lambarene in the Belgian Congo and introduced himself to Dr. Albert Schweitzer who ran a hospital for lepers and played Bach on an organ in the jungle. (I got my school class to collect money to send to his hospital. We were thrilled to get a thank you letter back with Congo stamps.) He travelled to India to meet Nehru; he walked in the park with Gandhi when he came to London; he had coffee with Max Beerbohm; he played chess with Aldous Huxley and Edward G. Robinson in California; he went to Mexico to spend time with Diego Riviera and Frida Khalo, He took me to meet Louis Armstrong and Ella Fitzgerald. He gave me a copy of Robert Frost's poems personally inscribed to me. He met Thor Heyerdahl and Bernard Shaw and Stravinsky. He was always pleased with himself if he managed to tell these luminaries something they didn't know. Not the most endearing of qualities. There was an unintended arrogance there which could be off-putting. Most of the friendships did not endure.

At the end of the Second World War we were still in London and I was five. 'I want my children to have oranges,' Dad announced. He managed somehow to borrow money from Mum's sister Judy and to arrange third class passages on the old Cunard liner *Queen Elizabeth* to America. On the voyage Mum announced that she was pregnant and feeling sea sick. I had the run of the ship bringing her whatever she needed.

An image that has remained with me all these years later was our arrival in New York harbour. As we sailed past the Statue of Liberty I'll never forget all the other poor, tattered 'steerage' class passengers weeping over the railings with joy and relief. The promised land at last. *'Give me your tired, your poor, Your huddled masses yearning to breathe free, The wretched refuse of your teeming shore. Send these, the homeless, tempest-tossed to me, I lift my lamp beside the golden door!'* says the inscription on the plinth from a poem by Emma Lazarus. It was true once.

I remember a long tiring wait in Immigration at Ellis Island then being collected by Mum's sister Bettie — now married to a wealthy architect. I had my sixth birthday at Bettie and Hugh's house in Lexington where she arranged for Father Christmas to arrive in a helicopter which landed in their garden in the snow with a sackful of presents. America! Did this happen for every child?

Then a year in a tiny, dingy brown flat in Stuyvesant Street where homeless drunks slept under the stairs. We couldn't play outside and had no friends but I was a strange child and would rope Zu in to act out the Greek myths with which I'd become obsessed. Mum remembers coming back one evening to the flat where we'd been left with a hapless babysitter. I was on the kitchen table being Prometheus, having my liver torn out by an eagle in perpetuity sobbing pitifully, 'Bring me the key, little sister! Bring me the key!' And poor Zu, aged four was crying because she didn't know where the key was. Mum, as she always managed to, made the grotty place into a temporary home with a checked table cloth, candles and flowers on the table, Rachmaninov or Mozart on the radio even if dinner was only tinned spaghetti on toast and a glass of milk. Hudi was born on April 16th 1947. We visited our new baby brother in the hospital bringing a modest present, a little soft hairbrush, from FAO Schwartz — the famous dazzling toy emporium on 5th Avenue, where we could never have afforded the toys, — and adored him from the start. I've since heard that Stuyvesant Street is a very smart 'historic' neighbourhood today.

One day Dad took me to visit the flat where Paderewski — the great Polish pianist and statesman — had died in 1941. Dad told me that, back in the days before he had left for England leaving my mother and me in New York he had carried me there when I was a baby to pay his respects to the dead. Even if I would never remember the occasion, he thought it was important for me to have come within the orbit of such a brilliant man. He had strange ideas about age appropriate things to do with children. He would often ask me what I was reading and when I answered 'a Donald Duck comic' he would be shocked. 'Lali, you must read Zola', he'd say. Or Dostoevski or Tolstoy. He gave me *The Brothers Karamazov* for my seventh birthday.

So now it was 1947 and after a cold harsh winter in New York the promised oranges had not yet materialised. 'California,' Dad declared. He'd also heard that a movie being made in Hollywood starring Claudette Colbert was auditioning children to play her as a child. One of his daughters would surely be the obvious choice so money was borrowed from Bettie, professional photographs were taken, tickets to Los Angeles were purchased and we boarded the train. Was it Grand Central station or Penn station? Did the journey really take three days? Mum was breast feeding Hudi.

Our first home in the golden west was a shabby tenement. Grandview, in Downtown LA where the fathers wore vests and drank beer out of cans and the mothers had curlers in their hair all day. Zu and I were agog. Our dad never even owned a pair of jeans and always wore nicely pressed trousers and a tweed jacket. Mum played the classical radio station KFAM at top volume drowning out the prevailing popular music of the day in a snobby attempt to establish our superior taste. Encouraged by the pack of feral kids Zu and I chucked milk bottles down the fire escape and ran wild in the dusty yard. There was a communal tortoise called Tortaruga we all loved who burned to death in the incinerator where he had mistakenly chosen to hibernate. All of us kids were distraught when one of the dads raked his blackened shell out in the spring. It still makes me sad to think about his gruesome fate.

Alas, after a crushingly dismissive audition – two amongst hundreds of much cuter little girls with ambitious mothers – we were not to become movie stars after all but Dad realised that with his wide ranging knowledge perhaps there might be a job for him in the film business. He found temporary employment on a Cecil B de Mille blockbuster biblical epic where his role was to spot continuity inconsistencies and historical inaccuracies (gladiators with wristwatches; a bicycle propped up against a hovel; an extra wearing spectacles…). He couldn't stand it for long. He'd hoped to influence the big Hollywood producers in a film idea of his own – a biopic of the great Polish poet Julian Tuwim – 'an iconoclast, a revolutionary, a Jewish mystic who had turned to communism in order to escape anti-Semitism …' he said. Where was the money in that? he was asked. Disillusioned, after a year in Grandview Dad decided a rural childhood for us would be preferable to the questionable influences of our current neighbours so money was borrowed from a sympathetic rich Jewish movie magnate and the next move was to a rented chicken farm in Van Nuys in the San Fernando Valley.

It was back-breakingly hard work for Mum who hand reared the tiny fluffy yellow balls that she collected in cardboard boxes from the railway station, carted around the wheelbarrows of chicken feed, cleaned the cages, collected the eggs, culled the non-layers, and drove miles through the canyons in the old Pontiac loaded with carefully graded eggs to sell to the movie stars homes. She was a huge hit with her English accent and her flaming red hair. Sometimes we were allowed to go with her and ogle the rich and famous. We once saw Mitzi Gaynor dancing with her lover in their sitting room. Dad, meanwhile, sat in his armchair and read books on chicken farming. I never saw him do anything practical. But he did make up wonderful stories. Our favourites were his tales of Bimbo the magic monkey and Kimbo the giraffe. He just pulled them out of the air and we were enthralled, begging for more when they ended on a cliff-hanger.

I do clearly remember one event that included Dad as it was so rare for us to go off for the day for a picnic as a family. We never went on holiday but for some reason when I was about eight we had a day out and drove in the old Buick to Lake Elsinore. We rushed gleefully into the water in our baggy homemade knitted swimming costumes and there, floating in the shallows was a hessian bag full of drowned puppies. A terrible image of death and horror that intruded into our perfect day and clouded the memory forever. Who could do such a thing? Those sweet little newborn faces. It still haunts me.

Another Dad story… In one of my comics I read about a competition to name a horse – a beautiful Palomino. The prize would be enough money to buy a horse of one's own. I chose 'Goldie'. Dad vetoed it immediately. 'Far too common,' he said. 'Boring! Be original. Name him 'Rocinante' after Don Quixote's horse.' So I took his advice. Of course the winning name turned out to be 'Goldie'. We longed for a horse but a horse would be far too expensive and where would we keep it anyway? So we were fobbed off with a donkey instead. Dipsy was an evil animal who refused to budge when we tried to ride him but galloped like the wind when it was time to go back to his stable in the evening knocking off any riders under a low branch into a patch of stinging nettles. But there were peach trees and grapefruit trees and lemon and orange trees to climb and an old barn, reeking of DDT where we had to take care to avoid the black widow spiders and jump from the rafters onto an old mattress. We had a dog who had nine puppies in a hole in the ground where half of them suffocated and a cat named Eggery who cleverly gave birth to her litter of kittens in the storm cellar where mum sorted the eggs. We walked barefoot to school down the grassy middle of the boulevard. It was the happiest of times. I even made a best friend. Sharon. I loved Sharon straight away because she told the boys to fuck off, rode her bike like a maniac and gave as good as she got in a fight. No chicken farms or orchards exist in Van Nuys today and our grassy boulevard is a multi lane freeway.

One night there was a terrifying storm with crashing thunder and ferocious wind whipping the branches about. As we looked out of our bedroom window a bolt of lightning struck the enormous walnut tree in the front garden and it fell stopping short of demolishing the house by a matter of inches. As soon as the rain stopped and the dawn arrived I made some jam sandwiches then persuaded Zu to come with me. We climbed out the window into the cold, wet horizontal fallen giant and sat there rather miserably trying to feel adventurous. Mum made us come in and later some men came with chain saws and carted it all away. It was all rather disappointingly sad and should have been much more thrilling.

One unforgettable day, when I was eleven, there was an open day at the Mt Wilson Observatory in Griffiths Park. Dad took me and we queued up to look through the giant telescope to see the rings around Saturn. It was beyond awe inspiring. I was speechless with wonder. Dad just put his arm around my shoulders and told me that Einstein once said, 'If the universe is like clockwork, I would like to meet the watchmaker.' It gave me a lasting understanding that even the most rational scientific mind could leave room for the mystery. Dad may have been a terrible provider but what he gave me was far more valuable. He introduced me to wonder and magic.

It ended all too soon. The price of chicken food went up and the price of eggs went down. A neighbour's dog got into the enclosure where the baby chicks were. Tiny, half eaten bloody little bodies were scattered everywhere. I can still see Mum's white knuckles gripping the fence and her grim face as she surveyed the carnage. Dad heard of the vacant position for a Reform rabbi in the seaside town Redondo Beach …

We moved into an old wooden house with eucalyptus trees in the yard where I made a tiny clubhouse out of an abandoned piano crate. It was really uncomfortable to squeeze inside but it was mine and I made a flag to fly from the roof, 'Sparrow Club. Private. Keep out!!', and a skull and crossbones. Zu wasn't allowed to join nor was Sharon's sister Tina. I was eleven.

Mum became the Rebbitzen and we had to morph into the rabbi's children and behave properly in the synagogue. Dad had no actual qualifications for the job but could legitimately claim that all his papers had been lost in the holocaust. We had to answer the phone saying 'Dr Honig's residence'. Dr Honig wrote interesting sermons, had a beautiful cantor's voice and took seriously the counselling of his congregation. We learned the Hebrew prayers and songs phonetically – "Barukh ata Adonai Eloheinu, melekh ha`olam … …" We celebrated Passover and Chanuka as well as Christmas. We adopted Bozo the best dog in all the world who appeared one night on our porch with a wounded paw. He let us dress him in a baby bonnet and push him around in a doll's pram. He could do a few tricks and won second prize in a dog show at the school playground during the summer holidays.

I liked to hang out at the penny arcade on the pier and try my hand at darts. If you scored a bull's eye you could win a hideous plaster Alsatian dog. I loved them and got quite good at darts. Mum hated them and said they were bad taste and common which made me love them more. I also liked to feel clever and different from other children and remember taking myself off to the seaside cinema on the pier where they were showing Laurence Olivier's Hamlet. Superior taste, surely. And possibly why, apart from Sharon, I didn't have any friends.

Around this time a letter arrived from the immigration department reminding Dad that we had vastly outstayed our original visitors' visas. The fact that Hudi, born in New York, was an American citizen had complicated the issue but now was the time to get legal. We would have to leave the country and apply for proper immigration status. The choice was Mexico or Canada but we had no money to pay for the trip. What followed was probably the only knowingly dishonest thing Dad ever did. He created 'Family X', a poor destitute Jewish family in need of support and invited members of the congregation to donate generously to a fund. When enough money had been raised train tickets to Vancouver were bought and off we went – a marvellous trip up through the russet autumn foliage of the Pacific North West where I saw a brown bear standing on a rock.

Zu and I loved Vancouver and went everyday to the seashore where we tried unsuccessfully to build a raft out of drift wood. Just as well since neither of us could swim. Allowed to do whatever we wanted and with no school to go to, we invented adventures in Stanley Park the magnificent natural West Coast rainforest on the edge of the city until one day, idling along a forest path, we were scared half to death by a totally naked man who jumped out from behind a tree and chased us. We ran back to the entrance gate and never returned. I remember there being no one else around. Today it is a popular tourist attraction with entrance fees.

We re-entered the United States as proper immigrants and moved to a nice home on 23rd Street in Santa Monica with hummingbirds in the garden. Dr Honig set himself up as a Psychologist (whose Ph.D qualifications had also, alas, been lost in the war). My best friend Sharon and I used to lie on the floor with enormous pillows to stifle our giggles while we eavesdropped outside the double doors to his consulting room. During the time we lived at this address I had two years of schooling at Lincoln Junior High but never quite fitted in.

I was only good at music. Lousy at sports. Last to be chosen on any team. I begged my Mum to let me cut off my waist length plaits. I wanted a curly perm. I hated my name. I ditched Allegra and called myself Sally Honig. None of it really helped. I was never going to be a 'popular' girl who wore a twin-set and saddle-oxfords, a boy's signet ring on a chain and his football letters on her jacket. My dad was an embarrassment. He wore squeaky handmade leather shoes to parents' meetings and kissed the teacher's hand.

Dad actually wrote a play during this time which mum typed for him at night while also working at her day job as a receptionist. *Take Now Thy Son* – a modern take on the Abraham and Isaac story from the Old Testament. This was performed by the Maurice Schwartz Yiddish Arts Theatre Company at the Pasadena Playhouse. Mum got him a wooden cigar humidor for a first night present with the words 'Take Now Our Love' engraved on a little silver plaque. But the play wasn't a great success and only ran for a week.

He and Mum rowed a lot about money. He would come home with expensive gifts for her or bottles of Chateau Lafitte. I remember a saucy lime green 'baby doll' nylon nightie they nicknamed 'the Kinsey' after a popular sexologist. She ripped it up and threw it at him. She would rage that there wasn't enough to pay the gas bill; the children were going to school barefoot … and he would laugh. She would throw the dinner on the floor and storm off in the car. Zu and I would creep around like good little mice doing the washing up to placate her. Then she'd screech back into the driveway and they'd kiss and make up. They always kissed and made up. And they didn't hide much from us. One night I was woken up by alarming cries coming from Mum's bedroom (they always had separate rooms). I was worried but not enough to go busting in. In the morning I brought Mum a cup of tea in bed and asked her what she had been crying about. She patted the sheets next to her and invited me to snuggle in. 'Sometimes darling, grown ups get a bit carried away when they are making love,' she said. 'I'm sorry if we frightened you. Daddy and I love each other very deeply. It's all perfectly natural and you will experience the same thing one day when you love someone very much.' I have always been grateful that she honoured me with the truth and didn't try to fob me off. Instead of being embarrassed, she managed to turn the occasion into an opportunity to tell me about the joy of adult sexual pleasure. In fact she'd always answered any question about sex and childbirth truthfully much to the wide-eyed amazement of my school friends who were still being told gooseberry bush stories. I can't remember a time I didn't know the facts of life.

But our time was running out again and less than two years after we'd become official immigrants to the United States and settled into Santa Monica we had to give Bozo away and took off for Brazil.

Chapter Two

I was a dreamy, romantic child and the first man I was in love with was Beethoven. They used to play the Emperor Concerto at my nursery school during 'rest time' when I was three years old. I came home singing it. Forever hooked on classical music. My parents bought me a book about him. It made me cry. If only I could have been there for him! How terrible to be deaf. How tragic. How unthinkable. Not even able to hear his own music. No wonder he looked so sad in his portraits. I would have made him happy.

My next huge love affair occurred when I was about eight or nine. I was taken to the Hollywood Bowl to a concert – Leonard Bernstein conducting the Israeli Philharmonic. He was so gorgeous and the music so fabulous … who says children can't understand or appreciate classical music. I was overwhelmed with passion and adoration.

The next crushes were all for unattainable popular boys at Lincoln Junior High school in California. The Bonnies, the Cindys and the Carols all had 'steadies'. No one chose me. I guess to any outsider I was an overweight, bossy know-it-all with the wrong stye of clothes and the dreaded pigtails instead of the longed-for curly perm. But it masked such a different me. Appallingly unsure, mortified at the prospect of making a wrong move that would brand me uncool. I mostly took out my bad moods on playing the piano which Mum cleverly intuited would provide an outlet for all my pent-up passion. I did have one particularly wonderful piano teacher. After a terrible one who tried to make me learn ghastly tunes with names like 'Little Blackbird on the Fence' Mum found Greta Cohn – a Jewish holocaust survivor whose husband had died in the camps. 'What would you like to play?' she asked me at my first lesson and when I said 'Chopin's Revolutionary Study', she sat down and played it for me. 'Might as well start here then', she said. Of course it was completely out of my league but cleverly made me yearn for more. For my birthday she gave me sheet music inscribed, 'To my gifted student'. I wish I had been more gifted to please her. She understood my combination of ferociousness and longing. I also vented my frustrations by being mean to poor Zu. I had collected a huge library of comics – everything from Captain Marvel and Donald Duck to teen romances, ghouls and horror stories. They cost a dime but Zu had to rent them off me for a nickel if she wanted to read them. (If only I'd had the foresight to keep them. Vintage American comics sell for about £20 each wrapped in cellophane today.)

The agonising year of being thirteen I spent in Brazil which sounded exotic but was just the same old insecurity in an exotic place. Every morning I looked in the mirror and made pacts with the devil if only I could have one day without spots or even one inch of my face that was completely clear. Brazilian girls had all-over tans and wore bikinis made of dental floss, their hair like tossed chestnut manes.

For our first Carnaval I was sent off to a family in the countryside with a fazenda near Campinas. Some contact of Dad's. It was thought that I needed to 'make friends.' They probably wanted to remove me from the mayhem and temptations of Carnaval in Rio. I shared a bedroom with two lackadaisical sisters much older than me who lay around with no clothes on in the afternoon heat, painted their toenails red, smoked non-stop and threw their fag ends into a full chamber pot under the bed. They didn't get up till noon and spent ages doing their make up but they taught me how to samba and at night we danced in the street following the bands and everyone sprayed each other with ice cold 'lança perfume' from pressurised aluminium cans. Red earth, bougainvillea and banana trees. I can smell it still. The parents, normally models of Catholic rectitude, were away for the entire five days of unlicensed revelry having a year's worth of illicit foraging. 'You can do anything you want for five days,' said the sisters. 'Then you give it all up for Lent.' "Vai todo mundo pra resaca! Resaca, resaca, resaca!

Ninguen aguenta mais, Eu vou manda para. Vai tudo mundo pra casa curar. Sei que voce gusto muito d'ela. Mais e bon qui não esqueça, que ela não e amiga. Deçe pra barriga, depois sobre pra cabeça." (I'm remembering the words from nearly seventy years ago.) We pranced along in a gang, dancing in the street, singing with our arms around each other until we could hardly walk and stumbled home. In the morning there were a couple of young men sprawled asleep in our beds. I'd lain awake with rigid limbs, thumping heart and quivering eyelids pretending to be asleep while they fucked two boys in their double bed and then swapped over. I wasn't ready for sex yet so nothing could have budged my thigh-clamped virgin territory. It felt daring just breathing their abandoned air. I had to push one off me in the middle of the night but it was all fairly good humoured and I was still a virgin when I got back to Rio. Was that being sexually assaulted? I was certainly not traumatised. I'm not sure my parents understood that the mayhem of Carnaval extended everywhere. The evocative smell of the cheap ice-cold perfume aerosols, cooling the sweat and the fever, the lust and the fantasy – they're with me still. I longed to be older, prettier, freer, more sophisticated but I was just 13 year old me.

Our apartment in the red light district provided endless hours of fascination. In this new world where we hadn't yet learned to speak the language or find our way around Zu and I used to kneel up at the window on turned-around chairs resting our chins on folded arms and amuse ourselves looking down on the street life five floors below. It didn't take long for us to realise that the same women stood waiting and smoking in the same places every day. Men would come up and talk to them and they'd go off for a while. Sometimes they'd stand there for hours and nobody would approach them.

'They're whores,' said Mum, 'and that's not a term of abuse. It's a good honest Biblical word for an honourable profession of ancient lineage. They make love with men for a living and don't you ever think badly of them for doing it. Any woman worthy of the name would do the same if her children were hungry. Remember, never judge someone until you've walked a mile in their moccasins.' Or high heeled gold mules in their case.

From then on we were rather in awe of them. At that age, sex was a pretty disagreeable prospect and the thought of such heroism for the sake of their hungry children was motherhood at its most selfless. We each adopted a favourite and kept score watching anxiously from the window, sometimes for hours until she'd had at least one customer.

"Mine's got one! 'Hooray,' I'd cry.

'I think mine has too, a man's talking to her. Oh no, he's gone off again!'

Mum had a great friend in Los Angeles who'd been a prostitute in wartime London and had married one of her clients, a Dutch business man who was besotted with her. Norma was loud, generous, vulgar and humorous. I thought she was wonderful and she showed me how to put my hair in pincurls so I could look like Debbie Reynolds. She wore amazing red snakeskin shoes with bows on and carried a red snakeskin clutch bag to match. Mum said she most likely hadn't given 'it' up entirely and occasionally kept her hand in, so to speak.

Mum was full of good advice on being a woman, rather out of fashion in today's world but daring in its day. 'A good woman should be able to be a lady in the drawing room, a char in the kitchen and a whore in the bedroom,' she'd say dramatically, giving us the concept quite early on that womanliness was a subtle, complex thing not to mention hard work. 'A good woman plays the hand she's been dealt with dignity and to the best of her ability.' She'd certainly lived her own life by these precepts and enjoyed a very unconventional creative marriage for forty-five years as well as being a working wife and bringing up three children.

One day, as we watched the street life from the window, Dad came and stood behind us. He put a hand on each of our shoulders and told a poignant story from his time as a journalist in 1937 in the Spanish Civil War. As an innocent, idealistic young man he had been appalled at the numbers of women reduced to working as prostitutes in Barcelona. The fact that so many were young and beautiful seemed to make it worse. He wanted to find out what circumstances had caused them to seek their living on the streets so he approached one, agreed to her price and followed her up a rickety staircase to a curtained cubicle.

Upon hearing that he only wanted to talk she looked at him quizzically, rebuttoned her blouse and sat down for twenty minutes. She couldn't afford to waste too much time, she hinted delicately, as she could cater for several more clients before the night was over. Dad said he would like to take her out for tea on Sunday and she readily agreed.

When he arrived for the assignation at the botanical gardens, he hardly recognised her. There she was demurely dressed in a high necked blouse and shawl, not a scrap of makeup, her river of thrilling, black, waist length hair neatly confined in a single plait. She was accompanied by her mother, her grandmother and two aunts. An invitation from a young suitor of serious intent required chaperones and they followed along behind at a discreet distance the whole afternoon fanning themselves.

Dad had been deeply moved, he said, by the way the family still maintained their deep traditional protective regard for their daughter while accepting the reality of her life. Mum disagreed and said it was sad that they were such hypocrites. Why did she have to maintain the fiction of being a virgin by day while she was a whore by night? A man wouldn't have to keep up such a pretence. Or maybe they just had no idea about her double life.

Mum's great heroine, about whom she once wrote a play that sadly never got published, was Aspasia, the most famous of the Greek hetaerae, and lifelong partner of Pericles the leading statesman of his time – the Golden Age of Athens in the fifth century BC. The hetaerae held very honoured positions in society as the mistresses of the country's most powerful men. Aspasia successfully combined intelligence, political astuteness, sexual expertise and motherhood. She taught and spoke in public. She was universally loved, respected and acknowledged. She didn't have to choose between being a good wife or a fallen woman. She was who she was. Mum admired her because she appeared to integrate so many of the female archetypes – The Mother, The Whore, The Priestess, The Goddess – into one total woman. And this was to be a huge influence in my own life many years later when I came to write my books.

São Paulo was a small, manageable city in the 1950s. You could ride a 'bondi' (tram) into the centre of town and wander about getting a 'churasco' (steak sandwich) for lunch for a few cruzeiros. Zu and I often went to the matinee at the seedy picture house on our own to watch Superman and Batman movies. When mum found out that the cinema was frequented solely by men in dirty raincoats she put a stop to it. I decorated my bedroom with film stars pictures torn from movie magazines – Tony Curtis, Janet Leigh, Doris Day, Debbie Reynolds and Eddie Fisher – and hung up a banner with the legend, 'I Love you California' but as soon as I met Mauricio de Oliviera the swimming instructor from the local pool I suddenly became interested and enthusiastic about learning Portuguese. He was eighteen and I was thirteen. Apart from Dov Grossman who lived next door and dumped me after I let him put his hand inside my t-shirt, Mauricio was the first boy who seemed to really like me. I invited him for tea and he arrived in an electric blue polyester suit and shiny pointed yellow shoes. Mum was horrified and morphed into her Dame Edith Evans persona completely destroying the poor lad with her chilly English aristocratic hauteur. 'Not good enough for you darling,' she announced after he'd fled but she approved of the talented conducting student Isaac Karabtchevsky from the Escola Libre de Musica and I began to really love Brazil. I grew into my body and came to terms with my face.

Many of the teachers at the Escola were emigres from Hungary and I had to play a lot of Bartok which I didn't particularly like but I adored singing and joined a group that rehearsed in the local Catholic church. We sang motets by Palestrina, Thomas Tallis, Gesualdo and William Byrd. I'd never heard such glorious music or experienced such soaring emotions. Pointed yellow shoes was quickly forgotten.

About forty years later when visiting Venice I saw a playbill for an opera at La Fenice. The conductor was none other than Isaac Karabtchevsky, my long lost heartthrob from the music school. Alas, the opera house was closed for renovations after a fire so I never got to see him. But I looked him up online the other day just before leaving for the Amazon and found that he has had a wonderful international career 'one of the living icons' of Brazil, according to the *Guardian*. And now directs, in Italy, masterclasses for conductors from all over the world. That made me happy.

In retrospect, being taken out of the teenage scene in California with its Soda fountains, Happy Days, cheerleader squads, Beach Boys, high school proms …was probably the luckiest break I could have had. It set me on a different path for which I am grateful. I reconnected with the real me – the romantic, passionate child who was in love with Beethoven, who lived for classical music.

Through Dad and his knack of making friends with interesting people, I met the explorer Peter Fleming who gave me a copy of his book Brazilian Adventure. He was one of those droll, self-deprecating old Etonians with superb manners who radiate absolute confidence. Dad loved his laconic style of humour and told him some Jewish jokes. They couldn't have been more different but seemed to really get on. Into our circle of acquaintances also came a young English Anthropologist and his Danish wife. David and Pia Maybury-Lewis. They had been doing fieldwork living with the Xavante people in the far reaches of the Amazon headwaters. At that time indigenous rights were not on anyone's radar. David was an extraordinary person – the most brilliant I had ever known. Quietly spoken and modest, he was fluent in 9 languages yet he and Pia always had time for a fairly clueless teenager. Pia would have tea parties and invite other young people to meet each other. I thought she was incredibly courageous. She'd gone out to live for long periods of time with her baby amongst the indios in the jungle and soon realised that it was much less trouble to go naked like the other women rather than provoke endless curiosity about what she was hiding under her clothes.

Many years later I learned that David became professor of anthropology at Harvard in 1960 and in 1972, he and Pia founded Cultural Survival, an organisation committed to guaranteeing indigenous people a voice in the policies affecting their lives, a sustainable means of livelihood and the means of adapting their cultures to change. In talking about the indios, David said that although their rich heritage gave plenty of meaning to their lives they were constantly being coerced to join the rural poor or follow the missionaries, 'Nobody mentioned the other option,' he said 'that they might retain their lands and enter the Brazilian economy while modifying, but not abandoning, their own traditions.' Part of the reason I wanted to return to Brazil this year was to honour their wonderful work and to learn something about what had happened to the people they had championed.

Back then, Dad somehow became involved with the PEN conference being held that year in Brazil and asked me if I'd like to accompany him. It was a long bus ride and I sat next to David. When he heard that my family were shortly going to England he asked me to deliver a message for him to his brother-in-law Tony Thompson a documentary film maker working for British Transport Films in London. How could I have possibly imagined the train of fate that this moment set in motion.

London in 1957. Fleeing once again. Nowhere to live so Mum and Dad and Hudi stayed with Mum's eldest sister Sheila in Swiss Cottage and Zu and I had bunk beds at our cousin Xenia's house in Golders Green. Sheila had studied singing in Russia where she had met her husband Benio Szladkowski a piano student. In fact it was at Sheila and Benio's house back in 1932 that my dad first met my mum – "Sheila's sister Pat" – that he writes about in his own memoir 'The Wanderings of a Wondering Jew'. They held wonderful musical soirees in their home and were friends with the great musicians of the day: Piatagorsky, Heifitz, Horowitz, Huberman, Schnabel, Myra Hess. I auditioned for the Guildhall School of Music and Drama and fortunately got a place to study piano and viola though still only 16.

One day, up in central London I went into British Transport Films to say Hi to Tony Thompson and deliver David Maybury-Lewis' message. 'What a bit of luck,' said Tony, 'we were just looking for a couple of girls to be in our latest documentary – *The Travel Game*. Would you and a friend perhaps be interested?'

I could hardly believe my ears. Was this how it happened? A film? We'd be discovered! Fame? Stardom? Alas, none of those things but my friend Gina from the Guildhall came along with me to audition and we got the job. £5 and a new frock each. British Transport Films was a prestigious company begun in the great days of British Documentaries – headed by Edgar Anstey. Originally it just produced films on the subject of British Transport but also made such classics as *Night Mail* with music by Benjamin Britten and words by W H Auden, 'Terminus' directed by John Schlesinger and *Wild Wings* narrated by Peter Scott which won an Oscar.

Our film *The Travel Game*, was one of their travelogues extolling the virtues of places which could be accessed via the British Transport network. In this case a train from Liverpool Street to Harwich. Then a ferry to the Hook of Holland and from there …Europe spread before you. Endless possibilities. The theme of the film was that the narrator was playing a little guessing game with himself – where were all these passengers going? A lonely looking sailor; a family with small children; a business man; a mystery woman; and two girls with a large ungainly piece of luggage and a guitar (me and Gina) … Our ungainly piece of luggage turns out to be a collapsible canoe which we will assemble on the banks of the Rhine, paddle and drift along, visit Koblenz and Heidelberg, attend a jolly wine festival and be seen drinking a glass of Riesling in the sunset.

Neither of us had ever been in a canoe before so we were given a couple of lessons on the Thames at Eel Pie Island and then let loose on the enormous and terrifying Rhine trying to avoid getting mown down by towering cargo vessels and tourist boats. We adored every minute and flirted with the film crew. The only heart stopping moment that intruded into this idyll was one day driving along the Autobahn and seeing a road sign casually pointing to Dachau. This was only just over a decade after the end of the war. All still so recent. I was Jewish and here we were in Germany.

Back in England we were dying to know what we looked like on the screen so I stopped by the cutting rooms in Soho one day. Well, unbeknownst to me, while we were away filming in Germany, young Richard Taylor had joined British Transport Films as an assistant editor and, as I learned much later, he had been beguiled by my screen image – specifically one shot of me playing the guitar and singing a Brazilian carnival song sitting on my bunk on the ferry to Hook of Holland. When I came bouncing in to the office wanting to look at the rushes the editor Ralph Sheldon tactfully suggested to Richard that he might show me around. And that was it. Our eyes met in the crowded corridor and our life's journey of sixty years together began at that moment. All because of sitting next to David Maybury-Lewis on a bus in Brazil.

Richard arranged to show me in their little in-house cinema one of BTF's films, *The Elephant Never Forgets*, about the last tram in London on its final journey to the depot at Elephant and Castle – historic archive film set to old music hall songs. It was so poignant I cried all the way through, mortified to be blubbing in front of this handsome stranger but he said afterwards that this was the clincher – I was romantic and sentimental as well as attractive.

A few days later I got an invitation to accompany him to a Beckett play at the theatre to which he 'just happened' to have a spare ticket (he bought it after I said yes). The following week I sold him a ticket to my choir's concert – Walton's *Balshazzar's Feast*.

I ruthlessly dumped Tony my very nice chartered accountant boyfriend. We sang in the same choir and used to queue all night to get arena tickets for The Proms. Ever since, I have felt terrible about my youthful cruelty – 'I've outgrown our relationship,' I told him loftily. Shame. Shame. And have always wanted to apologise to him. Tony Shepherd, if you ever read this, I'm sorry. You deserved better. Please forgive me. I hope you had a nice life.

When I finally introduced Richard to my parents. Mum was scathing. – 'a bearded beatnik, an angry young man. Living in Soho!' Not the violin virtuoso, chess playing, Oxford educated Jewish lawyer she'd had in mind. She collared him at the first opportunity and said she'd personally kill him if he interfered with my music studies as I was going to be a great pianist. She had always shown stubborn faith in my modest talent although I knew that I would never be good enough or hungry enough for a concert career.

I was still sixteen when Richard asked me to marry him. He was twenty-four and I was seventeen when we married the next year with no money, a single mattress on the floor and an orange box table. Everyone predicted disaster. A magazine even featured me in a piece about the folly of teenage marriages. Dad cried tears of shame: 'Ah my Lali. What kind of father am I? I have nothing to give you. Not a house. Not a horse.' I didn't want anything from him. They'd given me the only thing I've ever needed in this world – the certain knowledge that love was possible and that I was lovable. We got £100 in wedding present money and decided to spend it on a honeymoon rather than a bed. We went to Ibiza for our honeymoon. Travelling by train down through France to Valencia sitting up in Third Class, sleeping on deck on the ferry, knocking on little old landladies doors for a room. No rave scene back then. No flights. We both got jaundice from drinking the water and spent the first few months of our married life in separate hospital isolation wards. I was eight months pregnant when I took my finals at the Guildhall – scarcely able to reach the keyboard to play my Brahms Rhapsody.

£6 a week rented us a tiny attic flat in West Hampstead. We had a single mattress on the floor, orange boxes for furniture and a baby grand piano. We both worked all hours to afford it. Ralph Miliband lived in the flat below with his two little boys David and Ed. Doris Lessing used to visit. I had a job in a grotty omelette bar in Shepherd's Market, Richard operated the spotlight in a Soho strip club at night in addition to his day job in the film business. We ate a lot of fried spam and sardines on toast. Our little bumble bee was born at Queen Mary's Maternity Home on Easter Monday 1960 with the sounds of the Hampstead Heath Fair outside drifting in through the windows on the warm breeze. A perfect baby boy. I was overcome with bliss and delight – contented as a cow.

I wrote this in heartfelt gushing teenage prose;

I am nineteen years of age and it is Easter Monday 1960. Outside the open window I can hear the steam calliope of the old-fashioned merry-go-round puffing and blowing, clashing and tooting. The Bank Holiday Fair on Hampstead Heath is in full swing but I am lying on a hospital bed on clean, starched sheets and my new baby son, my firstborn, my precious bumble bee is in my arms. To anyone else he probably looks like just an ordinary baby, a stewed apricot even, but I know he is the Prince of Peace and I am the Goddess of Spring. I am tired after 6 hours labour to bring him forth, to give him birth but I have never been so happy in my life. I am the Earth and the Moon. I am the river and the sea. I am the cave and the mountain, the she-wolf, the doe. I am a cornucopia of milk and honey, of figs and pomegranates. My ripe, round body has given him life. I am in love with myself for my brilliance, my fecundity. He grew in the nourishing darkness of my womanspace One by one his fingers appeared, his features, his toenails. He changed from a tadpole to a boy, from a frog to a prince within my secret cauldron of transformation. He grips my thumb with his tiny fist and I know that I would kill for him, would die for him. I am life but I am not afraid of death. My genes will continue. I am immortal.

CHAPTER THREE

After my unconventional childhood I assumed I'd married into a different life – one with a steady income, a bit of stability and a permanent home but within six months after Ben's birth we moved to Nigeria for three years. A fantastic opportunity offering the enormous salary of £4,000 a year. Richard had been offered a job by Rediffusion Television to be part of a team going to Ibadan to start up the very first television station on the whole continent of Africa – WNTV – Western Nigerian Television and to gradually train Nigerian technicians and producers to take over. Richard flew out a few months before me while I packed up our belongings and our baby son, caught the boat train from Euston to Liverpool and boarded the passenger liner *ACCRA* of the Elder Dempster Line bound for West Africa. I was still only nineteen years old.

This was the crest of the wave time to be in Nigeria. 1960. On October 1st the independence movement succeeded in peacefully gaining Nigeria its independence from Britain. The beautiful new hospital had just been built. The new University of Ibadan was attracting first class professors from all over the world. Wonderful writers such as Chinua Achebe and Wole Soyinka were beginning to reach an international audience. Art historians like Uli Beier were cataloguing and preserving the wealth of traditional wood carvings and bronze sculptures. Art and music were thriving. There was a large community of Lebanese traders, loads of shops selling everything you could possibly want and a huge produce market. Richard's job was Head of the News Film Unit and he loved it, He quickly gathered a team around him who became and remained close friends for life. Most of the time they were out travelling around the country filming newsworthy stories determined, in spite of pressures to the contrary, to establish the difference between 'news' and a social diary of ministers' cocktail parties.

As a 'wife', I soon understood that nothing had changed much from colonial days. The place was full of bored ex-pat women with nothing to do. Everyone had servants. I was expected to employ a 'steward', a 'small boy', a gardener, a night watchman and a nanny. Horrified – I had no idea how to handle 'staff' – I declared I would manage without. I was promptly lectured about my responsibility to give jobs to people who needed them; to provide a livelihood for local families; as an employer to be available to intercede on their behalf in health matters or disputes … . In other words, it was really weird and selfish of me to refuse this duty. So, in the end, a compromise. Christopher came to work for us as 'steward' and cook and Elias, 'small boy' who was actually a grown man, as his assistant. They lived on the premises in the servants quarters. I was uncomfortable being a 'madam'. Even Richard's workmates who called him by his first name called me madam no matter how many times I asked them not to. Most of the other wives belonged to the Club. I don't know if it was policy but there were only European members. *'I know we're all supposed to be equal now,' complained one Shell oil-driller's wife with a gin and tonic in her hand, 'but I'm sorry. Really?!' 'I know,' said her friend. 'Every time I see a black hand come round the door I just want to slam it shut.'* They played cards and read magazines sent out from England and lay by the pool and drank.

It was impossible to get a work permit and I was going stir crazy. We had been allotted a company car and I learned to drive – taught by a Nigerian policeman. Richard and I had taken some wonderful trips driving around the country with baby Ben staying in old Government Rest Houses: Enugu, Benin, Oshogbo, Akure, Abeokuta, Ilorin, Ife, Calabar. Both of us loved the traditional wood carvings and began collecting them. Many modern church-going Nigerians seemed slightly ashamed of this 'primitive' art and its association with the old Yoruba religion. They preferred shiny new decor in their homes and were happy to sell the carvings to us.

One day in May 1961 I drove out to a little mission hospital run by Irish Catholic sisters in the nearby village of Oke-Ofa with the idea of offering my services as a volunteer. It was immediately apparent that this poor little place was overcrowded and understaffed. There were sick people lying on filthy cots outside in the sun and a queue of others waiting. 'What can I do to help?' I asked. The head sister invited me in. *'Well, come and see these twin babies that were left here a few weeks ago.'* Their mother had died in childbirth, she told me. The father and the other children in the family all saw her haemorrhage to death on the bush path while trying to get here. She wasn't expecting twins and had gone into labour prematurely. *'The father brought them in and begged us to take them then he disappeared leaving a false name and address. They weighed 3 lbs and 4 lbs. at birth and it's a miracle that they are still alive. We just haven't the time to look after them but we have had them baptised so they will go to heaven when they die.'*

And there they were; lying in a cot, tiny, miserable, naked twins – a boy and a girl, now eight weeks old and still only the weight of a normal new-born baby, seven and eight lbs; they had bottles propped up in their mouths. I picked up the little girl and she went rigid with fear and screamed. No one had ever cuddled them. Total maternal deprivation.

'Well, how about this?' I said. *'Rather than standing around rolling bandages, why don't I take these babies home with me and get them fit so that when somebody comes back to collect them they will be alive instead of dead and gone to heaven?'*

'What a good idea,' said Sister Brigid. And put them in the back of my car with a bag of old nappies. No one ever claimed them and that was fifty-nine years ago.

What sad little sprouts they were in the beginning. They both had contracted malaria, skin infections and horrible boils and sores on their bodies. Luckily I had a really good family doctor who came everyday to help me bring them back from the brink.

They couldn't manage a complete feed so I fed them every half hour with a doll's bottle. Our pet monkey, that I'd bought for ten shillings from a hunter who'd killed its mother and was walking down the road swinging the poor little creature by its tail, became insanely jealous of the babies and climbed up the curtains shrieking and peed in their cot. So Lisa, the Mona monkey, had to go as she would have been a danger so off we went to Ibadan Zoo who gave her a home.

I would fall asleep on the sofa drip feeding the babies. I was so tired I sometimes couldn't remember which one had been fed and which needed changing. They cried all the time. It was terribly unrewarding. Richard thought I was mad and went around looking bemused having gone off to work one morning thinking he had one baby and coming home that evening to find three babies. He always let me get on with whatever I wanted to do just as long as I didn't expect him to babysit. To his eternal credit he accepted the situation and always supported me. I explained that it was only temporary as their family would surely want them back soon. Gradually the twins, Taiwo and Kehinde (traditional names for Yoruba twins) named Thomas and Ruby by the hospital and Timothy Joe and Olufemi Claire by us began to grow into healthy, bonny babies and one wonderful day when they were about six months old they smiled. I had three little kids sitting up in high chairs at my twenty-first birthday party. In Yoruba society, the second born twin, Kehinde is the senior one having sent the first one, Taiwo, out into the world as a scout to see if it's an auspicious time to be born.

Our time with WNTV in Ibadan came to an end and Richard began working for the Shell Film Unit based in Port Harcourt. The twins, Tim and Femi, came with us. After a year the job moved us to Lagos where we spent another year. When it was time to return to England nobody had come to Oke-Ofa looking for the twins. They were now so much part of the family I couldn't bear to just leave them behind so we applied for permission from the loosely named Social Services, who had never taken the slightest interest until there was an opportunity to be officious, to take them out of the country and subsequently adopted them officially through the British Courts. They were 2½ years old, Ben was 3½ and I was pregnant with Matt.

But I'm skipping ahead.

Lagos was where I first became interested in the old Yoruba religion. Groups of women clad all in white would congregate on the beach drumming, singing and make offerings to the spirits. We had now been collecting Yoruba wood carvings and masks for three years and most were associated with the Orishas or deities of the Yoruba religion. Bunmi, the lovely older woman who'd joined us as a 'nanny' in Lagos was a practitioner. We became very close after she caught chicken pox from my children and became terribly ill. I nursed her back to health again with cool baths and calamine lotion and while she was recuperating I asked many questions about the Orishas and the various practices. She said I could come to a ceremony with her. Twins, in the Yoruba language are called Ibeji and there is also an Orisha who is connected with them. Many tribes in Africa have historically regarded the birth of twins as bad luck and even gone so far as to kill the babies or leave them in the forest. Not so the Yoruba to whom twins are a sign of good fortune. Statistically, more twins are born to the Yoruba than anywhere else in the world. When a mother gives birth to twins the family will often commission a *babalawo* (priest or oracle) to carve a set of small wooden Ibeji. These figures are known as *ere ibeji* (literally meaning *ere*: sacred image; *ibi*: born; *egi*: two) and should one of the babies die, the mother will carry around the statue representing the dead baby next to her body so that its live twin will not feel lonely. There is a high mortality rate amongst twins and Yoruba mothers are often faced with the death of one of the babies. The carving remains a memorial and a point of connection to the spirit of the one who died. Some of these carvings are exquisite. The mothers will care for them like a living baby. They are ritually washed and oiled and sung to and danced. They are carried everywhere wrapped in cloth on the mother's back. They may have special little clothes of cowrie shells and necklaces of beads.

The fact that Tim and Femi had been abandoned must have meant great sorrow and hardship for their birth family as Ibeji are regarded as extraordinary beings protected by Shango the deity of thunder. No one would give them up willingly. They are believed to be capable of bestowing great fortune on their families and bad luck to those who do not honour them. I only discovered many years later that Joseph Omoniyi, their father, had brought his family from another town many miles away looking for work as a market trader in Ibadan. So when Felicia, their mother, died giving birth to the twins there were no nearby aunties or grandmothers to help take care of the children. The father, with four other motherless children to worry about, did the only thing he could think of and left them at the mission hospital.

I knew none of this when they first came into my life but powerful spirits they indeed turned out to be. How lucky we were that they became part of our family. The twins grew into beautiful, gentle youngsters. Their shaky start in life seemed to have given them an extraordinary drive and determination to make the most of every opportunity they were given. Femi became a beautiful dancer and has had a glittering career. She trained at the London School of Contemporary Dance and the Alvin Ailey Dance Company in New York and went straight into roles on the West End stage and now earns a good living in television, films and theatre. Tim became a jeweller making exquisite things in gold and also an excellent sportsman. He held the Amateur Light Middleweight Boxing championship of Great Britain for two years running and boxed all over the world for England.

But always through the twins' lives ran the sadness of exile. 'Who am I?' 'Where do I come from?' 'Where do I belong?'

It was to be twenty years before Richard, on a visit to Nigeria for the BBC, discovered the whereabouts of their birth family … a happy story which I will relate in due course.

My Ibeji were my entree into the world of the Yoruba religion – called *Candomblé* in Brazil; *Santería* in Puerto Rico, Cuba and Trinidad; *Voodoo* in Haiti and cleverly disguised amongst the Catholic saints wherever the diaspora took the captured Africans in the New World. It was this connection that I hoped to make on my return visit to Brazil.

Meanwhile in Lagos, I went with Bunmi one evening at sunset to Bar Beach (notorious later on in the 70s during the time of military rule as the site of public executions), a tranquil place of soft sand and tall palms back then. Out from the surrounding shadows, dressed in white and blue with white head ties came the followers of *Yemaya* – a very powerful nature spirit, Goddess of the living ocean, Mother of All, protector of fishermen and boats travelling on the sea. She is sometimes depicted as a mermaid. I have a tie-dyed batik art work of her riding the waves on a giant crab.

I was greeted by everyone, made welcome and allowed to watch but as I was not initiated I couldn't take part. The energetic drumming by four teenage boys sent everyone into a trance. One large mama seemed to be the priestess in charge. They danced and sang on the edge of the surf summoning the spirit of Yemaya, offering her little gifts of crystals, sea shells and food (NOT fish, apparently, as she is the mother of fishes). A headless chicken in a straw basket was brought and thrown into the water with white flowers. If I wanted to follow this custom and petition the spirit, I was told, any small natural token will do. You toss it in moving water with your wish; the water should be flowing toward you if you wish to manifest energy and flowing away from you if you want to carry away problems. Some women in the group became possessed and fell to the ground hollering out loud – their eyes rolling in their heads. Others tended to them and held them until the seizure had passed.

The whole event took about an hour by which time it was dark, candles were lit and the group gradually dispersed – little lights glowing and fading in the distance. I was grateful to have been allowed to attend though not tempted to become an initiate. I felt the power of the belief and the enormous strength of this religion to have survived in spite of everything – endured being ripped from its home of origin and dispersed across half the world; how it sustained its followers and kept its essential identity through centuries of hardship and suppression. I would track some of its permutations in the coming years.

Bunmi (pronounced Boomee) was convinced that the Orisha of Ibeji had blessed and protected Femi and Tim from the moment of their inauspicious entry into this world and would continue to guide their steps throughout their lives. Whatever it was that kept my twins alive until that day when I first met them it was nothing short of a miracle. To have survived, born prematurely weighing three and four pounds with no incubator or special care, they brought with them only an extraordinarily powerful life force and an appointment with destiny.

Matt was born in Lagos in 1963 – the only baby we actually planned following a miscarriage the previous year and our daughter

Francesca in London in 1965 (conceived the night Richard returned from making his film about St Francis of Assisi.) Those five children all grew up together (five under six years old) and went to school in London. We bought a little house in Twickenham and my adventures were confined to looking after them and obtaining a London University B.Ed degree in music and philosophy at a four year part-time course. I set up my own little music school teaching piano and guitar from home after school hours and on Saturdays and also began writing articles for women's magazines. It was great training: I'd be sent to interview some well-known person: Vidal Sassoon; Cilla Black; Christian Barnard; Anita Roddick or write about a subject of interest or adventure: women in engineering; parachute jumping courses; dinghy sailing; sex therapy; marriage counselling; new young talent in the arts and so on.

My Dad, meanwhile, slowly surfaced from the bottomless pit of depression into which he had sunk after the Brazilian fiasco. While Richard and I had been away in Nigeria he descended into a state of hopelessness and lay every day on his bed with his face to the wall *'waiting to die'*, he said. Mum let rooms to the ballet students from Zu's ballet school and did her best to keep the family together until one of the children got nits and the ballet mums deserted en masse. She then got a job at Grodzinsky's a Jewish bakery in Golders Green and a stint as a barmaid in a pub. She refused to have Dad sectioned and never stopped believing that he would fully recover. Manic Depression they called it then (I think it's Bi-Polar now). Anyway, a wonderful friend from our days in Brazil, the Irish writer Frank Tuohy now living in London, never deserted him and came frequently to visit He passed a few little translation jobs Dad's way which gradually restored his confidence and when the manic phase arrived he was unstoppable.

Dad was actually the first person to uncover the story of Oscar Schindler – the German industrialist who had saved so many Jews from the concentration camps. I don't know how he came to learn about it but it was many years before the Australian Thomas Keneally wrote his Booker Prize winning book *Schindler's Ark*. Instantly energised, Dad formed The Martin Buber Society – a sort of forum for the Humanities with a magazine, *I and Thou*, as its mouthpiece.

As usual, with Dad, he went about everything the wrong way. He had headed notepaper printed with Igor Stravinsky as its honorary president (neglecting to seek his permission first). He also faced some resistance from Martin Buber's estate who also hadn't been consulted. The initial aim of the society was awarding a prize to Schindler for his humanitarian work. Dad wanted to hire the Albert Hall for this event but even he could see that filling 6,000 seats could be a challenge so he hired the Cadogan Hall instead. J B Priestley was invited to present the prize; a Jewish pianist who had survived the Holocaust was to give a recital; Dad, himself, would meet Schindler at the train station … you can see what's going to happen: I'm at the door greeting people, Priestly is waiting in the wings, the pianist has been playing for over an hour. People are beginning to fidget.

No sign of Dad or the guest of honour. Mum gets up on stage and says there must have been some sort of delay. We wait another half hour. Priestley gets up, fuming and walks off in a huff, kissing me viciously on the lips and slamming the door on the way out (WHAT!). The Hall is only sparsely filled anyway as invitations were sent out too late. Everyone disperses. I take the bottles of wine home in a taxi. Later I hear that Dad had gone to King's Cross instead of to St Pancras. He hadn't been able to find Schindler who had got fed up waiting and gone back to his hotel. Mum has to work overtime to pay off the rental for the Hall.

Next, Dad hoping to interest Dino Di Laurentis in a film idea of Schindler's life goes to Ciné Cittá in Rome where he gets the run around. *'Mr Di Laurentis regrets …'* Never gets to pitch his idea. He takes the train to Paris to revisit some of the haunts of his time there with Mum before the war and checks himself into the George V but after one night leaves without paying his bill. He is traced to another hotel and promptly arrested.

Three o' clock in the morning Richard answers the phone in our little house in Twickenham. It is the British Consul in Paris: *'Terribly sorry to disturb you, sir, there's probably been some mistake but we have your father-in-law here and he appears to be in a spot of bother.'* Richard flies to Paris to bail Dad out of the nick. Dad comes out looking a little sheepish but laughing and joking – regaling Richard with stories about his interesting night sharing a cell with a murderer (slight embroidery perhaps?).

Dad abandons the Martin Buber Society idea and comes up with another idea – a magazine to be called *The Mediterranean Review*. This is pure genius and the perfect retirement hobby for an elderly gent. Leaving aside the fact that his board of directors and honorary president are, again, luminaries who have not been consulted, Dad himself is the Editor-in-Chief; he is also the Record Reviewer and gets sent all the new releases; he is also the Literary Reviewer and receives all new publications; and best of all, he is the Travel Correspondent enabling him and Mum to go on annual Mediterranean cruises for free. They take me with them for a marvellous trip one year on a Greek ship to Dubrovnik, Corfu, Crete and Cairo. I've no idea who ever bought the magazine. I think perhaps a few universities had subscriptions. Printing costs turned out to be a bit of a stumbling block but once again, Mum managed to pay off the debts in dribs and drabs and by now they were living in a Housing Association flat near Primrose Hill and were happier than they'd ever been. No more pressure to earn a living. He could, at last, do what he was best suited for – sitting in a chair and reading books all day. The Manic Depression seemed to find some sort of equilibrium and they lived peacefully until his death at the age of seventy-one in 1977. Dad, who knows why, had requested a traditional Orthodox Jewish burial after all those years of wanting to leave that part of his life firmly in the past. And what a glum business it was. Bushey Orthodox cemetery. No flowers; no music; mumbled prayers from a rabbi who didn't know anything about him; Yehudi, our brother saying kaddish; all of us trundling his coffin on a hand cart to the graveside and shovelling in the earth. Acres of hideous headstones in black marble with the Levis in the front row. I was very out of sympathy with the whole thing.

Mum wanted only to follow him as she'd always done. She lost all interest in continuing life and just begged me to drive her to the cemetery as often as possible. She realised with horror, that she would not be permitted to be buried next to him, as was her wish, because although she had been a rabbi's wife and taken up the burden of the

Jewish people with a fierce passion and considered herself Jewish, she was not an Orthodox Jew so it became her mission to convert. It took her five years to be allowed to join that exclusive religious persuasion. (The Orthodox never proselytise. You must be born into it or go through a gruelling acceptance procedure.) Mum had to keep a kosher kitchen; learn the Hebrew prayers and take the ritual total immersion bath – known as a mikveh – for spiritual purification. She was totally focussed on the task she had set herself – 'waiting to join my Camille' – just as she had in 1941 badgering the consul in New York to find her a transatlantic passage in the middle of the Second World War. Shortly after she qualified as an Orthodox Jew she died quietly all alone while watering her house plants in the kitchen of her little flat near Primrose Hill. By her bed, in her wavery handwriting was this note:

4.45 a.m. ad infinitum
Glow without a flicker clear and beautiful blue light.
Through the night keep watch over our love that never dies.
Penetrate through my heart your clear blue light.
Telling me of our eternal flame,
Our eternal love
That will never fade
That glows more brightly
More truly
More surely
As the days slip by
And the nights.
Little blue light that shines through the night
Undying as your love for me – stronger and purer
As the days and nights of my life fade slowly away
Bringing me nearer to you with every failing breath
Of mine.
Oh give me that light to lighten my alighting
From this life
To my life agin with you
For ever more.

On the one hand I was glad for her and moved by the unwavering constancy of her conviction, but also saddened and enraged by her wilful refusal to perceive of life as worth living without my father. But she'd done as she'd always done. Packed up and followed him. At Bushey Orthodox cemetery we wheeled the little hand cart with her coffin to the grave she had reserved next to his. On her headstone it reads:

'Fidelia' (his name for her)
Ruth 1:16
(Whither Thou Goest, I will go …
Whither thou diest, I will die
And there will I be buried')

It was a triumph. She'd won.

Chapter Four

M y life now and for a few years centred around bringing up the five children and teaching piano after school and at weekends. Richard's career as a documentary film maker went from strength to strength and he worked as a senior staff producer for the BBC for the next twenty-five years, making some of the first films to highlight important social, political and environmental subjects such as the cutting down of the forests in India: 'The Axing of the Himalayas'; The relationship between the black community and the Metropolitan police: 'Equal Before the Law?'; The damaging effect of tourism on small Caribbean islands: 'The Price of Paradise'; 'The Unleashing of Evil' (1988), which examined the complicity of Western democracies in the use of government-instigated torture around the world; The closing of the British shipyards: 'The Fight for Clydeside'; films about ecology and population pressures and desert encroachment, the Bhopal gas disaster; 'Nigeria: A Squandering of Riches': about the misuse of the oil wealth and many more.

I often joined him at the end of a location and was thus able to travel to Syria, Bali, America, Nepal, Kashmir, the Arctic Circle … where I began to try my wings as a writer and journalist. Freelance jobs included articles for the *Guardian*, *The Illustrated London News*, *Traveller Magazine*, *Woman*, *She*, *Annabel*, *19* and *Choice*. Always wanting to explore a subject in more depth I wrote a proposal for a book about healing : 'I Fly Out With Bright Feathers – The Quest of a Novice Healer'. For which I would travel around the world spending time with traditional healers in different cultural contexts – shamans, medicine people, witch doctors – and asking; 'In places where Western allopathic medicine is not available or not trusted, what is the healer offering? What is the patient hoping to get out of the encounter? Can anyone be a healer? Can I be a healer?

There are now hundreds of books about healing but this was one of the first to be published by a mainstream publisher. It was 1989, my children were old enough to leave and Richard was very supportive. My agent got me a publishing contract and small royalty advance with William Collins and with that I bought a round-the-world-ticket and set off on my own for three months.

With the explosion of tourism today 'round-the-world' means nothing – Gigantic cruise ships like floating apartment blocks with 3000 passengers on board crowd the ports of every city but thirty years ago it was more of a big deal. I had a few potential contacts but mostly it was to be an unfolding story of following up chance encounters – the story of my own idiosyncratic journey of discovery – not an academic thesis or encyclopaedia of techniques but a personal search for an understanding of the healing phenomenon. There were many highlights but one of the best was returning to the land of my birth – Australia.

I had never before felt any particular desire to go to Australia but there was always the intriguing mystery of why a Polish Jew and his Irish-Scottish wife, unable to have children for eight years, should have sailed half way round the world in wartime to give birth to their first baby under the Southern Cross and then gone back again to the air raids in London. Having spent only the first few months of my life there, I remembered nothing of my antipodean infancy, except that I've had an unaccountable feeling of well-being whenever I've chanced to be lying on my back looking up at a blue sky through eucalyptus leaves – an imprint of some primal pram memories?

An astrologer friend once told me that he believes each soul deliberately chooses its incarnation, complete with the parents it will have and the place where it will incarnate which fits in rather well with the delightful Aboriginal version of the gooseberry bush. The story goes that little spirit children wait around in the bushes until they see a woman who they think will make a good mother, then they jump aboard and begin life as a human being.

49

The mother I picked turned out to be a wise choice but why Australia? Working on the book 'I Fly Out With Bright Feathers' awakened in me a powerful gravitational pull to know my native soil and explore my relationship to that ancient land and its indigenous inhabitants – the Australian Aborigines – the oldest surviving Stone Age people in the world – a people intimately attuned to their environment. How did they practise their healing and does the tradition still continue today?

For 40,000 years they have been wandering across this vast, isolated three-million-square-mile landmass in the Southern Hemisphere. Their lack of communication with the outside world while they lived in an arid and inhospitable terrain, gave rise to a remarkably successful and harmonious way of life with a rich mythology and elaborate ceremonial customs. They have a beautiful concept which they call The Dreamtime, to explain the mysteries of creation. Their stories tell of giant mythical beings who rose out of the featureless plain or came across the water from the direction of the sunrise and created the landscape and laws. The places where they walked and rested became rocks, waterholes, sacred sites to be tended in perpetuity by their descendants. And so it continued, unchanged and unchanging, world without end, until the arrival of the first European settlers only eight generations ago set in motion the forces which have all but destroyed the first Australians. The Aboriginal population today is half what it was then.

I wanted to try, before it was too late, to listen to a medicine person or sorcerer whose ear is still tuned to the voices of the ancestral dreamtime beings who passed down their legacy of wisdom and knowledge to those who tread in their footsteps today. Would it be possible? Where would I start?

So, away into the night sky for a two-day flight. We crossed the International Date Line on the way, and the whole of October 17th disappeared into nowhere. Maybe I can ask for it back at the end of my life. I mused about the capricious nature of time; if we can't make sense of it as it exists on this little planet of ours, how are we supposed to come to grips with the timelessness of eternity? It's the oddest sensation to travel through that time warp, and arrive in a place beyond one's wildest imaginings. A land with grey trees, birds that laugh, animals that bounce and furry ducks.

I came to Victoria because a cousin lives there and it seemed as good a place as any to start. I asked my cousin about the Aborigines. First surprise: I learned that he, like most other white Australians, has no contact with them at all. He could show me lots of interesting books about their art and culture but he didn't actually know any and thought they lived mainly in Arnhem Land up in the north near Darwin rather a long way from Melbourne (the distance from southern Turkey to northern Norway, in fact). I borrowed a car and went into the city. Maybe there is no hope for the continued existence of these ancient people. Everyone kept telling me that they're not making it, their ways cannot survive the 'fatal impact'; but surely there must be something they have stayed so long to pass on to us, if we can grasp it. The baton in the human relay race? But everywhere I asked, nobody could tell me anything about them: 'Try the Aboriginal Handicraft Shop, the museum, the Aboriginal Study Centre.' All run by whites.

Once in the city, I went to the Aboriginal Artifacts Gallery – a dull little shop on the ninth floor of an office building and staffed by little old ladies with tight perms. They sell a few tourist boomerangs, hand-made string dilly bags at exorbitant prices and koala printed drying up cloths. They didn't know any Aborigines. I walked around Melbourne and felt haunted by the *absence* of those first-born heirs to the soil. Do their spirits watch us brash, loud usurpers who have built car parks on their sacred sites? At the museum the Aboriginal exhibit was shoved in the corner of a poorly lit room – a few dusty, tatty artefacts badly displayed – to make room for the tinselly razzamatazz of 'One Hundred and Fifty Years of the State of Victoria'; all popcorn, corsets and stagecoaches. It gave the uncomfortable general impression that Australia only really began then. Nothing of the life, customs and astonishing miracle of the first Australians who had been surviving here for so long, intimately connected to the land and the web of life. Certainly one doesn't want to be overly romantic about the nobility of their Stone Age lifestyle but there must be lessons to learn from such a direct connection to the origins of Man on this planet; a connection and a memory as yet not totally lost by the overlays and refinements of civilisation. In their dreaming may they not still have the pulse beat of the universe in their blood? What knowledge have they brought with them from beyond the rising sun and what do they understand of the proper balance between spirit, mind and body?

At a dinner party one evening, I raised some of these points. A guest at the table brayed loudly, 'It's a primitive, backward culture and I agree with an early explorer who described the Aborigines as the miserablest people in the world who hardly differ from brutes. Have you seen them lying around drunk in the gutters? Whites who claim to have an affinity with them are pretentious, self-seeking show-offs. It's impossible to understand them or presume to speak up for them. Stone Age chic,' he added dismissively.

Well I'd have to find out for myself. Then, after a good two weeks of disheartening, frustrating dead ends someone mentioned a chap in Adelaide called Djangawu, a white man who says he is an Aborigine and who has given workshops in Aboriginal healing techniques. Nothing to lose, I called him up. 'Come and stay with us,' he said. So, ten hours on the bus rolling along the Western Highway to Adelaide. A further train ride out to their suburb and I turned up on their doorstep where he and his partner Omega welcomed me warmly. Djangawu is a red-headed, thin white man with a beard and long curls who says he is an Aborigine. What then, is an Aborigine? I asked. Do you have to be born one? Can you be adopted? Or adopt yourself? Is it a state of mind? Is this what that guy meant by 'stone age chic?' He sat on his haunches and spoke about 'attunement' and a feeling of 'oneness' for the land and the dreaming. It was hard to get a straight answer. Omega added: 'If ever you ask an Aborigine a question you might have to wait a long time for an answer – days even. They are afraid of giving away their power. Theirs is a history of having been lured into white man's settlements and missions with promises and threats only to find themselves utterly unmanned, victims of diseases for which they have no immunity, and sickened by 'white man's tucker' that doesn't suit their digestive systems.'

Separated from their land with its myriad symbolism and sacred ancient meanings, they have been cut off from the source of their power – the Dreaming. Fences and highways sever their great ancestral pathways and the delicate balance of their fragile interaction with the environment is ruined. So, yes, they are wary of being conned and guard jealously any secrets which are still known. But I didn't know what to make of Djangawu. He sat on his haunches, totally naked with a faraway look in his eyes, his wild curls tangled about his head. He spoke in riddles and gave cryptic answers. He told me that he and I are connected and have shared many lifetimes before. He said we come from beyond the solar system which makes us both Aborigines because we still remember our connection to the 'source' as they do. Being born in Australia has given us both an instinctive understanding and connection to the great red centre of this ancient land and we have travelled a long way through space and time to meet once again in Australia on our way to whatever comes next.

Perhaps this was as far as I was going to get. It was all a bit hard to grasp. Djangawu is a very strange person – almost alien – an impression he likes to foster. He says he has travelled to other planets. I'll never know how much of his legend about himself is imagination but I don't think it really matters. He is a gentle person to have in the world and whether he has arrived at his present state of mind by some traumatic event, or by epilepsy, mental illness or inter-galactic travel, where he is now is what counts. He has extensive knowledge of native plants, nutrition and medicinal herbs and, by his very silences, he implied some useful things: that there really is no way of rendering Aboriginal concepts into a language-bound frame of reference. Their philosophy of life has been very inadequately translated into European terms. We use words and rely on them to convey meanings so much that we've almost forgotten some older methods of communication: telepathy, empathy, intuition, which are second nature to many primary peoples. Djangawu's very enigmatic qualities turned out to be an essential staging post for me on my journey to the Aborigines. He made me listen to silences; slow down; question assumptions; open myself to unfamiliar concepts. Without meeting him and Omega, I don't think I would have been so well prepared. Lovely, peaceful people they have started a little Centre for Human Awareness where they are trying to put their principles into practice and devoting their energies to bridging a tragic gulf. They understand what being Australian really means – why Australia is unique and not just England in a sunny place. In order to live here in harmony people must find the wholeness and oneness that the Aborigine had before the white invader came.

Omega could see that I was finding Djangawu's cryptic utterings somewhat frustrating so she took matters into her own hands and phoned an old friend, David, a teacher in Arnhem Land. Yes, he knew a couple of Aboriginal health workers in the local hospital who were trying to introduce traditional healing into the settlements. Yes, I could stay with him if I needed to and he'd point me in the right direction. At last!

The catch, of course, was the ferocious cost of long-distance travel. Darwin was four thousand miles away but I knew it would be stupid to have come all this way and not follow it through. I bought a ticket on my credit card and built in a four day stop-over in Alice Springs on my Kangaroo Air Pass so that I could climb Ayers Rock and a see something of the Outback. I flew up to Alice Springs across a Martian landscape of iron-red desert. If you look at a map of Australia it is covered with lakes and rivers and you might well wonder why everyone keeps telling you the place is so dry. In fact the names like Lake Disappointment and Lake Hope are the clue to the devastating realisation that except for five minutes a year when it rains, the lakes are salt and the riverbed totally dry.

From the air the landscape bears an uncanny resemblance to Aboriginal art – concentric ripples in red ochre, primal patterns of land and life. I used to regard their paintings as merely primitive squiggles and spots – nothing more than abstract patterns – until it was pointed out to me that they are maps, explicit, sophisticated, stylised descriptions of identifiable locations and myths, bird's-eye views showing the great dreaming tracks of their ancestors. By this method the young would be instructed in the topography of the landscape as well as in the creation stories and the laws and customs of the people. The drawings were made in the sand with a stick or on the walls of caves – constantly renewed and refreshed – enabling a person to walk across vast tracts of empty desert where he'd never set foot before. His mental maps would tell him where the rainbow serpent had created the water-holes, what the night-sky looked like, where the kangaroo women sat by their campfire. When first taken up in an aircraft to help government surveyors plot the sacred sites of the Northern Territories, tribesmen could easily transcribe their ground drawings and point out the Dreaming sequences.

Ayers Rock – Uluru, the Aborigines call it, the world's largest single stone – was as memorable as I hoped, beginning with a three-hundred-mile drive through the Simpson and Gibson deserts. A surprising amount of vegetation grows here: desert oaks, mulgas and red gum trees, spinifex grass and even some greenery at that time as it had rained about three weeks before, but it was all very dusty and dry. The Finke River which we crossed is the oldest river bed in the world – it has never changed its course, probably because there's never any water in it. The oldest fossils have been found here (Australia is full of superlatives) and the sand goes down ninety-six feet before you hit rock, so it was costly to build the unimpressive little bridge that spans it.

My travelling companion, driver and guide was a very knowledgeable old bushman who'd spent his whole life in the Outback working on cattle stations. Cattle stations out here are huge properties – one hundred square miles as a small one, and forty to fifty thousand square miles not unusual – almost the size of the whole of Great Britain or the state of Texas. Old Bill had a great love and respect for the canny Aborigines of the central desert area and had been rescued more than once when lost. They never got lost, he said, and lived in perfect accord with this hostile terrain. They survived by integration rather than domination. And there seems to be a moral here for us and our lack of harmony with the environment. Our ruthless drive to control, to conquer, to subjugate, has been a prominent characteristic of European civilisation and may even finish us off once and for all. Not only the many species of wildlife heading for extinction already; not only human beings but the planet itself is threatened with annihilation and is screaming out at us to change in time.

The Aborigines were once described by Charles Pearcy Mountford, a white man who lived with the desert nomads for many years, as a courteous, happy, considerate people. They had no organised warfare, no worship or pacification of a supreme being. Maintenance of the eternal life-giving forces of the land was assured and achieved by performing specific ceremonies that caused the animals and plants to increase and the rain to fall.

'Through the ages,' he wrote, 'they have evolved a code of laws so well-balanced to their mode of living, so equitable to one another, that in general they live in peace with each other and with their environment.'

Old Bill kept me entertained on the trip with stories of how the Aborigines taught him the way to live off kangaroo, lizard and witchetty grubs ('swallow them headfirst so they can't climb back up,' he advised me for future reference.), the way they systematically fired the bush to clear the undergrowth, flush out the animals and germinate the seeds that only burst asunder in intense heat, the way they always know how to find water.

A highly intricate system of sexual taboos used to ensure that the population was kept to a manageable size for the food resources – well thought out, simple and effective. To contrast this with the town Aborigines of today breaks your heart. Dispossessed and demoralised, they look old and broken-down before their time. Syphilis is rife and twelve-year-olds get pregnant as soon as they can with no proper family structure to care for their babies. Sleeping with an Aborigine woman is insultingly referred to as 'rooting a djinn'. There are many half-caste children but few mixed marriages.

Since Uluru has been handed back to the Aborigines, all the brash, disrespectful, jerry-built motels that used to cluster around the base of this most sacred of sites have been abolished and all visitors have to stay at Yulara, an unobtrusive tourist village where there are varying standards of accommodation from campsite to luxury Sheraton. I stayed at the modest Ayers Rock Lodge.

Everyone goes to the sunset viewing point for the famous show as Uluru turns blood red in the glow of the dying day. This is a hilarious spectacle as over two hundred people are ranged along the sandhill vantage point with their coaches waiting, each one getting a once-in-a-lifetime picture of the great wild wilderness, the loneliest place on earth – rock, sky and rugged desert. If they'd point their cameras the other way they would get a truer picture – a mob of amateur photographers all tripping over each other's tripods to get the best shot.

Human antics notwithstanding, it is an awesome sight, magnificent enough to withstand any indignities. You can't believe the mighty size of the thing until you see it for yourself. The worlds largest monolith – one single stone three hundred and forty-eight metres high, five and a half miles round the base and they reckon nine-tenths of it is still underground; all we can see is the tip. The colour becomes more intense, like rare roast beef, like the cut-out heart of the earth itself and then, suddenly, its all over – just a huge brown rock sitting there at twilight.

I was lucky enough to be able to climb it (it has subsequently been declared off limits to tourists) – setting off just before dawn the next day. I was very moved by a sense of belonging; of coming home to the great red centre of the land of my birth. Reaffirming the choice my spirit made to incarnate on this strange continent.

If Uluru was revitalising, Alice Springs was depressing. Baked and dusty, it's still a miracle that it's a town at all, two thousand miles from anywhere in the middle of the hottest part of the driest continent in the world. The town is deservedly proud of its local history – the first telegraph station and other such triumphs of the pioneering spirit. But what they don't tell you in the guide books is how many derelict aborigines are lying drunken in the streets. Rudely awakened from the dreaming, there is nothing here for them – no need for their skills. Their inherent virtues of patience and endurance are redundant in time-keeping town life. They shamble like lost woolly mammoths from another age. People feel contempt for them and laugh at them, stripped of their power and glory. And they do look wretched, in filthy clothes with matted hair and hordes of mangy dogs and snotty children. This was my first contact with any aborigines and it was very shocking to see them, these once-proud nomads of the desert, in such a piteous condition.

I was glad to fly away to Darwin and take a connecting flight to Nhulunbuy, a mining community in the north-east corner of Arnhem

Land. My little plane made one brief stop at the manganese mining town of Groote Eylandt in the Gulf of Carpentaria where lots of 'real men' with workboots and tattoos stood around the airstrip looking predatory at the rare sight of a woman on her own.

CHAPTER FIVE

D avid kindly met me at Gove airport and put me up for the night. First thing in the morning I went over to the hospital to look for Aggie, one of the community health workers. David told me I would find her sitting with a large group of women and children who were camped nearby. The authorities don't really approve but they tolerate these bands of relatives who keep a constant vigil. They stopped talking and stared at me. Aggie, forewarned of my arrival, detached herself from the group and came forward.

After all this time in Australia this was the first Aboriginal person I had spoken to. David first met her because she was one of a group of kids deemed extra bright who were sent to a government boarding school where he taught ten years ago. Now married with two children of her own, she works in an office in Nhulunbuy, lives in the town and is attempting the difficult feat of straddling two cultures.

She was a little reserved to begin with but relaxed after a while as I tried to get across my reason for coming here – not to pry, not to study, not to preach, but just to learn about traditional healing methods and share old wives' tales. Aggie suggested I sit down under a hibiscus bush for a while and she would call her auntie, a traditional midwife, over. A ragged old woman with broken teeth and wild hair came across with a baby draped round her neck. Gradually others drifted over until we were about fifteen sitting under the bush. The women had been out hunting that morning and brought some bush food for the old lady's daughter who is a patient at the hospital and the reason for their vigil. Turtle meat, turtle eggs, yams and mangoes. Yesterday they caught a stingray and sometimes, with luck, they harpoon a crocodile. 'We always know which are the good foods for our people to eat,' said auntie. 'Only when we eat *balanda* (white man's) food we get sick.'

Everyone tucked in, sitting under the hospital bush. It was all very jolly and companionable and rather tastier than the regulation semolina I remember from my own periods of hospitalisation. I showed my kids' photos around and motherhood provided a wonderful starting point for getting on friendly terms. We sat under the trees all day, our words spinning a web from birth to death – from how to stimulate breast milk production and which foods a nursing mother should eat, to which songs to sing to a dying person. As they talked the older women passed a pipe of tobacco around and the younger ones practically chain-smoked cigarettes.

When Aggie's children came out of school in the afternoon they joined us. Her husband, Sam, a police worker, stopped by the hospital to pick us all up in their beat-up old truck and we drove to Yirrkala, the mission settlement. The whole of Arnhem Land is actually an Aboriginal reserve. The first great land rights case was fought and won here and now no one is supposed to enter without a permit. I was taking a chance coming without one but I thought it would speed things up to apply in person if necessary. Most of the Aborigines in this area live in or around Yirrkala Mission where there is a church, a school, a clinic and a store established by Christian missionaries fifty years ago. They have been spared the worst excesses of the European invasion because nobody took much of an interest in north-east Arnhem Land until recently when the bauxite was discovered. But like Aborigines all over Australia, they have suffered profound upheavals in their way of life as a result of settling at the mission. Their health is affected by crowding, poor sanitation, impoverished diet, alcoholism and smoking (I've never seen anyone smoke as much as Aboriginal women.)

On the way I asked Sam why alcoholism was so prevalent. 'Because people feel whitefella control their lives,' he said, and added that this morning he had picked up two boys suffering from brain damage as a result of sniffing petrol. Aggie said that on the outstations where people have gone back to live on the land, you don't find those addictions. Young kids are sent out to hunt their own food and help build shelters for old people. Their dignity, worth and sense of responsibility are slowly restored.

She also told me she vividly remembered the first time it occurred to her that white people can sometimes be wrong. She had an argument at the hospital with a white nurse who said it was disgusting and unhygienic for the grandmother to be 'slobbering all over the baby'. The usual reaction, said Aggie, is for Aborigines to devalue their own knowing – immediately to presume they are the ones who have got it wrong. 'But I know baby needs grandmother's love. It's not always our thinking that's upside down, sometimes Europeans upside down.'

At last it seems the tide may be turning. A few people are beginning to speak up for traditional indigenous ways in an attempt to reverse the lamentable downward spiral of Aboriginal health. There also appears to be a mass exodus from the towns back to the outstations and homelands as more and more people feel the desire to re-establish the old harmony. 'Our land and our good health go together,' said Aggie. 'Otherwise our people get sick.'

She charged off into the bush came back with three samples that she uses all the time: a bark which is scraped into water, boiled and used for sores and open ulcers; leaves which are used to rub on sore muscles; a type of eucalyptus leaf and bark used to make an infusion to drink for back pains. Everybody uses bush medicine, she said. Women make it for their families and pass on the secrets from mother to daughter. You wouldn't consult a medicine man for this kind of thing – they deal with more serious matters such as sorcery and divination.

The self-governing local Aboriginal council has imposed a strict liquor ban in Yirrkala. Its a serious offence even to drive through the neighbourhood with alcohol in your car. The people asked for this restriction themselves as they appear to have such a low tolerance to alcohol's toxicity. Two beers, and their metabolism, which is so exquisitely tuned to the harshness of the environment, just breaks down.

One constantly hears the opinion expressed by local white residents from the mining community that 'Abos' have no concept of doing a day's work, they don't take care of material things, they make no provision for the future, they have no idea of time. There may be some truth in that, but it does seem ironic that the average Aussie miner or stockman, for example, works hard all his life at a backbreaking dirty job in order to buy himself a little air-conditioned suburban box, while his idea of the perfect holiday would be to go hunting or fishing and living rough, cooking over a campfire and sleeping under the stars without any of the frustrations or conflicts of the modern world – exactly what the nomadic Aboriginal bush life has always been!

Next morning Aggie arrived with the news that in order to visit Yirrkala I am expected to have a permit. I was afraid this might happen. No stray Europeans can come into Aboriginal territory without written permission, which can take up to four weeks if it's granted at all – not a foregone conclusion by any means. Of course its a good rule as it keeps out unwelcome intruders and stops tourists coming to gawp but I hoped having an invitation from David would enable me to slip through he net. Aggie called the president of the Aboriginal council that decided these things and he agreed to see me so we piled into her rusty heap and bounced off down the dirt road to Yirrkala again.

About halfway there we ran out of petrol and had to sit by the roadside until someone came along who would take our jerrycan into town and leave it at the petrol station, then wait another hour until someone brought it back and we could proceed. David had warned me that nothing here goes according to plan. At least I was learning to be patient and philosophical. While we sat under a bush brushing the stinging ants away, it was another good opportunity to talk. There were two people Aggie wanted me to meet, she said. Her uncle, an old medicine man who had pushed off to an outstation – nobody was quite sure where and Liyapidini a much respected elderly woman in charge of the Women's Resource Centre in Yirrkala.

We were eventually rescued by a mechanic with our jerry can and carried on our way to the council president's office. I launched myself into an impassioned declaration of my sincere purpose of furthering understanding of traditional healing practices and he gave me the benefit of the doubt, granting me permission to stay. He'd actually seen me in town yesterday sitting under the trees outside the hospital.

Liyapidini Marika, the old lady Aggie had mentioned, was there in her Women's Resource Centre today – a little concrete and corrugated-iron building with signs on the wall saying 'Grog is Tearing our Families Apart' and 'Boozers are Losers'. The little place has a sewing machine, a cooker and a video player. A few women and children were lying on the dirty floor watching *The Life of Jesus*.

Liyapidini is a tiny, dignified woman and everyone seems to come to her. She is besieged all day long. She has worked twenty years at her job – giving practical advice and teaching hygiene and nutrition. Two years earlier she had received the Order of Australia in recognition of her services. She is also a devout Christian and a lay preacher. She believes strongly that she was called to do this work and asked me, rather accusingly, if I had received Christ in my heart. I started to explain, in a long winded way, about the kind of healing I was especially interested in and she grabbed my arm. 'You mean spiritual healing? she said solemnly. 'I do this work also.' I carried on stating that I understood the Christian willingness to be of service, the surrender and dedication, to be the very same thing I was trying to do but that I was not actually a Christian. The search for a sacred healing space; communion with the source of life; longing for oneness – to me it was very exciting to discover that all over the world people had the same basic goals and tried to make sense of the mysterious and the occult in so many varied ways according to different cultural traditions …

Perhaps I should have just said 'Yes'. She cooled off me a bit after that but I was just trying to be honest.

Liyapidini then asked me if I would like to go with her and another of the Aboriginal church elders to a Pentecostal prayer meeting. I didn't know what to expect and was curious so I went gladly. But it was a most sinister and bizarre event and gave me an insight into the way some missionaries operate. We gathered on the lawn of the missionary's house overlooking the beautiful tropical paradise beach and sat around in a circle. Five missionaries, the two Aboriginal ladies and me. They prayed and sang evangelical style, with talking in tongues and lots of fervent 'Thank you Jesus. Bless you Jesus', hands uplifted, faces ecstatic.

Then one of the missionaries started working herself to fever pitch. "We ask you, blessed Jesus, to set these people FREE from the darkness, FREE from the superstitious cultural traditions that bind them. FREE from the work of the devil. FREE from the ignorance of their religious beliefs and FREE to submit themselves to YOUR DOMINATION, Lord'. Everyone was off in a sort of trance.

When the fervour had calmed down a bit I introduced myself as a learner healer writing a book about healing and curious to discover and understand things of value in traditional Aboriginal methods. The five missionaries smiled like a row of piranha fish. 'Jesus is the only healer,' they said. I replied that I certainly believed the spiritual element was an essential part of any holistic health philosophy. 'The only spirit is the Holy Spirit,' they chorused, still smiling. Not much chance of a dialogue there. Liyapidini and her friend just stood mutely by. As we walked away I said to them indignantly, 'Do you really believe that you have to reject your own culture in order to be a good Christian?' They just shrugged. 'It makes those ladies happy.'

Aggie was waiting under a tree to drive me back to town. I said I was really upset that two venerable grandmothers had to sit there and be told they were benighted, backward and ignorant. I thought it was obscene and inappropriate; insensitive and culturally aggressive. She just shrugged as well. Later I was again quite shocked to see how differently Aggie herself behaves when she is being bossed around in her office – patronised and told to run errands – from when she's with her family and friends; in the one role dumb and subservient, in the other confident and animated. As Isak Dinesen wrote in *Out of Africa*: 'It is more than their land you take away from people, whose native land you take. It is their past as well, their roots and their identity. It brings about the degradation and demoralisation of the human spirit.'

The pace of life crawled along. I learned that there's a fairly large gap between the theoretical plans that get made and the mind-blowing inertia and non-happenings of everyday life here. Aggie promised to pick me up next morning and take me hunting for crabs and oysters but she never showed up. I had turned down a fishing trip with David and some of his friends in favour of a genuine aboriginal experience and sat at his house all day feeling cross and miserable. When the phone rang and I heard her voice, I asked what had happened. 'Argument,' she croaked in a harsh whisper – no other explanation, no apology. She said she'd come the next day after breakfast instead but by midday she still hadn't come.

My time was beginning to run out and no matter how hard I tried to be philosophical and laid back, I was finding it terribly frustrating to be so dependent, but only through Aggie did I have any entree into the society. I liked Aggie – she is a warm, affectionate woman – and I think she liked me but there is a considerable dichotomy – almost a schizophrenic split between how she talks about her life, the aspirations and ideals she has for herself and her children, and the rather sordid reality of her violent domestic home life, inadequate education, inability to think in a straight line, emotional volatility. I never saw Aggie again but I heard later that her husband beat her up after an argument about another woman and she was too embarrassed to tell me. When I tried to seek her out, I know she was at home but she wouldn't answer the door.

Feeling disappointed and useless, I walked off up the beach and stopped to talk to some of the women who camp out under the trees. They were cooking hermit crabs and making carved didgeridoos and shell necklaces to sell at the craft centre. They beckoned me over. One was the mother of a baby who'd wandered too close to the fire. The clinic had bandaged his raw feet but they were already filthy and covered in flies. They have a hard life, earning just enough from selling their craft work to provide for themselves and the young children at the camp. Further up the beach is the drunkards' camp and young men from there come and take the women's money to buy illicit alcohol which is still available in spite of the ban.

They talk about the old days when things were good. 'Yo! Too very much sick when people sad,' said one old lady shaking her head. Utopia was yesterday and tomorrow.

I wished I could go to an outstation and see for myself. Also although talking to the women was interesting and valuable, I really wanted to be able to contact Aggie's uncle, the old *Marrnggitj* (the

Yolngu or Aboriginal word for a native healer). I kept hearing stories about him but no one has been able to tell me where he was, or maybe they just didn't want to. It was quite difficult to find anything out as the concept of objective facts doesn't really exist here. What you are allowed to know depends strictly on who you are and who is telling you.

To ensure that I didn't waste too much of my remaining time, I thought the best course of action was to appeal directly to the council president who had granted my original permit and throw myself on his good will. I hitched a lift into Yirrkala and sat on the steps of his office waiting for it to open.

Suddenly, like a vision, a beautiful old man appeared, an Aborigine version of my father, with a long white beard and a wise, kindly face. He joined me on the steps and asked me what I was doing there so I poured my heart out to him. He listened and then sat there for a while in silence smoking his pipe. 'The Marrnggitj lives on Bremmer Island,' he said finally. 'About an hour's journey from here by speedboat.' My heart quickened and then sank. Like a mirage, the nearer I got the faster my goal seemed to recede just out of reach.

Then the old man introduced himself – Wandjuk Marika, OBE, tribal elder and artist of some repute, decorated at Buckingham Palace by the Queen for services to aboriginal culture. By a felicitous coincidence it just so happened that Bremmer Island was also his own native homeland and he was going out to visit his sisters there that very day. Everything began to come together like the interweaving voices of a fugue. He suggested we call them up on the short-wave radio to see what was happening. They said they were already expecting me and were wondering when I would make contact!

I just had time to buy some fruit and within an hour I found myself in a little outboard with nothing but the clothes I stood up in, flying with tremendous speed over the waves with a boatful of Aboriginal men I had never met before. We sped past the sacred mountain, Mt Saunders, past the rock that sticks up out of the sea to mark forever the place where an ancestor was speared in the Dreamtime, and past the last point of mainland Australia. I dismissed from my mind a passing thought of the possibility of capsizing in those shark-and-crocodile-infested waters surround by a plague of deadly box-jellyfish, and instead allowed myself to enjoy the thrill of adventure and to savour the excitement of doing exactly what I had come all this way to do.

We arrived at Bremmer Island without incident and pulled the boat up on the shore. Right there on the beach was the family camp – a couple of awnings stretched between the trees, a little campfire and three or four women, one old man and a few children lying about on mattresses. I somehow thought an outstation would be a sizeable settlement but apparently most of them are just family camps. Wandjuk's three sisters, Laklak, Dhuwarrwarr, and Banyygul go back and forth between the island and their beach camp on the mainland, living where the fancy takes them.

Laklak welcomed me and we settled under the trees to talk. The old Marrnggitj, whose name is Barrparr, was away attending a council of elders but would return later, she told me. They were reluctant to speak on his behalf, preferring for me to put my questions directly to him, but they did say that for about the last two years he had lost his magic due to the effects of alcohol and the reason they kept him over on the island now was to try and take care of him, remove him from temptation and hope that his powers would be restored to him in due course.

They boiled me up a billycan of tea and we dozed the hot, humid afternoon away in the shade. When evening came they took me for a walk to see the sacred waterhole that miraculously seeps up from underground in the middle of this small island, providing fresh water clean and sweet, right through the dry season. It was created by a snake, they said, the rainbow serpent, in the Dreamtime and has made this the home of their fathers' fathers' fathers since the beginning of time. I dipped my bucket and drank from their enchanted fountain of life. Their ancestral family lands include the area of coast from Yirrkala to Nhulunbuy, Bremmer Island and Yelangbara on the Gulf of Carpentaria.

Laklak used to be a health worker herself – a job from which she'd only recently had to retire due to 'pressure' from living in the mission settlement. Everyone talks about this unnatural stress. She worked mainly in mother and baby clinics, giving first aid, teaching community hygiene and nutrition. The most common problem in the town, not surprisingly, is diarrhoea. The standard of hygiene is appalling, with litter everywhere and scabby dogs that eat excrement. (David told me he once saw two starving dogs growling and snapping around a poor little kid's backside trying to eat the stuff as fast as it came out.) But since moving out to Bremmer Island, the children have been much healthier.

Laklak, like most of the women, makes all her own herbal medicines and only consults the doctor when all else fails. She, herself, had a bad back injury a few years ago and her elder sister Banyygul successfully treated it with one of the steaming treatments which seem to figure quite prominently in traditional remedies. One of the children here has a spectacularly runny nose and scabies sores on his feet. They treat the sores by collecting green ants, crushing and burning them and applying the paste to the skin. It stings, apparently, but heals effectively.

Just before sunset the boat carrying Barrparr, the old medicine man, arrived. He is a fine-looking old fellow and came over to shake my hand. In the fading twilight we sat around in a circle in the sand and I introduced myself as an apprentice healer seeking to learn what I could from traditional aboriginal ways. He asked me what kind of healing I did and if I had magic powers. I said I felt I could help people by laying my hands on them and becoming a channel for spiritual power and that some things made that power stronger: dream images in my mind; sometimes crystals, colours, sounds … . He nodded and lit his pipe.

His method was to use thoughts and visions, he said, to tell what was wrong, and to put his hands on the ailing part – sometimes massaging the sick person, sometimes sucking out an offending object. Perhaps he would use some special spells or one of a variety of magic stones, quartz crystals or pearl shells that he kept in a little bag, and pretty soon the person would begin to recover. He was very interested in my large Mexican amethyst ring. I told him that some people believe that purple is the colour of healing and transformation and that the amethyst crystal helps to attract and distil that colour from the rainbow to strengthen the healing energy flowing through my hands. He wanted to try it on so I placed it on his little finger. He closed his eyes and jammed his other fist in his armpit, then felt up and down the veins of his arm. The arm began to vibrate dramatically. Finally he pronounced that it was, indeed, a magic ring.

I asked him if he would tell me how he first got his power. There was silence in the camp and even the youngest children moved in closer to listen. Everybody loves a good story. I wrote it down word for word by the light of a torch. It went on for nearly two hours, a very involved story of meeting a spirit in a lonely place while out hunting, being very frightened, tussling back and forth in a life-and-death struggle while trying to escape and finally surrendering himself (dying to the old life?), being borne aloft and transported across the water on the spirit's back, acknowledging that he now had the spirit's power within him.

Suddenly, there was a lot of excited talking amongst the gathering in their own language and Barrparr informed me that while we were sitting there, the spirit came among us and warned him that it was unwise to speak of these things. They could all hear the spirit voice – only my ears and eyes were closed because I was a stranger. Everyone was telling me politely not to ask any more questions as it might threaten his power – some things are better not revealed. Only during lengthy secret initiation ceremonies is this sacred knowledge passed on. And quite right too.

I promised to respect and honour his confidence and I was touched to see how tenderly the family protected him, a poor old washed up medicine man, both from the indignities of being misrepresented by alien snoopers and from destroying himself with alcohol. We sat in the firelight, passing round a half coconut shell of kava – a potent beverage – and some of the men started to play their didgeridoos. The didgeridoo is a huge, deep-toned, long tube – made from bamboo or a eucalyptus branch hollowed out by termites – into which they blow. This is a most haunting, spine-tingling sound that seems to vibrate up through the earth, enter the soles of your feet and shiver your timbers. It speaks of ancient connections to the land when our lives were not separate from the life of the natural world. With skilful circular breathing the sound is a continuous zum-zumming drone and can imitate the cries of birds and animals. Then the women took up an ethereal high-pitched chant and clapped sticks rhythmically together. It was magical and *familiar*. It must be among the earliest instruments known to man and sounds rather like the shofar or ram's horn that brought down the walls of Jericho. How can I, a white woman born in Sydney, *know* this sound and know that it exists somewhere in the rivers of my bloodstream. I can float in it. I was transported. I read somewhere that whatever landscape a child is exposed to early on will remain a filmy gauze through which she will see and hear the world forever after.

Meanwhile Laklak kindly prepared a mattress and sheet for me under the stars and one by one people drifted away to their sleeping places. There is a convention that if any lady wishes to relieve herself in the night she whispers the word to the other ladies and they all decamp together in a toilet party. It would be unthinkable to leave the firelight circle on your own for anything might happen in the dark: *galka* (malevolent sorcery) attacks, the appearance of evil spirits, snakes or crocodiles. Privacy is not an Aboriginal concept so we walked along the beach just out of sight of the men, then all squatted down and peed companionably in a circle, chatting away the while. People were slightly anxious for two jolly good reasons – one, that someone had been bitten in the heel by a death adder while sweeping the camp out a little while ago and, two, that a wild buffalo had been tramping about in the bush all the night before, keeping everyone awake. Finally in desperation, one of the men had chucked a spear at it wounding it in the leg, making it even wilder. The worry was that the wounded buffalo would rampage through the camp again tonight.

I must have slept a bit because I know I was dreaming some of the time but I was chilly in my shorts and singlet, I kept imagining I could hear the certain sound of thundering hooves and crashing horns bearing down on my flimsy bed and mosquitoes pestered me all night long totally unrepelled by my insect repellent. In spite of everything, the pleasure of being here watching the silent heavens revolve in splendour, gazing at the immeasurable field of stars, smelling the delicious woodsmoke-scented air as the tide gently lapped in, made it one of the most memorable nights of my life, and I awoke at dawn to the glory of a tomato-coloured sky splashed across the Arafura Sea.

Above and around me the miracle of morning happened. Every camper knows that feeling, of course, but it seemed to be invested with a special meaning for me lying on the dawn shore of the land of my birth, listening to the whispering sounds of the Earth waking up. A thin wisp of smoke arose from the campfire, dishevelled bundles began to stir, a dog stretched, a parrot screeched, interminable insects hummed and whizzed, the tide, at its lowest ebb, was almost motionless. In my feeling of intense happiness and completeness, a heightened clarity of vision was mine for an instant. The boundaries between temporal and external experience vanished and I escaped from my usual time-bound self.

I had come home to my earliest experience of life on this planet and felt as if I was being shown a fundamental truth racing through the corridors of my mind, hearing the murmuring of my own DNA, listening to that part of the collective unconscious which is stocked with the accumulation of all our evolutionary experiences. I was standing between two mirrors with my arms outstretched, touching the infinity of my soul's existence – right to the vanishing point of the universe. I was in a dimension of time and space that echoed my beginning and my end – my alpha and omega- enfolded in the certainty that the river of life never stops and we are connected to one another by an invisible thread. *This* is what Djangawu could see: part of me is rooted here with the people of the sunrise, on a coral island in the southern seas, vibrating with the myths and legends of creation. The rainbow serpent which gave it form and continues to provide it with fresh water slept, coiled, beneath my feet.

Dazzled by these mighty insights, I walked over to where Dhuwarrwarr was cooking a giant clam one of the women found in the night when she went to move the boat off the rocks. It provided a couple of mouthfuls each, eked out with snails and oysters. Its unthinkable not to share food – almost the worst crime you could commit. People subsist on remarkably little. A fish spear is always at the ready. Their eyesight is astonishing and they can distinguish the grey underwater shadows from all the other dancing patterns of light on the surface of the sea. But very often they have to go without.

As we sat round the campfire after breakfast, there was a general consensus that I ought to belong to an Aboriginal family and have a tribal name – partly because they can never remember 'Allegra' from one minute to the next and partly because it's almost impossible to exist outside the complex web of interrelationships. Both they and I need to know where I stand in relation to each member of the group. A person without a family simply doesn't exist – here a casual friend is unheard of. In view of our shared profession, they decided to make me a member of Barrparr's family; his daughter in fact. My Aboriginal name was to be Bararrtji and Bremmer Island is my homeland. Dhuwarrwarr, Laklak and Banyygul are my sisters and Wandjuk my brother. I was very pleased with this gift which enhanced my feeling of belonging. Everyone was much happier now that they knew where I fitted in and what my status was. Even babies who used to howl when I clucked at them now stretched out their little arms.

Around noon when some of the men decided to cross over to the mainland I was offered a ride back. I would have liked to stay longer but as I was so ill-prepared it seemed a sensible idea. In one way I think they liked me and were curious about me. One the other hand, one of the main reasons they've dispersed to the outstations in the first place is to get away from people poking into their affairs. With the best will in the world I am an intruder, I don't understand the etiquette or the language, and life is probably simpler and less stressful when they're not having to entertain (and feed) an outsider. I made a terrible gaffe earlier – sitting in a mixed group, I started to ask Laklak some questions to do with pregnancy and birth. Someone clapped a hand over my mouth and with a great deal of giggling and whispering explained in my ear that it is forbidden to talk about such things in front of a brother. Everyone goes to great lengths to preserve the fiction that men are not permitted to know about women's business. In reality, of course, they do. But it's very rude and ill-bred to be ignorant of these elaborate refinements.

Back in Yirrkala, I spent a lot of time sitting with Liyapidini at her little desk in the Women's Resource Centre as she coped with the sorrows, problems and muddles of the mothers and kids she works with. She is a very compassionate serious person and feels everything very deeply. What impressed me most about her as an effective healer is the holistic approach she instinctively takes without ever having heard that trendy word. she works on three fronts simultaneously. Using her rudimentary barefoot paramedical skills she can administer first aid and tell when an emergency needs hospitalisation. Using her strong faith and genuine love and concern for her patients she attunes herself to the spiritual dimensions of their needs. Using her traditional knowledge of Yolngu customs and bush medicines she can brew up some local remedies that everyone believes in and reinforce confidence and pride in aboriginal culture.

She tries to encourage others to work in the outstations in the same three-fold way, and stresses the importance of going out hunting for fresh food involving the whole family in a shared activity and not relying on shop purchases. She is also concerned with getting families to understand the importance of such things as post-circumcision hygiene and she counsels women not to hit themselves (an alarming ritual in which women bash their foreheads violently with rocks or lumps of wood to display grief and mourning).

From having been friendly to begin with, Liyapidini, at a certain point, became quite reserved. I noticed her watching me quite a lot and looking rather stony. After a while she suddenly blurted out, 'Those missionary ladies say you are a witch!' So that was it. The two evangelical fundamentalist fanatics who had been translating the New Testament into the Gumatj language had apparently been warning people to beware of me – telling them that I was an agent of darkness. I must say I was flattered that they took me so seriously, but it was a frightening indication of their ignorance and paranoia. You can see how witch hunting caught on.

Ever since that prayer meeting I had been intent on reassuring Liyapidini that my modest aspirations are merely to exercise whatever gifts I may have and make myself into a channel for 'God's' healing power (whatever that means). However, it was a good thing that she told me about the accusation in the first place. They watched me at first to see how I would take it and when I laughed they all joined in. 'Yo! Umm!' they cackled, wiping away tears of mirth. 'Nobody is perfect. We can all try our best to serve God in our own way.'

One morning Liyapidini took me out with her to gather some special leaves to make a bush remedy for a sick baby. I never realised how many different types of eucalyptus leaves there are in Australia – over five hundred different kinds with different uses. The one she chose was a melaleuca which had been burned in a bush fire and was putting out bunches of new growth. An important feature in the selection of bush remedies appears to be the choice of a *particular* plant which resonates with the patient. 'Seeing with inside eyes', it's called. These were the mysteries to which Djangawu had begun to introduce me. A plant growing in a certain grouping; flowers at a certain stage of maturity, all add symbolic and metaphorical healing properties to whatever biochemical merit the substance might have. This sensitivity to and appreciation of the land and its bounty is what binds the people still so inextricably with the myths and legends of their dreamtime and makes it impossible to separate off their healing practices from the rest of their life.

We picked several handfuls of leaves and returned to the centre. The mother arrived carrying the sick, miserable baby – Daisy, nine months old but very small for her age. We crushed the leaves by pounding them with a rock on the cement floor then stuffed them in a billycan and boiled them up to a greenish brew which was then tipped into a tub with sufficient cold water for us to be able to put the baby in. A pungent, delicious aroma of eucalyptus oil arose in the steam and we bathed the tiny girl, pressing handfuls of the leaves onto her chest and back while she breathed in the vapour. The child actually stopped crying and splashed happily for a few minutes.

After the healing some of the women and children went down to beautiful Shady Beach so I tagged along. Aboriginal children are exceptionally pretty with huge black, liquid eyes, fine soft blond down all over their dark skin and lovely hair – sometimes tumbley curls, sometimes dead straight. Occasionally you see a child with astonishing flaxen Nordic hair which occurs quite naturally. The teenagers are still graceful and fine featured but as they get older they seem to spread and broaden. You see them hanging out on street corners sniffing glue instead of hunting and fishing. By thirty they're pretty broken-down looking like Aggie, and with few exceptions are unhealthy, overweight and bashed up. In their natural nomadic state they retain their characteristic thin legs and arms and lithe wiriness, but the awful town diet they eat of take-away food, alcohol and white bread gives them vitamin deficiency, skin diseases, obesity and rotten teeth. The ultimate consequence of colonial genocide and exploitation. Very sad to see.

I had brought a watermelon and we shared it round, sitting on the beach. It was times like these that I learned most about their customs, feelings, gossip and relationships. I learned which twigs you chew for toothache, which fruit is good for clearing the stomach after eating too much shop food. They use green ants and wild honey (sugar-bag) for colds. White clay and raw oysters for stomach ache and diarrhoea. Flying fox for asthma and TB. Goanna fat for rheumatic fever. Breast milk for sore eyes and ears. Charcoal for cleaning teeth. Stonefish gall for neutralising the fatal stonefish sting. If a person is bitten by a scorpion or other poisonous insect, the insect is crushed and rubbed into the wound (a forerunner of homeopathy?)

The hottest item of gossip on everyone's lips was the recent violent death of a man in Gurrumurru, a neighbouring outstation. Some said it must be murder, others suicide. 'How could he shoot himself in the back?' enquired someone. 'It must be *galka* attack.' Barrparr should look into it, they all agreed, because he 'sees'. He could visit the dead person in a dream and find out what happened. He could see the spirit of the murderer hanging around the corpse … he could tell if sorcery had made the man shoot himself … . The speculation went round and round.

In marked contrast to everyday practical medicine provided at a family level, in the private domain by the women, the role of the Marrnggitj, it seemed, was in healing the threatened stability of the communities as a whole – spectacle, magic and ceremony operating in the public domain. The combination of missionaries and alcohol had fatally damaged this self-healing mechanism.

Talking with a Western-trained Aboriginal health worker at the government clinic, I thought, would provide an interesting contrast to the folk cures. So I paid a visit. A nice girl in a clean, crisp uniform showed me round. It started out being a brisk tour of where they kept records, medicines, radio, snake-bite serum etc until I asked her in a casual sort of way, if they managed to incorporate any indigenous beliefs and remedies into the overall system of health care they offer. Her eyes blazed. 'What makes me so angry,' she said, 'is the doctors just give medicine because they think everything is caused by germs. They never look for the real reason.' In other words something or someone has upset the equilibrium. Nothing in life can be separated from the life of the spirit. When a person becomes detached from their true nature or spiritual beliefs – their knowledge, spiritual practices and creation myths dismissed as 'primitive' – they will be appallingly vulnerable to illness.

She wanted to know what I thought should be done when a person had been subjected to *galka* attack (malevolent sorcery). I said I thought they could obviously benefit from both kinds of treatment simultaneously – the skills of medical doctors to work on the physical illness, and the skills of the Marrngitj who understands things of the spirit, working more on the underlying causes, exorcising evil spirits and extracting troublesome foreign bodies by magical means. He knows the stories that the patient understands which give meaning to the disease or affliction. What heals is not confined to a doctor's drugs or scalpel blades. It is rooted in their belief system. This, of course, is Barrparr's department, but he was once humiliatingly thrown out of a hospital ward by a matron for 'molesting' a patient when the family had called him in – all of which no doubt contributed to his descent into depression and alcoholism.

After fifty years of missionary influence, most people here have been converted to Christianity. They also deeply believe in magic and sorcery. I see no reason why Christianity, medical science, herbalism and magic can't co-exist reasonably harmoniously so long as each faction respects the world of the others.

In the late afternoon I went down to the mainland beach camp where Dhuwarrwarr and her kids were now hanging out. I came to ask her advice. I had brought with me from England a ring with the intention of possibly giving it to an Aboriginal healer valued by his community. I had decided to give it to Barrparr, not because he's the greatest healer in the world, but because he symbolises the magical healing tradition in this culture and its continued relevance in keeping people in touch with the powers of creation and renewal. I wasn't sure if he would find the gift acceptable so I wanted her to enquire for me to make sure I wouldn't be breaking any taboos or committing any clangers of etiquette. She nodded but I couldn't tell from her expression what she thought of the idea.

I went back to Dhuwarrwarr's beach camp in the morning to check out the progress of my Bremmer Island saga. The message was that Barrparr had been informed of my gift and would be pleased to accept it. I could travel over the following day.

For my second stay on the island I borrowed a sleeping bag from David and a few supplies so as to be a bit better prepared. The boat, I was told, had first to go and pick up a turtle speared by Wandjuk then it would come and get me – I was to wait down at the beach camp … I sat there scanning the sea for a sign of the boat, fully realising that I might well be waiting all day – or forever, but it was a better place than most to wait … It's so pleasant down there at the beach camp, a cool breeze blows continuously. In contrast the Yirrkala dwellings are squalid and stifling, designed originally as little bungalows for the white mission staff and now all broken down and almost buried in litter, fly-screens busted, doors hanging off. Most families just sleep outside on the ground anyway, except in the wet season.

Urgency is not an Aboriginal concept, therefore getting impatient or frustrated is a totally useless waste of energy. There is no better way to attune oneself to the rhythm of life here than to listen to the spaces between events. Waiting is such an inseparable part of life that it's essential to experience the full flavour of it. I watched a man fishing as I sat and waited. He stood motionless for about two hours, just watching the sea, then suddenly he began a long-legged loping run along the shore, spear poised in his woomera. Elegant, powerful, graceful, he tracked the fish through the waves and then flung the spear with tremendous propulsion into the water and there was a three-foot-long kingfish writhing on the end of it. My city-slicker's heart leapt in admiration.

They chopped it into three sections, stuffed it into a billycan of sea water and boiled it up right then and there to eat. Although cooking isn't always so rudimentary. On another occasion I saw them make a sand pit and a very hot fire with rocks laid on top. When the rocks were almost red-hot, they took them out, lined the pit with fragrant leaves, laid the fish in, put the rocks back and finally packed sand on top with a few holes poked in through which water was poured to steam the fish. Delicious, if a bit gritty.

When we finally made the crossing to Bremmer Island late in the afternoon, the wind had got up and it was very rough. The little boat crashed along over the waves, drenching me in stinging spray as I gripped the sides for dear life. One of the boys had killed the wounded buffalo to everyone's immense relief, but another one had appeared to take its place, rather magically. In fact they can, and do, swim over from the mainland, which is very clever of them, as if they missed the island the next stop would be Papua New Guinea. The camp had moved from the beach to an inland site for some reason. Maybe the litter had got too deep. Also the population had doubled since I was last there. Apparently people always come and go in this way Even when there's no one here for some time, its still a homeland or outstation. This erratic nomadic occupation of the land was exactly what enabled the invading Europeans to justify helping themselves. How could the Aborigines prove it was 'their' land? Where were the villages? Where were the farms? Where were the fences? It's just a different concept of land use.

Barrparr seemed pleased to see me. After a seemly interval, I sat down facing him in the dust, cross-legged and solemnly presented him with the ring saying it was a mark of my respect for his work as a healer and as a man of high regard in his community. I had heard many stories of his power and skill and, as one healer to another, I was honoured to have been made a member of his family. I explained that the fire opal is a stone which can reflect and augment the rays of the sun in its fiery colour and if ever a healer might feel his powers were weakening, the ring could help to strengthen him again.

He was clearly pleased with the gift; his eyes shone with the light of far-off magical deeds, and although the ring didn't even fit on the little finger of one of his huge hands, he said he would wear it on a string around his neck. He gave it to his toothless old wife for safekeeping and then everyone launched into a collection of wondrous stories of people he had healed: Wandjuk's son once had a split vein in his leg and was bleeding profusely. Barrparr put his hands on it and the bleeding stopped. A woman dead for two days was restored to life. Barrparr had also on many occasions removed stones and sharp objects from people suffering the effects of sorcery or *galka* attacks.

I don't know how many of the stories are true or to what extent they are embroidered. The significant factor for me is that he is very much loved and revered by his community – almost like a holy relic. In the never-never land, in the once-upon-a-time, he was a dragon slayer, legendary foe of demons. The reality of this poor old man who sleeps under a tree all day and whom nobody consults much any more isn't really relevant. He is a symbolic hero and his deeds live on in the collective memory.

As twilight fell my new sisters spread out a large tarpaulin and showed me where to to put my bedroll. Instead of being off by myself as I was before, my status as a family member meant I was now in a row with the other married ladies there without their husbands. It would be unthinkable to just doss down anywhere. The taboos are very intricate. Every tree has special significance (someone's grandfather once slept under it) and therefore only certain people can camp there.

Everyone who brought food shared it with those who didn't have any and we ate supper in little groups. The great self-sufficiency nostalgia is really rather a myth. People talk romantically about the pleasures of hunting all their own food but the reality is quite often one small fish to go round ten mouths. Proximity to the mission also means they are always within easy reach of junk food. However, this time there were plentiful turtle eggs and I was given one to try. You bite a little hole in the leathery shell and suck out the contents – a rich grainy-tasting yolk and a white that never sets no matter how long you cook it so the consistency is a bit watery, but the experience wasn't as startling as I'd feared. You can't be fussy about food and some of it is rather alarming. I managed to avoid eating snotty gubble, black lip and duggle duggle, but I did try a mangrove worm – not as bad as it sounds- and a witchety grub. (I remembered old Bill's advice about swallowing it head first, but that's not how you do it – you're supposed to bite the head off and suck out the insides!) I reflected that most of us are very illogical about the foods we find repulsive, and are quite happy to peel a prawn, for instance, with all its wavy legs and crunchy exterior, but would rather die than eat a beetle or a locust.

After supper, some the men started to play the didgereedoo and clapsticks. The tiniest children got up one at a time and sang little songs in piping voices. It was enchanting. Everyone encouraged them and laughed delightedly. Every so often one of the women would leap up in the firelight and do an impromptu stamping dance, wagging her bottom with comical eroticism. Each exhibition was greeted with gales of laughter and applause. As the full moon rose and we sat in a circle passing round the half coconut shell of kava the teenage boys encouraged the little children to dance to the music. A tiny three-year-old boy did his sacred goanna dance – crouched over to imitate the animal's movements, he shuffled forward in a series of stiff-legged hops and skips and tricky footwork. Slowly at first, as the didgeridoo began its sombre, mournful pulse, then as the clapsticks speeded up and the rhythm got faster, the little spindly knees started going madly from side to side. Everyone clapped and cheered.

In the moonlight the children looked like little matchstick figures drawn on a wall – miniature sacred cave paintings come to life. Once again I slipped through a crack in the curtains of time to some place where the fragments of my ancient consciousness survive, weaving myself into the tapestry of 'everness' by this eternal thread. In the enchanted, transfigured night-time you could forget the dirt, the rubbish, the tedium and frustrations of everyday reality. Here, under the stars, with molten silver lunar light bathing the sea and the firelight casting shadows of dancing children on the sand, you could be half a million years away in the country of dreams.

The fire burned down to a glowing pile of embers and the kava gradually laid everyone out. It was hard to sleep on the unyielding ground with the full moon shining in my eyes as bright as daylight and one of the old women snoring like a traction engine in my ear. But I must have dozed off because the next thing I knew was the island sunrise illuminating the daytime reality of the twentieth century again. Rather a squalid sight by the dawn's early light – bundles of sleeping rags and old Coke cans, disposable nappies and plastic bags lying about – the detritus of the consumer culture. In the old days people's possessions consisted of a string dilly bag, a spear, a woomera and a grinding stone.

There's nothing romantic about the reality of these outstations. They bear as much resemblance to the idyllic noble fantasy as modern-day 'traveller' campsites under inner-city flyovers do to the golden earrings and gipsy violinist image evoked by a Brahms Hungarian Rhapsody. But I loved what they stood for: a defiant pride and the desire of the Aborigines against all the odds to be once again the masters of their own destiny, connected by an unbroken line of perspective to the origins of life on Earth.

As the men got ready to leave in the boat, I realised how lucky I had been with the timing. By the next day there would be nobody there. Everyone was going to Gurrumurru for the funeral. It was the cue for me to say a final goodbye to my new family. Laklak gave me a parting gift of a delicate shell necklace to remind me forever of my hamfistedness when I had tried to make one, and I sped away from my dreaming island, watching it until it was just a shimmer on the horizon.

A friend sent me this poem, torn out of an exhibition catalogue. I wish I knew who wrote it and I hope they won't mind me quoting it:

> *I am of the Dream time which is Now but not Here.*
> *I am of this sacred place which is Here but not Now.*
> *My people have been recalled to the Earth, Mother of all things.*
> *To be replaced by those who do not know*
> *That which is the right of all to know.*
> *Yet I remain lest one or two of the not knowing*
> *Might seek to know.*
> *For these I watch. And these I will watch over.*

I flew down to Sydney to spend a few days visiting the sacred sites of my nativity, immortalised in faded white ink on the black pages of my baby album. Little scalloped edged snapshots of that buxom young mother and that dark-haired father with their new-born, first-born wrinkly baby, in Rushcutter's Bay Park; Wooloomooloo; McCleay Street; the Botanical Gardens ... . Tears slipped from my eyes as I made my pilgrimage, lost in an amniotic reverie. Those young parents – younger than my grandchildren are now – who had been through so much; lost so much; seen so much. Bless them. I went to a performance of the Messiah, which I knew they had heard on the night before I was born. They often used to sing me, 'Unto Us a Child is Given'. Going to the concert didn't make me sad as I had feared. It sort of brought me full circle to the strange fact of having been born here in passing. It made me happy.

Years later, on an island in Greece where I was giving a course in creative writing I asked my group to pick a character from the past who had never made it into the history books and to write their story in twenty minutes. The only rule is pick up your pen and don't stop. Forget grammar, spelling, syntax just keep going. If you write yourself into a corner just write. 'what I really want to say is ...' and carry on. I always did all the exercises with them and we read them aloud to each other at the end of the twenty minutes.

Remembering the dancing Aborigine children in the firelight and the way it made me think of the rock and cave paintings that have been found in so many parts of the world from France, to Arizona to Australia I wrote this:

Forgotten by History

The embers of the dying fire are glowing softly in the dark, The others are asleep in the cave which is our home. Today was a good day. We filled our bellies with fresh meat from the antelope my man brought home. Many times we feel the terrible gnawing hunger and exist on berries and insects. We grow thin and scrawny. Our teeth fall out. The young children sicken and die. Winters are hard and we follow the wild game hoping the men will outrun a buck or spear a fish. The spears are a wonderful invention. It was my man who thought of it A sharp stone tied to a stick with some strong animal gut. It can be thrown to bring down a large beast from a distance. He is the leader of our little group and many times has protected us from attack. Once when a lion took one of the children, he tracked it without sleeping for three days and nights until he killed it. Now he wears the lion's skin. But he is a rough bad-tempered brute and often hits me. He drags me by the hair when he wants to mate. I respect him but I also fear him. I am happiest when everyone is asleep like this. My newest baby is thriving. The last one died after three moons. My body ached for him and water flowed from my eyes. The milk flowed from my breasts. Inside me I feel a great longing to leave some record of my time here and the things I know. Nobody has seen me do this but sometimes I take a stick from the fire and make marks on the wall of a deep empty cave not far from here. I try to show the excitement of the hunt. The men with their spears, the animals leaping and running, the great ball of fire in the sky, the beautiful moon whose rhythm matches my own. I have found some reddish clay which makes the pictures look more real. Maybe one day someone will find them and say, 'A life was lived here.'

Chapter Six

My mother told me this story when I was maybe five or six years old. Her Auntie Violet, my grandmother's youngest sister, was a beautiful woman renowned for her very long reddish–gold Titian hair that she wore pinned up in an elaborate bun. In the First World War she became a nurse and was much loved by the wounded men she looked after. Violet Long OBE Deputy Controller of Queen Mary's Army Auxiliary Corps was serving on The Warlida a hospital ship transporting casualties from the front back to the UK when, on the Second of August 1918, the ship was torpedoed. As she was flung into the water her gorgeous hair came loose. She was being crushed between the lifeboat and the sinking vessel and her foot had become entangled in some rope. One of the soldiers who had lost both his arms in the fighting saw her going down for the third time and valiantly tried to keep her afloat by grabbing her golden hair in his teeth but they both drowned. It was the saddest thing I had ever heard but so brave, so romantic. I could make myself cry whenever I wanted to just by imaging the scene. Violet is part of the family mythology. A story of heroism and selfless dedication. But there are other stories too …

What of Violet's sister, my grandmother Ethel? I never knew her.

She died of breast cancer long before I was born. In fact my mother was only eight at the time. All I have of her are stories and photographs. A wild, wilful, beautiful redhead of aristocratic birth, she was married at sixteen to Sir Gordon Guggisberg, Governor of the Gold Coast – a dedicated, cool colonial servant twenty years her senior. A marriage so unsuitable, so unhappy, so confined, constrained and catastrophic that after she had born him the first and second of her daughters she did the unthinkable. Tearing off the Edwardian straight jacket she escaped. She ran away to India with the vicar – handsome John Moore. She left the children. She socially dug her own grave. She defied everything that being a woman, feminine, ladylike, motherly, decreed. 'That whore!' they whispered. 'Trollop!' Her husband and his family closed ranks behind her. Her name was not allowed to be spoken. She was never again to be granted access to her little girls Ena and Nancy who became prisoners in a stout, square stately home presided over by a starched housekeeper with twenty-seven other servants to tend to their infant needs. I have a faded, sepia photograph of their forlorn little presences arrayed in front of the house with an elderly widowed aunt in a basket chair and the staff standing at attention on either side.

Only a kindly governess would take them for walks to the bottom of the estate where their mother – my grandmother – who had been tipped off, was able to wait behind a tree and watch them from afar with their butterfly nets and summer bonnets. Maybe she never recovered. To fall foul or transgress the rules in those days was to reap the whirlwind. A fallen woman might as well have been dead. In fact she was remarried to her handsome John. He got a job teaching in a school in Simla in India. She bore him five more daughters before she died at the age of forty-four. Sheila was only fourteen, Judy twelve, Betty ten, Pattie eight and poor little Dickie Bird only a baby. The second youngest, Pattie, was my mother

I never knew any of my grandparents. They all died before I was born but sometimes I'd try to imagine what they might have written to me if they could have foretold my existence. I'd combine what little I knew about them from family stories with filling in the blanks with my imagination. What message would they want to pass on to me their unknown, unborn grandchild? Who knows what ancient echoes might still sound in the hidden codes of our DNA.

I often gave this idea as an exercise to my creative writing groups and we would share our stories afterwards. The only rules: pick up your pen and don't stop for twenty minutes. Don't think too much. Don't agonise and don't worry about spelling or grammar. It was amazing what wonderful pieces came out of this: A grandfather who had been a lonely lighthouse keeper and drowned in a storm; a grandfather who was a circus trapeze artist; a grandmother murdered by a crazed stalker in Northern Ireland; a grandmother who became the first female medical student: a drunken neer-do-well grandfather who abandoned his family: a grandmother who had finally tracked down the daughter her parents had forced her to have adopted … …

Here's one of many that I did. What I didn't know, I made up so the stories are half fact, half imagination: Here is my grandfather, the infamous vicar:

Ernest George John Moore born in 1870. What can you tell me?

What would I like to leave you, dear granddaughter, whom I will never know, child of my beloved Pattie. I will start with my garden – the only place I ever felt at peace. The selfless beauty and uncomplicated being of trees and flowers, the sound of running water in my little streams and fountains, the solidness of rocks and earth … I would bequeath you all this because the rest has been failure. I know I haven't long to live but strangely I don't want to talk about it. I always told my daughters to be honest with me and to tell me if I was dying but Pattie tried to bring the subject up the other day and I diverted the conversation. She is a headstrong girl living in sin with some Jewish intellectual but she seems happy. A little robin – my gardening companion sits on my window ledge every day looking at me lying here. It's as if he's saying, 'Come on! You should be out here in your garden with me sitting on your spade.' My garden. What a balm and a solace its been these last comparatively peaceful years. I do not imagine I will ever sit out again under the willow and will have to content myself with the view from the window of all that I have created that was good and beg forgiveness for the rest. You know the story …I was a quiet country vicar trying to look after my flock when into my church and my life one day came the wild, captivating, childlike Ethel. Distraught with grief over the death of her newborn baby. She'd had scant sympathy from her cold, Edwardian diplomat of a husband who actually seemed to blame her for the loss of his longed for son. I listened and comforted and by and by my arms were around her. We kissed and I did the unpardonable. We hatched a plan to run away together. Of course the consequences were dire.

The doors of propriety closed against us and we were on our own. We fled to India where I got a job teaching school in Simla and our first two daughters were born out there — Sheila and Judy. Then eventually back in England in Pimlico we had Betty, Pattie and Dickie Bird — the baby. It was a life of stress and struggle but my deepest shame, which only now that I'm at the end of my life, can I begin to admit to myself, is that I wasn't very confident with real adult love between a man and a woman. I couldn't resist my perfect little girls with their perfect little bodies. I never thought to harm them, only hold them and touch them. I'm so sorry now that I know how wrong I was.

My beautiful, fiery, impossible Ethel died of cancer at forty-four and I didn't know what to do with all these daughters. I farmed them out to various relatives which seemed a good idea at the time but in retrospect it was a terrible mistake. I should have kept the family together. Please God release me from this guilt and torment. Anyway, I'm not long for this world and the garden is what I hope I will be remembered by. It is the best of me. Pattie forgave me but the others never did. Little Allegra who won't be born for a few more years — I long for you to think of me in my garden. The trees, the beautiful trees will outlive me and maybe the streams and fountains will purify my memory in your eyes ...

★

Well I luckily chose a good man to be my life's partner. He supported our family and he always encouraged me to do my own thing. 'Don't expect me to babysit,' he said 'but I always want you to be free to follow your own passions.' He even gave me contacts from his old film locations if I needed a place to stay.

So I went to America. Friends took on the kids and I did the same for them when the time came. After a few days with cousins in New York I decided to visit an evangelical preacher and his wife in Nashville Tennessee with whom Richard had made a film some time before. It seemed imperative to me that you had to arrive in Nashville on a Greyhound bus. 'Don't do it,' said my cousins. 'It's a horrible journey. Why don't you fly?' but my mind was made up. The bus station at Port Authority Terminus is really the arsehole of the world. Full of junkies and weirdos, hot as hell, and crowded even at midnight which was the scheduled departure time for the Nashville bus. I queued for nearly half an hour for my ticket and only just made the bus struggling down two flights of stairs with all my luggage. A young man helped me put my stuff up on the rack and sat down in the seat by my side.

That was the start of an extraordinary journey that affected me deeply for a long time. We just started talking as the bus travelled out of the night city across the Verrazano Narrows Bridge into New Jersey, through Delaware and Maryland and on down towards Washington DC. He was back from living seven years in Korea where he is a parachute instructor. He was on his way to Dallas to do a training mission experimenting with much lower altitude (300–400ft) parachute jumps – no time for a reserve chute. He loves Korea and has a house there off the army base and doesn't want to come home to crazy, materialist America since he has discovered oriental religion, philosophy, food and lifestyle. He plays the flute and has studied the Korean language and Japanese music. He was probably only about six years younger than me. But it felt like he could have been my son.

I asked him if he had been in Vietnam and that started him off on a series of horror stories that curdled my blood. He had been in a loving relationship with a Vietnamese girl with whom he had a child. Fraternising was strictly against the rules but he had enjoyed the clandestine thrill of their secret meetings and come to love the beauty and simplicity of traditional Vietnamese culture. He was planning to marry her and bring her to the United States. One day an American helicopter gunship (suspecting enemy hiding in the village) came over and strafed the place to pieces. His little family were killed. When he heard about it, he said, he went berserk. 'The emptiness was deafening. It's the loudest silence you'll ever hear and I wanted to fill it with rage.'

After that he volunteered for all the most dangerous missions and didn't care if he lived or died. A shard of ice seemed to penetrate his heart. He said he became a cold, efficient, brutal killer – enjoying the exhilaration – making up little games to play to keep the killing interesting. 'I've killed 1,400 individuals and that's not pressing buttons.

That's hand to hand. That's one on one. I was good at it. Good at my job. I was invincible. Nobody could kill me.'

I asked him if he thought about what he was doing. 'Didn't think about it at all. I was a bad, hard person. Not angry, not crazy, just efficient. I'd been raised in an army family. Army was the only thing I knew. Jumping out of planes and killing people was my job. I was wounded quite badly twice. Never even felt the pain. I'd learned how to shut off physical pain. I was anaesthetised.' Then something happened which changed his life ...

'I remember the exact moment. I was alone on sentry duty and suddenly came face to face with a Viet Cong soldier. We saw each other at the exact same instant. We were not more that five feet apart. He released his safety catch and I released mine. There was no way either of us could miss. If either of us fired we would both die. We looked straight into each other's eyes and I knew I didn't want to kill anyone anymore ever again. He was just another young man doing his job. So we smiled at each other and I let him go his way and he let me go mine.

'I'd been there for three and a half years by that time – never even wanted to go on leave but this day I went to my commanding officer and said, "I've had enough." He said, "Why don't you just take a long leave? You're tired." But I wasn't tired. I wasn't suddenly filled with disgust or shame or revulsion. I was perfectly calm and perfectly sane. I had suddenly seen the senselessness of it all and I just knew I never wanted to kill another person again. And up till now I haven't.'

The bus travelled on all night and all day down along Highway 81 right the way through the state of Virginia. Sometimes at rest stops he'd walk off on his own pacing about, sometimes he'd come and sit by me. Sometimes he'd be very silent hardly answering when I said something to him and then sometimes the flood gates would open again and the dark thoughts poured out. He talked about how much he missed his mother who'd died three years ago while he was abroad. And his father: 'My father was always the Colonel, never Dad. He set the highest standards. Failure or weakness of any sort was not tolerated. He was strictly authoritarian and would not countenance sentimentality. A mistake was a "strategical misreading". I never got to talk to him about my feelings on war and life. He got blown apart before I ever got to talk to him at all.' He talked about learning to be self sufficient. "I like my own company. I've learned how to leave my body whenever I want with meditation and yoga – like, I mean, I'm *gone*.'

Both Carl and I were pretty tired – he much more so as he'd flown from Seoul the same day. We drifted off to sleep with our arms lightly touching and his head on my shoulder. My whole body ached with the knowledge of his pain and the tragedy of his life. I ached to hold him. I ached from the proximity of his beautiful body and his troubled sleep. I wanted to rock him and ease the sadness in his heart. But his spring was wound so tight.

All the maternal tenderness in me overflowed. The feel of his skin against mine, the smell of his body and the look of his sleeping head with his dark, handsome Italian/American features on my shoulder … . He had learned to survive alone and maybe I should have held him, maybe I should have trusted my instincts. But somehow the time was not right. I didn't sleep at all but watched over him as I would one of my own babies.

'I sure wish I had a family,' he said when he woke up. 'It's all I've ever wanted my whole life. Christmas time is the worst. Sometimes I'm the only person left in the barracks. That sure is lonesome.' He talked about his feelings of re-incarnation and death. He is sure he will meet his lost love and his baby again just as he was sure when he first met her he'd known her before in another life. He talked about his dreams and nightmares, He is frequently tormented by haunted nightmares filled with the faces – always the faces – of people he'd killed. And his recurring dream is of a beautiful seaside cove, a horseshoe bay with three red fishing boats. Always the same, no place he's ever been though he's looked for it up and down every coastline he's ever been near. A girl is standing with her face to the wall of rock and never turns round. One day he knows he'll find it.

He is terrified of another war. All he wants is to see out his eight remaining years in peacetime so he can retire on full pension and teach music to children – maybe live in Australia. He said nearly everyone he knew back in Vietnam was permanently stoned on one sort of drug or another. 'There was no other way to deal with it – you didn't know why you were there or even who you were fighting. The whole thing was insane. Once on a night patrol we came across a group of enemy soldiers. We killed them all. I recognised three of them as guys I knew real well by their first names. During the day they fought on our side, at night they changed into black pyjamas and killed us. The Viet Cong would wire children up with explosives. Living hand grenades. They'd stand by the side of the road and ask American soldiers for gum and blow up when you touched them. Five of my friends were killed like that in front of my eyes one day. I was the only survivor splattered with the brains of the detonated child."

He said, in spite of everything, you couldn't fail to have respect for the tenacity and endurance of the 'enemy' especially their underground tunnel system. Once his platoon discovered beneath a blown-up hospital a whole network of chambers and tunnels that went on for miles. People lived down there for months.

He was also disgusted with the way the US troops pulled out when they did. The whole world knew but the South Vietnamese didn't. Neither did the ordinary American soldiers. The ones with American wives were told so that their families could be evacuated but they were sworn to secrecy. Guys with Vietnamese wives – hundreds of them, were flown out with no warning and many of them never saw their families again …

All this and more. The abscess of horror drained away through the long day. He said how much he now hates and fears any sort of violence; how he has to put his hands in his pockets if he's having an argument because he knows how easily he could still kill somebody; how he runs away if there's any kind of fight because he can break someone's neck with a single blow; how once when a guy tapped him on the shoulder because he thought he knew him he'd spun around and knocked all his bottom teeth out in a reflex action; how he still believes in the essential goodness of mankind even though he's seen so much evil …

We reached Nashville at 9.30 in the evening where I was getting off. Two women were crying and hugging each other; people were kissing children; lovers embracing; men punching each other's arms.

'I love to watch families saying goodbye and greeting each other,' he said, "even though it makes me feel melancholy. Nobody's come to see me off since I was seventeen.' I gave him my address saying that I would gladly share my family with him if ever he needed it. I kissed him and wished him happiness and he was gone from my life. I never saw him again. Whether his stories were wholly true, partly true or entirely invented I will never know but I completely believed him at the time. The anguish and the damage seemed real enough and for that brief, intense moment in time I loved him with all my heart.

CHAPTER SEVEN

When I left Cal at the bus station in Nashville Tennessee, he went on to Dallas and I was to embark on another adventure.

Dottie Snow was there to meet me at the bus depot. A gorgeous Nashville Barbie Doll with a cascading blonde wig like Dolly Parton and a perfect figure, married to the Rev. Jimmie Snow, the pastor of the Evangel Temple. She once said to Richard during the filming, 'I might be the only Bible these folks ever read so I need to look this good.' He was making a series of short 'portrait' films for the BBC about women's lives in different cultural contexts – Mexico, Ghana, Israel – and I had written to Dottie asking if I could come and visit. That night was the only night of the week when the 'Grand Ole Opry Show' is on and you can't come to Nashville and not see it. It is the mecca of Country and Western music lovers the world over. Dottie and her family have been in the entertainment business all their lives. She took me straight backstage where she knew everyone from the doorman to the stars and we watched the show from the wings. Even if you've never really been a fan of Country and Western music you could not help but be impressed by the high level of musicianship of these artists. Fabulous fiddle playing, banjo picking, guitar strumming. First class. At midnight we went on over to Ernest Tubbs' record store where they broadcast a continuous version of the same thing out of hours. Although the style is very different from African American Blues music the sentiments are pretty similar: faithless lovers, loss, misfortune and broken hearts.

Next morning was the start of a week-long Revival at the Evangel

Temple. People poured in, the place filled up fast and on came the band and a large choir including Dottie. The Rev. Jimmie Snow seized the microphone and got things rolling with a rousing hand-clapping gospel song. America is a profoundly religious country and the deep connection between the entertainment business and the religion business here in the Bible Belt is at its most obvious in Nashville. The Rev Snow's father was Hank Snow, the famous Country Music artist who recorded 140 albums, sold 8 million records and was the first person to invite Elvis Presley to appear at the Grand Old Opry. When he was young, Jimmy was a singer himself, making plenty of money and travelling all over with Elvis and other artists. He told me that back then he was into bad company, and bad habits. 'I've woken up in every motel in this town,' he said. Then he saw the light when he was twenty-two, became converted, began preaching and has been at it ever since.

A young curate led the next few numbers: 'I used to be a heroin addict,' he cried. 'Now I'm a Jesus junkie! Praise the Lord!' Then a visiting musician from Fort Lauderdale Florida did a solo number. 'How many of you people want to hear some good old fashioned Holy Ghost organ music?' Shouts of Hallelujah! from the congregation. 'C'mon! Smoke it boy!' yelled the Rev. and one of the women came up and fanned the keyboard to cool it down. 'How about that? C'mon y'all. Let's hear it for God! Give him a big hand now.' Then Brother Snow began his sermon. He is a charismatic preacher, working the crowd, ever the entertainer, pacing up and down the aisles, orchestrating the crescendos. His theme was a verse from the Bible which states something to the effect that, 'Happy is the man whose sins shall not be charged against him.' He preached for an hour exhorting us to let Jesus take the load off you. The only way to get to heaven is to unburden your sins on Jesus – doesn't matter what you've done. He finished off in quite a lather, his shirt soaked with sweat, rivulets running down his face, his pale blue ultra-suede jacket long since removed. He jumped up and down like a pogo stick on the stage yelling, 'I been SET FREE by the blood of the lamb! There are no sins charged to my account! Jesus has put them on his American Express credit card and he has NO CREDIT LIMIT!'

Shouts of Hallelujah!, Amen! and Praise God! People certainly had a good time. It was a great show with plenty of audience participation.

Afterwards Jimmie Snow didn't feel it had it had gone all that well. He looked tired and said he wasn't really on form but wanted to play me a tape of Country music he had just put together where he has done all the arrangements and Dottie the back-up singing.

The Snows were kind and generous hosts. They took me to lunch at the Opryland Hotel and implored me to let the Lord into my heart. At seven the evening service began. It started off in the same way with people singing and clapping. Jimmie was doing nothing special to whip them up but gradually a huge emotional tide filled the room. One by one people had tears rolling down their cheeks. Those standing next to one another reached out and held each other, arms were lifted in praise, some people fainted clean away and others sat beside them with joyous faces holding and rocking them. Middle-aged men comforted each other's tears. Little children lifted their arms and asked Jesus to come to them. The congregation – conservative, white, working class, blue-collar folk – sang and danced and jumped and cried as if some universal life force had possessed them. A spontaneous combustion of love and faith and joy and the music played on. A total cathartic orgasmic release. An opportunity for a shared experience of uninhibited surrender. A relinquishing of self and willingness to let the tide of it sweep them up. Yes, you can see this kind of crowd phenomenon at a football match or with teenage girls at a Beatles concert. But this seemed really loving and caring. Even a naturally reserved, sceptical British onlooker couldn't fail to feel the energy. Jimmie never even tried to preach his sermon. He could see what was happening and he just let it roll.

Gradually it died down, people composed themselves a bit and stood around talking with their arms around each other marvelling at how happy and comforted they felt. Maybe what most of us are looking for is the opportunity to express – without embarrassment or judgment – our capacity to love and be loved.

Jimmie said it had been over a year since he'd seen such spontaneous lift-off. Afterwards I talked to a woman who had designed the stained-glass windows for the church. She told me her story:

Seven years ago her daughter and son-in-law had been having marital problems. He was abusive, she left him and in a fit of jealous rage he and a buddy hijacked a plane, kidnapped the daughter, landed at some airport and were stormed by the FBI whereupon the son-in-law killed both himself and his wife. They left a three-year-old daughter which this woman and her husband had adopted. She'd had a hard time coming to terms with this horrible tragedy and tried going to her old church. But everything seemed cold and meaningless until a friend brought her to the Evangel Temple where the warmth and strength she found here have healed her.

Tribal life in primary cultures always had occasions for ecstatic release – drumming, dancing, chanting, mind-altering substances. Today's rave culture has reconnected with the same phenomenon. Maybe we all need to find it somewhere. At the Evangel Temple it is prayer and surrender. Even a sceptic such as myself has to admit that there seems to be a power for good here. The church services today could have been an easy target for ridicule but there's no substitute for being here and experiencing the atmosphere. I'm glad I saw it with my own eyes.

Later I asked Jimmie Snow wasn't he worried about the vulnerability and exploitability of the people in his care. He said the difference between him and someone like the infamous preacher Jim Jones (the American cult leader who ordered his 900 followers, including their children, to commit mass suicide at his jungle commune, Jonestown, in Guyana) was that while he, Jimmie, remains a humble medium for the spirit he tries to pass on, Jim Jones assumed the mantle. The power made him drunk and he started to believe he was God – the spirit incarnate. Since that didn't really answer my question he conceded, yes, they are very vulnerable when they are first converted because all they have is an intimation, an emotional glimpse without any backing to give it substance. They need about a three month period of Bible study to consolidate their faith, he says, and root it in facts. (Is the Bible a source of 'facts'?, I could argue, but I let it go.) Jimmie's showmanship is part of him and part of Nashville. The fact that he uses it as a tool just means he has to use it with care. It is a huge responsibility.

Next morning a family friend and star-struck church member came over to fetch me. She was kindly giving up her time to show me around the sights of Nashville- (mostly a far off glimpse behind a high, chain link fence of the homes of Country Music stars) We visited Johnny Cash's House of Cash – his collection of memorabilia, cowboy boots, guitars, family photos etc. Cash was a real wicked character in the past and he still has the face of a man much battered by life but he also got 'saved' and has spent many years now doing philanthropic work – playing his music in prisons and raising money for good causes at free benefits. At the gift shop his old Mama sometimes helps out distributing signed photos of herself and her son with little messages such as, 'It's better to be with the construction gang than with the wrecking crew'. We went to the County Hall of Fame and saw Elvis Presley's solid gold Cadillac and visited Centennial Park where there is a full scale replica of the Parthenon much prized by local citizens who are anxious to promote the 'Athens of the South' image.

Then Dottie and her little granddaughter Shandy joined us and Jimmie took us flying in his little plane. He loves any excuse to fly and I was very touched that he took the time to take me up. Then Darren, Dottie's fourteen-year-old son, and I went to Opryland – a huge amusement park with rides and shops and music everywhere. All top class quality. You don't get by in this town if you're a second rate musician. We heard a Blue Grass concert, a New Orleans jazz concert, a rock concert. Darren was a great guide and it was easy to forget how young he was. All the kids seem to ripen early down south. Dottie married at fifteen, her twenty-two-year-old son David has three little daughters already and is in the process of getting a divorce – has wife ran off with the church organist's husband. Lisa, Dottie's seventeen-year-old daughter, is married already and Donnie, her 'miracle child' – hideously damaged by a car crash three years ago, is now twenty-four and lives at home. He was married to Sophie, a fifteen-year-old girl, at the time of the accident and they had a ten-month-old baby daughter – Shandy. Sophie just couldn't cope with the situation and went home to her mother so Dottie and Jimmie adopted Shandy and she learned to crawl and walk at the same time as her father's rehabilitation. She calls him Daddy and her grandparents Mommy and Poppy.

Donnie was hit at high speed by a drunken driver and flung ninety feet off the road. His back was broken in two places and he had multiple contusions of the brain and at least two large blood clots in his head. He had inhaled so much blood that he had double pneumonia. The doctor told Dottie; 'They just don't make it when it's this bad.' He didn't die however and remained in a deep coma. Strange things happened then which Dottie is convinced proves the power of prayer: his lungs cleared up overnight without the aid of a respirator; when Dottie came and stood by his bed his heart monitor registered much increased activity. The doctor was blunt and told them Donnie would be lucky if he did die. Survival would mean a vegetative state and no motor control but against all the odds he kept improving. When they brought him home from hospital after six months he was wearing nappies and couldn't walk or talk. But together with his baby daughter he learned again and now, although he thinks and moves slowly, he has regained his memory, can talk perfectly with only a slight slur to his speech, hold a normal conversation and sing in tune. His great frustration is that he hasn't sufficient control yet to play the piano.

Music was always his first love and he was very talented on the piano. He played me some old tapes of jam sessions with him on the keyboard before the accident and it was heartbreaking to hear and to see him sitting there listening to it. He says it drives him crazy to be so clumsy. He never could read music and wasn't taught to play properly but he has composed a song called 'The Valley of the Shadow of Death …in Remembrance'. Although he can't play it, he has written it down almost perfectly, complete with harmonies. I played it for him for the first time on his Yamaha keyboard.

Donnie says that in spite of all the anguish he feels he is a much better person since the accident. He used to be a very selfish young man and in fact the very night of the car crash he was running off from his wife to go to California with a rock band. Now he thinks a lot about spiritual things, helps as much as he can around the house and takes care of Shandy. Best of all is his great sense of humour.

Dottie and the rest of the family kid him and joke about his ham-fistedness and he kids right back. His is such a remarkable story and I was deeply moved by the love and faith that has brought him back to life.

Dottie suggested I might like to go to the 'Women's Love Fellowship' lunch with her. Rows of ladies sitting at trestle tables daintily munching while the chairwoman, herself a minister, led everyone in prayer and Nancy at the piano sang 'He's the bounce bounce bounce in my step. He's the blue blue blue in my sky'. A guest speaker gave a talk entitled 'Who is God? and How do you know you're right?' Old Testament and New Testament prophecies figured largely in his argument and he arrived, unsurprisingly, at the conclusion that the Christian belief made the most sense.

Afterwards Dottie took me shopping. They don't have little High Street type shops here at all. Nashville is strung out along identical freeways bordered by petrol stations and fast-food chains. All shopping takes place in vast space stations – air-conditioned indoor piazzas surrounded by car parks. Nobody seems to go outside ever. Dottie runs from her air-conditioned house with the blinds pulled down and the curtains drawn to her air-conditioned car with her sunglasses on to the air-conditioned shopping precinct with the ever present background music playing. I think the Snows would be good candidates to blast into orbit when the time comes to vacate this planet. They wouldn't miss the Earth at all. They even have plastic flowers in the flowerbed outside their front door and plastic water lilies in their little fountain. They never eat real food at all. They drink cokes and instant iced tea. They use 'creamer' in their coffee and 'spread' on their bread and pick up junk food from a take away whenever they're hungry. It tastes quite reasonable but leaves you feeling icky. They never have fresh fruit in the house but eat bowls of Baskin-Robbins ice cream or pies warmed up in the microwave if they want a snack. All Dottie's clothes are made of synthetic material as are the sheets on their beds and they have arrangements of artificial flowers in the lounge and dining rooms. Their television is projected onto a large screen and they never turn it off. The teenage boys sleep with the radio on all night playing softly. The things I would pine for in outer space they have already learned to live without. The shops are all well stocked and dream like. Shoppers drift around as if in a trance lulled by the muzak. Nobody pays with money – they use credit cards.

NB: Reading this back all these years later I'm amused to realise that what seemed so surreal to me back then – shopping malls; credit cards: continuous music pollution – is pretty much the norm in England now.

Dottie took me to the wig shop where she buys her artificial hair. 'I never go out in my real hair any more,' she said. 'A wig is so much more convenient.' She has several spectacular ones. For a laugh I bought a curly mane of strawberry blonde and wore it to church that evening entering into the spirit of Nashville. Brother Snow was determined to preach the sermon that he's had prepared since Sunday. The congregation were pretty tired which gave Jimmie the chance to talk to a quiet, receptive audience. The theme was prophecies in the Bible and how they linked 'perfectly' – uncannily – with historical facts. He finished off by asking if there was anyone in the congregation who would like him to pray for them. I put my hand up because I knew it would please him and Dottie that I wanted to join them in something that means so much to them but also because we could all do with a heartfelt prayer from time to time. They were ecstatic to think that I had made a commitment. They wept and praised Jesus and held me and prayed. I was honest with them and said there was a lot I didn't accept, that there are many ways up the mountain towards the 'oneness' we all seek but that I valued their generosity and love and the warmth and energy of their prayers.

Later that evening back at the house we had a long discussion about philosophical and theological matters. Jimmie is a good arguer because he's heard all the questions before. Dottie is a gut-feeler and can prove everything with a personal experience. I said I would be very unhappy about relinquishing responsibility for my actions and unloading all my guilt on poor Jesus. Jimmie's answer is that you need a mediator between the ordinary sinner and the perfection and purity of God. That didn't convince me. I said it depends on your interpretation of 'God'. My understanding is that we all come from a unified consciousness which includes all people, animals, plants, air, water, the sun, the stars, the moon, the Earth, the universe. This is what 'oneness' means. There is no separation. No mediator is needed. Organised religion has done great harm by creating divisions and separation. I was unhappy about the Christians proselytising and thinking that their way was the only way. What about the other great spiritual and wisdom traditions trying to find answers to the great mysteries of existence arrived at by totally different means – Buddhism, Hinduism, Islam, Zoroastrianism, Judaism …? His answer, that the Bible proves it, in so many words, didn't satisfy me either. 'If you have doubts, and everybody does, just open your heart and ask God to *prove* to you that he's real,' begged Dottie. 'Just try it. Make that leap of faith and you'll see that it's true,' she said. My view is that asking pre-supposes the belief in the first place. They're convinced I'll come round and we left it at that. They gave me a beautiful leather-bound study Bible and a book of commentaries on it. I've been so touched by their concern and generosity. They think I was sent to them – and that the whole visit was fated to happen the way it did. Maybe that's true. It was a privilege for me to be welcomed into their world for a while and the experience was fascinating. A lesson in suspending judgement. I'd half been expecting something more like Pat Robertson – the fanatical ultra right-wing tele-evangelist with his own Christian television station, the Electric Church. The Snows were not like that.

Next morning my dear, kind hosts took me to the airport, we all hugged each other goodbye and I flew off on my way.

★

Another film Richard had made for the BBC back in the '80s was a documentary about the long-distance lorry drivers who criss-cross the United States in huge trucks hauling timber and such. I had been invited to be a guest at the Independent Truckers Annual Convention in Colorado Springs where I was introduced on the platform and it was jokily announced that I was hoping to get a ride to Portland, Oregon. A few whoops and hollers and a big show of hands. 'Gary Black need not apply!' said the chairperson. Loud guffaws. Afterwards a lanky, 6'8", bearded guy came over and said, 'I'm the badass they warned you about.' Gary – a drawl talking, rough riding, hard living cowboy wearing pointed fancy cowboy boots and a Stetson is a bachelor with a terrible reputation as a ladies man. The very spirit of self-employed free enterprise. Big-headed, egotistical, intolerant, prejudiced. I didn't really warm to him but, after I politely turned him down he went to some trouble on my account phoning Denver to try and get me a lift. No luck.

The man who featured in Richard's film *Truck Drivin' Man,* Karl, is the person I'd come to meet. and his co-driver Jim. Karl is an older man, very fatherly and feels responsible for my safety. When I got another offer from a guy named Dave who drives the most beautiful truck in the entire place – a black and chrome Peterbilt so shiny and sparkly it looks brand new – Karl vetoed it. 'Don't quite trust him,' he said.

NB: Writing now, over forty years on from the perspective of an eighty-year-old great-grandmother where lone travel as a woman is hassle-free, its easy to forget how different it was back then in my thirties. Back then I even once got a lift from a handsome guy in his private plane from the wrong airport where I'd mistakenly landed in the Caribbean to the other airport 500 miles away where I was supposed to be. That wouldn't happen today. After the age of fifty women become invisible. At thirty you need to be on your guard and handle things cleverly neither encouraging nor offending.

Karl is passionately involved in Independent Truckers' Rights. Things are pretty tough for them from what I gathered from the meetings and forums I attended. They get harassed by the police who try and pick them off for weight excess, exceeding the speed limit, overloading, insufficient permits … . Permits are hard for independent truckers to get. They have to apply to the Interstate Commerce Commission which has all sorts of hoops to jump through and regulations which the owner/operator has difficulty complying with. Everything is stacked in favour of big companies, agents and Teamsters Union drivers.

These guys feel they represent the true spirit of red-blooded American independence and resent State interference on their personal liberty to hustle loads when and where they like and drive them wherever they please. Most people here are like Karl – hard-working free spirits not irresponsible cowboys. They take pride in their trucks, some of which are very beautiful indeed, and feel that the bare living they scrape is still not too high a sacrifice for the pleasure and independence of being your own boss.

Karl, at the moment, is hauling illegally as a lot of them are because he was refused an I.C.C. permit on grounds of 'Public Need and Necessity '. In other words there are already enough of the large company-owned trucks doing business through the States he wants to travel. He says it is a fix and he can prove it and so it goes on. The Independent Truckers Association is the only body that really gives the Independents support – both moral and legal – and a voice for their collective grievances.

In the free time between convention events I got lots of offers to see the sights. A load is unhitched, two or three of us squeeze into a cab and we 'bobtail it' up into the mountains. Colorado is an exceptionally beautiful state. One time we drove to Royal Gorge, a steep, narrow gorge through which flows the Arkansas River spanned by the world's highest suspension bridge. We walked across and came back via the spine tingling cable car dangling 1,055 feet above the chasm. We rode the incline railway down to the bottom of the gorge so we could look up. I heard about their love of the gypsy life, the jealous fights with ex-girlfriends and how hard it is to maintain a stable relationship.

Another time a few of us went to a barbecue at the Garden of the Gods. Held in a big marquee with a Country and Western band – a feast of beans, baked potatoes and barbecued steak in a gorgeous setting among the huge rock formations of red stone and a bright moon above. I got cornered by a truck owner from Louisiana – a real macho, hard drinking, strutting, good-looking tough guy who told me how irresistibly drawn to beautiful women he was. His voice was full of smooth innuendo, his eyes darting messages as he postured in front of me. I was fascinated by his line. It was like watching a male peacock swing into his mating dance. After a while a hard-faced, attractive woman came up and macho man slipped effortlessly into neutral and introduced her as his wife.

Next day Karl and Jim took me up to Pike's Peak – the great scenic wonder of these parts. From Maniton Springs we caught the Cog

Railway to the top — a spectacular ride up through quaking aspen, ponderosa pine and spruce forests full of giant boulders up above the tree line to the bare, bald summit. We were there as the sun set and the evening light made the red rocks glow. I couldn't help thinking what unimaginable hardship it must have been for those early settlers in covered wagons who trekked across the Rockies.

Back in time to hear an unconvincing talk by some Senator oozing insincerity from every pore about doing everything in his power to help Independent Truckers (Karl says they are just here to canvass votes — they never do anything), followed by an ice cream feast laid on by one of the companies who supply refrigeration units. Enormous tubs of marvellous ice cream of every conceivable flavour and a table groaning with nuts and cherries and marshmallows and sprinkles and butterscotch to personalise your bowlful.

I got talking to Dave again who owns the beautiful truck. He's still offering to take me to Portland but I think wanted to sound me out about what reciprocal favours I might be offering. I was very straight and honest. I'm willing to pay my way by sharing petrol costs but I want no misunderstanding on his part that I'm dazzled by the glamour of the microwave, stereo, double-bed cabin etc in his passion wagon. He's built this showpiece beauty himself and also the boat he lives on in San Diego, California. Actually he's quite a nice guy when you get to know him. Divorced and on the make but not a bully and not aggressive. He used to airfreight important valuable art collections for the Tate Gallery. He's pretty good company and basically decent so I'd have been glad of the opportunity, if it arose, to travel West with him but I was not going to run after him and quite happy to go by bus if it came to that although it was going to cost $97 dollars and take 36 hours. In the end he turned out to be rather a dud and lost interest when he realised he wasn't going to score. He is a roly-poly, baby-faced guy and obviously relies on his beautiful truck to pull the birds. Karl thinks he must have a rich daddy or some other form of private income as he never seems short of money and his truck must have cost him a mint. He is generally resented by the other hard-up independents for being chosen, because of his beautiful truck, as the 'face' of independent trucking. 'Not a real trucker!' Karl scoffed.

Back at the hotel, a few of us went up to the disco and I danced all evening with lots of guys. There are about six of them who cluster around. Its rather like being a highly prized mascot. The women here are nearly all married to truckers and they're not that many of them anyway so being in the minority means I'm not short of admirers and attention. Good for the old ego for this mother of five!

Everyone keeps trying to persuade me to enter the 'Miss Independent Trucker' contest on the last day but I don't feel it would be appropriate and would certainly cause bad feelings among the real truckers and their ladies so I was asked to be one of the judges instead. A much better plan.

A friendly old grizzled guy named Burt with a rather beat up old truck offered to take me up to Seven Falls – a local beauty spot with more fantastic scenery. We walked all the way up the steps at the side of the falls and then off into the hills in the late afternoon sun. Clear blue sky and pine trees and beauty so intense I held my breath and I just wished Richard was here to share it. Burt sometimes thinks about retiring to a small piece of land he has in Kentucky and settling down, 'find me an ole gal and a hound dog', but is still reluctant to give up the freedom of the road. We had a nice day and he asked me about my life and what I was doing on my own without my husband. I told him he'd offered to stay home with the kids for a month so I could go travelling and experience meeting some of the people he'd made films about for the BBC. 'Good Golly Miss Molly, he must trust you!' he said. 'Of course he does, why wouldn't he?' I answered.

We got back in time for the Beauty Contest – 'Ms Independent Trucker 1980'. Five guys from different states and me were the judges. There were ten contestants ranging in age from fifteen to fifty. We devised a system of scoring based on one third looks, one third personality and one third involvement in trucking. The pretty little fifteen-year-old failed on the latter two counts, the grandmother scored highly on all three. We selected four finalists: Dixie, half of a husband and wife driving team; Joyce, a bouncy girl who runs the business side of her husband's trucking enterprise; J.J. the grandmother who has been married for twenty-four years, brought up three children and is deeply involved in the I.T.A.; and Dee, a solo lady trucker both tough and feminine. It was hard to choose but in the end I swung the voting in favour of the grandmother who was awarded her trophy and a bunch of roses. They also announced the winners of other various competitions at the final banquet supplied by Ford. Karl's old beat-up truck won first prize for the best veteran (he's done one million five hundred thousand miles). The lucky draw for the prize of a truck engine worth fifteen or twenty thousand dollars caused great excitement but the winner was disqualified since he had never registered at the convention and was hastily trying to do so after winning. They had to call everybody back and raffle it again.

Dee, the only solo woman trucker at the convention – petite and pretty – was most unusual and interesting. I asked if I could interview her for a possible magazine article (my first). If she'd known what a novice I was she might have had other thoughts but I plunged in. You just have to have the nerve to have a go and I sold the article to '19' Magazine when I got home. (Thus began ten years of magazine journalism which fitted in well with family life.) Dee had been working as a waitress in a truck-stop diner and realised if she couldn't be a horse which was what she wanted to be when she was four years old, driving a truck seemed the next best thing. Against all her white-collar family's aspiration, she took an automotive mechanics course and found a guy to teach her how to drive the 13-forward-gear monsters. Qualifying standards for a truck-driving licence are high – a practical driving test, an ICC physical examination and a written test on rules and regulations. Dee excelled.

She and her instructor went into partnership and someone gave them a beat-up old truck – their beloved Mack 1965 B73 Truck – free so long as they fixed it up. Dee stripped it and tinkered with it; adjusted, painted and pampered it. She put on a sleeper box and bud wheels, padded the doors with styrofoam and buttoned vinyl, and in no time it was going like a bomb and won first prize in a truck beauty contest and first prize in a truck drag race.

They acquired two more trucks and a third driver. Business was prospering but the relationship between the two of them deteriorated as he sank deeper and deeper into alcoholism. He was dangerous on the road and physically violent with Dee. She was scared of him, he ran all the trucks to death, left all the maintenance to her and drank them into bankruptcy. One day he took the original old truck, sold it for booze money and ran out on her.

'I figured, what did I need him for?' she said. 'Just to spend our money and beat me up? No thanks. I was a better driver than him, more responsible, better at business negotiations and a harder worker.' So, after four and a half years, she picked her 'ass off the floor' and started all over again with nothing. She went to work for another owner operator, this time learning to drive tankers. 'Its a very different technique handling a tanker. You mustn't make any sudden movements. A liquid load affects your weight distribution, your cornering, your braking, and your speed on steep gradients. There are also special dangers and precautions if you haul a combustible or volatile substances.'

Dee tried working with a co-driver but preferred being on her own. 'I like responsibility and I like being my own boss. I'm not tough. I don't like that butch image a lot of women truckers project. I don't swear and I like to be treated like a lady. I don't think a woman has to act like a man to prove she's equal.' She had to put up with quite a lot of resentment and hostility from male colleagues and once some real aggression from a guy who told her, 'Women like you should stay in bed where you belong.' 'But I've got gumption and resilience,' she said, 'and I'm pretty careful, always park under bright lights, lock my door, check under the truck for any stray legs lurking about when I come back to the parking lot.' Like most women working in a male dominated field she realised the necessity for being more than qualified for any job she applied for. This included keeping herself in top physical shape. She owned her own horse – a quarter bred Arab stallion and rode every day. She was also a scuba diver and a sky diver. When she got laid off her previous job, she went along to Shell and told them; 'This is what I can do, I'm good and I know I won't trash your trucks.' They hired her and currently she drives a huge 18-wheeler and hauls gasoline out of their terminal in Pennsylvania to deliver to petrol stations within a 350-mile radius – two loads a day, 1,500 miles a week. Working four 10-hour days and then three off. Time to spend jumping out of aeroplanes, saddles or boats, or with her (then) boyfriend – a toll-collector on the turnpike. ('You can guess how we met!')

Marriage, family life and trucking are hard to combine. There are uncommon pressures and long periods away from home. Apart from which, a lot of truckers are drawn to the life for its very hobo quality. The call of the open road, the promise of adventure, the lack of fetters and chains are strong pulls. Dee was in no hurry to settle down. Shell Oil Company paid for her to attend college and do a part-time BA degree in business administration, economics and management. One day she saw her beloved old Mack truck dumped in a junkyard all defiled and forlorn. Her ambition is to resurrect it and maybe one day start up her own business again.

'I'm proud to be a representative of the trucking industry, proud to be a woman and proud of my independence,' she said. 'I can watch the scenery go by and dream my dreams. That my idea of a good life.'

[N.B. I met up with Dee forty years later when she and her husband Don visited me in England. They live on a sailing boat and lead an adventurous life sailing the seven seas.]

I really admired Dee and was chuffed to have bagged my first interview and now it was time to leave the Independent Truckers Convention. Karl was still trying to fix me up a ride and felt bad that he'd let me down but it all worked out for the best. I'd met a lot of truckers, ridden around in the trucks and listened to a lot of their problems and grievances and now a bit of time on my own on a bus was welcome. Karl and Jim came to see me off and bought me a bottle of orange pop. I was very touched by their kindheartedness. The bus left Colorado Springs at two in the morning, headed up to Denver then West to Grand Junction. We drove over the Rocky Mountains and arrived in Salt Lake City for breakfast in a place right opposite the Mormon Temple. I would have liked to stay longer, look round the city and meet some Mormons. My impression was of a clean, puritanical, friendly and hard working community. They've turned this desert area into fertile farmland with an ingenious system of irrigation. Then we drove and drove all day across the endless expanse of Utah and Idaho. Sagebrush, lava fields, barren dunes and occasional irrigated sections where the staple Idaho potato, beans and sugar beet are grown.

Since I was sitting in the front seat, I asked the driver a few questions about the farming. Once he saw I was interested, you couldn't stop him. He came from a farming family himself and rattled on for hours pointing out everything we passed, telling me anecdotes about his old grandfather who at nineteen had been one of the workers on the pioneer railway. He knew every contour of the land we drove through and slowed down specially for me to take a photo of the Snake River Canyon when we passed it. The sheer enormity of the distances really brings it home to you when you try to imagine getting a covered wagon train across that inhospitable, waterless expanse. Twin Falls for lunch and Boise – the blessed wooded valley that must have heartened the pioneers – for dinner.

The bus driver came and sat with me in the diner wondering if I might be coming back this way and he could show me some of the beauty spots such as the volcanic Mountains of the Moon when he was off duty. Thanks all the same. He certainly helped pass the time and made it more interesting but I was quite glad when we changed drivers. At Boise a sweet little boy got on and sat next to me. Ten years old – the youngest of fourteen kids. Divorced parents. He's been a ping pong ball all his life. Now lives with his dad but was travelling home to his mom in Seattle Washington because he has to have an operation and she is the one with the medical insurance. An old-fashioned, hard-working, polite, honest 'Walton' type kid. His dad had given him $1.00 to buy food for the trip. Of course it only bought a couple of packs of gum. I gave him half a sandwich and bought him a slice of blueberry pie then we tried to settle down to sleep a bit but there was an extremely noisy, family of outsize women and kids from Louisiana who'd been on the bus for three days. They talked loudly, laughed, yelled and slopped up and down the bus with curlers in their hair and cheap talc on top of B.O., hooting with hysterics every time anyone farted at the back of the bus. Sleep proved elusive.

We stopped briefly for a coffee and doughnut at three am – my eyes red and stinging, ankles swollen, neck stiff. Two nights sitting up is really a bit much. I sat on the step at the front of the bus keeping the last driver company on the journey from Bend to Portland. At 4.50 am we finally hauled into Portland and there was Al Jubitz waiting for me. So incredibly kind to get up that early to meet a total stranger. The famous Jubitz Truck Stop was where Richard had filmed a large part of his Truckers film and while I zonked out for a couple of hours in one of their motel cabins, Al had set up a fabulous treat for me. One of his mechanics, Chuck, has his own private plane and Al fixed for him to take us up to fly over Mt. St. Helens, the volcano that had erupted so violently three months earlier in May. It was a startling and awe inspiring experience. The mountain is still breathing clouds of menacing steam. We flew up within ten miles of the crater. The peak used to be 9,677 ft. The eruption blew 1,300 ft. off the top of it and a square mile out of the side of it filling Spirit Lake with mud. By the end of its cycle of fire and fury fifty-seven people, hikers, photographers, scientists and folks living in the shadow of the mountain died including the old-timer and owner of Mt St Helen's Lodge Harry R Truman who refused to leave his home despite evacuation orders. Countless animals perished. The column of volcanic ash went 80,000 feet into the Earth's atmosphere, blocking out the sun and travelled across several States even as far as Oklahoma 2,000 miles away. The violence devastated the landscape, unleashing eight times more energy than was released by the sum total of every explosive dropped during the World War II including two atom bombs.

From the air, only 200 ft above the mountain, you can really get the full measure of the devastation – thousands and thousands of pine trees flattened and scattered like porcupine quills, filthy ash everywhere burying the beautiful scenery. Humbling and terrifying to be reminded of how totally powerless we creatures are in the presence of that kind of power. Chuck gave me a little flying lesson and let me steer the plane part of the way back.

Back at Jubitz I bought myself a pair of cowboy boots to join in the Line Dancing, decided to brave the bar and go hear the Country and Western band. I ate a hamburger in the diner and a tall, bearded trucker called Tom came over and started talking. He offered to buy me a drink and we sat at the bar talking for about two hours. I had a couple of whisky sours and he drank beer and talked like there was no tomorrow. A lot of guys I've talked to come on hard and tough to start with. I guess maybe its their protective covering. Karl Black was like that at first. Big, bad talk sounding me out on dirty jokes, and suggestive innuendo. Its a delicate balance to establish the conversation on another footing – on the one hand not to make them feel clumsy and oafish as if you're too much of a lady to associate with that type of behaviour, and on the other to make a clear statement of position, openly, honestly and friendly. I don't flirt and won't be a cock-tease, 'I am who I am. If you like my company I'm happy to make your acquaintance but reconsider your stereotypes please.' Stereotypes are a terrible curse and create the worst barriers between people. I wanted to know what he was like as a little boy, where his family came from, what he loved to do in his spare time. In the end we got along fine and had fun line dancing except that my new boots pinched my toes!

Next morning I went on my way. The end of this particular adventure. Before coming home I met up with Sharon, my oldest childhood friend, in Longview, Washington and we travelled together to the Olympic Rainforest. I also went on to San Francisco to stay with some cousins, to Los Angeles where I managed to connect with surviving relatives of my father's from Poland, met up with my daughter Francesca who was staying with a friend, took them to Disneyland, and then a long plane ride home together.

It has been very poignant revisiting these memories of my earliest solo travels; establishing my independence; trying my hand at writing my first magazine article. From then on I knew I wanted to travel more and write.

Chapter Eight

Since both my grandmothers died before I was born I have grown up bereft, with no models from our youth-worshipping culture to help me age with wisdom, confidence and power. All my life I have felt this loss acutely – no lovely warm, soft granny with a cat on her lap to dry my tears, tell me stories, proudly display my gap-toothed school photo on the mantelpiece, teach me how to bake; or perhaps a wild adventurous granny who went tango dancing and parachute jumping and rode camels across the desert ... . And then I became a grandmother myself. When the first of my thirteen grandchildren arrived the spirit of the grandmother awoke in me and I knew I would have to invent the kind of grandmother I wanted to be.

By now I was in my fifties. I wanted to write a book about this process – of becoming an elder – a quest in many parts of the world, for the crone in her many guises. I wanted to discover her, reclaim her, invent her, celebrate her. The crone represents the power of the older woman in her menopausal phase. She is the truth-teller, the weaver of webs, the keeper of stories; she stands at the crossroads, lighting the way, holding a lantern symbolising a time of decision and renewal.

In antiquity (and in those present-day societies where she is recognised as a valid image and not a useless object), the older woman had a unique function. She commanded respect and her advice was sought. Her community looked up to her and took her seriously. It was the medieval metamorphosis of the wise woman into the wicked witch the transformed her cauldron from a sacred symbol of regeneration into a vessel of poisons. It also changed the word 'crone' from a compliment to an insult and established the stereotype of malevolent old womanhood that still haunts older women in Western society today along with a legacy of fear and lack of identity. Because she was past childbearing age an old woman alone became the ideal scapegoat: too expendable to be missed, too weak to fight back, too poor to matter.

The terror of the Inquisition reigned for 500 years. In relatively permissive England alone, 30,000 witches were tortured and killed between 1542 and 1736. Witchcraft laws were still on the statute books until 1951. There is a growing recognition in the West that most witches were and still are, none other than midwives and herbalists; wise women who preserve in their collective unconscious the remnants of an older religion based on worship of nature and the feminine principle.

The Inquisition outlawed the ancient wisdoms of women and cut them off from their own spiritual vision. Denied any form of spiritual authority until 1992, when the Church of England synod finally granted them to right to become priests (not priestesses, mind you, and still serving the Father rather than the Mother), women have little confidence in their own mystery, power and magic except as youthful sex objects.

In Britain and America today, in the wake of the women's movement, the New Age movement and the ecology movement, there is a gathering groundswell of interest in women's wisdom, drawing on ancient pagan traditions, European folk traditions and Native American traditions. I wanted to explore this revival and the way it is helping older women regain their intrinsic worth. I wanted to go on a personal voyage of discovery to visit and learn from grandmothers in various parts of the world. I wanted to talk to old women about their experiences and listen to their wisdom, insights, secrets, stories.

Thus began the idea for my book *Older Than Time* – a grandmother's search for wisdom. Now that my own energies were no longer directed towards giving birth, rearing my own children and caring for my family, I was ready to connect with something eternal.

Paracelsus said that witches taught him everything he knew about healing. I would seek in the myths and symbols which are my inheritance, an affirmation of those skills and qualities which have somehow become downgraded and made risible as 'old wives tales' and 'feminine intuition'.

The crone (from Kronos, the Greek word for time) – 'the old woman who knows no master' would be my guide on this journey. She represented for me precisely the kind of power women need to find in order to counteract the war-mongering, empire building, rapacious, patriarchal power that has brought our planet to the edge of extinction.

Of course there were many wise women to be found at home so why travel abroad? My reasoning was this: because we live in a death-denying, youth-worshipping society, it is very hard to grow old with zest and confidence. I wanted to travel to such cultures as the Polynesian, Caribbean and Indian where old age is venerated. It would be a rite of passage for me – learning to befriend the loneliness and the darkness wherein lies our 'unknowing knowing' as Meister Eckhart put it. There's something about modern life that makes us think we can learn everything painlessly, quickly, greedily; get a video, hire an expert, have a briefing – but I wanted to take time to see things from a different perspective, to allow my perceptions to alter slowly, to let the unexpected slip in between my heartbeats. I would have to go away from everything I know.

In the end the quest became like a river. Once I launched myself it just carried me along. I encountered ancient traditions and occult wisdoms which have been repressed, forgotten, condemned. I met ordinary women and rare ones, artists and prophets, housewives and mystics, rich and poor, educated and illiterate.

But before setting off, a chance encounter with a friend who, knowing that I was wanting to meet wise old women, offered to introduce me to an English village witch. Until recently I had rather a dim view of modern 'witches'. My local 'New Age' shop had a whole section on the occult; pointed hats, bottles of 'All Night Long Oil', love potions, spells and runes. It was much frequented by young women with purple hair and long black fingernails and weedy, would-be wizards with plastic shopping bags. But beyond the fancy dress and the longing for a magic wand to make your dreams come true lies a deeper enchantment. Through all the centuries of persecution it has lain low but never completely disappeared.

Paddy Slade, the seventh child of a seventh child with a double first in English and Medieval History from Cambridge lived on a war widows pension in an ordinary little pebble-dash council house at the end of a muddy country lane near Bath. I don't know what I expected but it wasn't the sensible, humorous, ordinary-looking country woman in a woolly cardigan who opened the door to me. The only clue to her profession was a sticker in the window of her car parked in the drive saying, 'My other car's a broomstick', and a small plaque by the front door stating, 'Never mind the dog. Beware of owner.'

Paddy is a hereditary witch. Her mother and grandmother before her were witches and the knowledge has been passed down in her family for many generations. Her sitting-room and kitchen were like any other pensioner's with photos of her grandchildren on the mantelpiece and the smell of rhubarb crumble wafting from the oven but upstairs in the spare bedroom she has created a temple and this is where the magic rites are performed. She also loves to work outside in the garden or some other natural setting such as a field or a sacred grove. For a big community occasion, such as a seasonal rite, she hires the village hall. She is accepted by the locals (except her next door neighbour who is a Jehovah's Witness) as the village witch.

I spent a lovely day with Paddy enjoying her company and her wisdom. 'There's so much magic right here in these islands,' she said. It's all to do with "spirit of place". We can dig down into our past and find the magic that's there. The magic is in the stones and the springs. It is in the earth and the trees. That's what we have to find again.'

I wanted to ask her how the malevolent stereotype of the evil witch had become so prevalent. 'Pure propaganda!' said Paddy. 'Old women were such easy, defenceless targets, especially if they had a little bit of property that could be confiscated. The Church was incredibly greedy and twisted. The infamous *Malleus Malleficarum* (The Hammer of Witches – the Inquisition's handbook on witch finding, written by two Dominican monks) sanctioned any amount of torture in order to extract 'confessions' from the accused.'

Witchcraft, according to Paddy, mostly consisted of midwifery, herbalism and laying out the dead. Because it was to do with life and death it was seen as usurping the role of the all-male priesthood. And because it was to do with healing it was seen as usurping the role of the all-male medical profession. Women were not allowed to study medicine and could be accused of witchcraft if they were seen to gather two different herbs. Witches, like the shamans of other cultures were the repositories of ancient wisdom, symbolically riding the transforming powers of the elements, disappearing into different dimensions. None of this could be tolerated by the Church which fought back by literally putting the fear of God into people. Hundreds and thousands of witches, mostly old women, were tortured, hanged and burned at the stake. Even those who escaped execution were silenced by the fear which exists to this day.

'Witchcraft', she went on, 'grew out of worshipping the goddess and although the Church did a good job of crushing it they never entirely wiped it out. My family have been witches for as far back as we can go. They were country people from Kent, lived in the same place since the year dot. My mother taught me the earth was female, giving life the way a woman gives birth and was to be cherished. People came to my mother before they'd go to the doctor – for herbal remedies, for advice, for healing.'

Paddy's mission became that of spreading the word that witchcraft is an honourable, respectable profession and not to be looked at as an aberration nor something to apologise for or to have justify. 'I think of myself as a teacher rather than a healer,' she said. 'Its what I wanted to do ever since I was quite small. Now it has become urgent to put the record straight. Witchcraft is not about worshipping the devil. It never was. Satanism is clearly a manufactured idea, a refined, effete, upper-class pornography. It's a very male thing, the idea of devil-worship, and certainly these cults do exist today. A lot of it is to do with paedophilia, with coercive sexual power, with control. Admittedly the witches had a horned God but that's because he was Pan; he was Herne the Hunter, he was a fertility god – the ram, the stag, the goat – nothing to do with the devil. Why should the devil have horns anyway? Witchcraft, in its proper sense, has always been the craft of the wise. I call myself a witch because that's what I am and because I hesitate to call myself a wise woman. I wouldn't claim to have achieved wisdom yet.'

We talked about ways in which older women can begin to reconnect with their power. 'People are going to have to dredge up from their own deep residual memories what has been there all along,' said Paddy. 'Unfortunately women like my grandmother are dead now so I can't ask her but I learn a lot talking to any older women – chair bound, crippled, educated or not. So much wisdom comes from experience, from being a witness, from happiness and sadness. It travels via tendrils and networks as it always has done. We have begun to find the courage to own our own power.'

As for rites and ceremonies, we have to reinvent them. Paddy has created rites for the seasons and the festivals, rites for the land and the new moon. She has created a beautiful rite to reconsecrate the womb of a woman who has been the victim of rape. 'We older women, must help with our wisdom, our tenderness and our love to heal the emotional burden the victims of such an outrage carry.'

A lot of Paddy's work surrounds rites of passage. As the village witch she is frequently asked by local people to help them mark a special occasion. People come to her at transitional stages in their lives. 'We have done purification for a house, a blessing for an infant. We did a beautiful ritual for a young girl who had just started menstruating and recently a lot of older women have been asking for a post menopausal rite to mark the momentous transition after childbearing years are over. There's so much fear about losing femininity and usefulness but I know that this is the time we blossom and come into our own – the time when we can move into a celebration of our unique gifts and pass on things of value. The archetype of the crone, the grandmother, the wise woman should be welcomed into our lives. She is a very sure, strong woman. She is the way-shower, the lamplighter, the teacher – passing on the last of her knowledge.'

'I am a pagan in the true Latin sense of the word,' said Paddy. 'Paysan', peasant, country-dweller, rustic. You can be a pagan without being a witch but being a witch presupposes a frame of reference which is to do with the old religion, the nature gods and the goddess. Your whole life lived in reverence twenty-four hours a day. It informs everything I do.'

I asked Paddy if there was a rite for the protection of travellers as I was shortly to be leaving on my round-the-world pilgrimage. There was. She lent me a white cotton robe and she wore a yellow silken one. The idea is to take off your everyday clothes and leave them outside the room along with your everyday persona and your watch so that you are in a space outside time. We went into her inner sanctum painted to resemble a stone circle. Paddy mixed a special incense from mastic, benzoin, red sandalwood, cardamoms, frankincense, oil of lavender, mercury and lemon rind to burn in a little charcoal burner and gave me a thistle – the most protective of all herbs – to take with me. She lit some candles and called upon the god and the goddess. She invoked the powers of the four elements and the four directions. She said, 'We ask a blessing this day upon Allegra who is setting forth on her travels. We ask a blessing on the work she does, on the words she writes. and on the words she speaks. We ask for the strength of fire to sustain her, we ask for the stability of earth to go with her and to keep her on the path. We ask for the love of water and the intelligence of air to keep her mind and heart open'. She turned to me: 'State your case.'

'Ummm, err, I am about to leave on my journey to speak with wise old women from different cultures. I ask that I will have the courage, the understanding and the humility to deserve the confidences that I will be given. May I use them wisely and write well. This is what I ask.' Paddy gave thanks, the circle was closed, we disrobed and stepped back into our ordinary selves in ordinary time and space.

What moved me most about my encounter with Paddy was the generosity of her creed. It is so enabling and respectful. The American writer Starhawk has written wonderfully about this in her book *Dreaming the Dark*. Witchcraft and magic are based on a world view of 'immanence', a pantheistic conception of the Divine being present throughout the universe, of spirit and transformative power being embodied in the natural world. It is a set of tools, a philosophy of harmony with nature. It is about power from within rather than power over.

A short while later while visiting an international travel exhibition in Earls Court I found myself drawn to the stand about the delights of the Cook Islands in the South Pacific. I got talking with Dorice, the person in charge and when I told her the story of the time when my parents sailed back from Australia with me as a baby and my mother tossed her farewell flower lei over the railings into the ocean as the liner left Fiji with the prediction that if it floated back we would one day return to Polynesia she said, 'Come! I run a small guest house.'

So I went and there I was over fifty years later fulfilling the old prophecy. Alas, the age of ocean liners has passed. (NB *This was before the 21st century era of monster 3,000 plus passenger cruise ships*). No more the cabin trunks, the seventeen pieces of leather luggage, the crocodile travelling shoes, the mahogany deck chairs, the evocative whiff of salt corrosion and diesel … I joined the scrum at the airport check-in where my nostalgic reverie was interrupted by the sight a bullet-headed lad wearing loud baggy shorts and a T-shirt that proclaimed 'I may not be Hawaiian but I still enjoy a good lei.' Nonetheless my head was full of the romance of it all as I changed planes in Honolulu and settled down across three empty seats for the flight to Rarotonga.

Looking beautiful with a crown of orchids in her hair Dorice was there to meet me at the most enchanting airport I had ever seen – picnic tables with big straw umbrellas by the side of the runway, a chap playing the ukulele and singing a welcome song in the arrivals building. It was tantalising to hear the whispering surf and know the sea was right there but not to be able to see anything in the moonless night.

Dorice is a hereditary chief, or *mataiapo*, of the Cook Islands and, although not old enough yet to qualify as a crone herself, she had offered when I met her in London to introduce me to some of the elders on the island and invited me to stay in her house which is right on the beach. What an amazing offer. All through that first night I dreamed it was raining. I didn't want to open my eyes in the morning for fear it would be a disappointing day but the sounds I could hear were just the gentle rustlings of the coconut palms outside my window and when I peeked out, there was the washing-powder white surf breaking on the coral reef, the still, clear turquoise lagoon, the white sand and the sun shining. Could I really open the back door, saunter past a couple of hibiscus bushes and walk into the crystal waters?. Yes! It wasn't a mirage. I was doing it. I was actually doing it. I had always believed that one day I would find a way to return to the South Pacific and here I was. 'This is me in the South Sea Islands!' I shouted to the immensity before me as I stood on the shore, surprised at how loud my voice sounded on the empty beach.

Rarotonga is the archetypal fantasy island. In the centre the razorback emerald mountains covered in dense jungle, all around the edge the frilly reef like a lei. What will the world do for an image of the beatific life when there are no more 'unspoilt' islands left? The fantasy has nothing to do with reality, of course. Polynesians were and are good and bad like the rest of us and they sometimes ate each other in the not-too-distant past, but somewhere in the collective unconscious the illusion of an oceanic Eden, an island paradise, a garden of abundance and innocence shimmers like something once known and still remembered. As I looked out toward the horizon, the sensation of recognition flickered like a fish beneath the surface of my mind. Had this once been home before the fall?

I had read in my guide book:

'The Cook Islands are overwhelmingly, enthusiastically Christian and at no time more apparent than at a Sunday morning church service', so, after my ecstatic swim, I was glad of the opportunity to accompany Dorice to her local church. She, like most of the other women, dressed in white and wore one of the lovely wide-brimmed hats that the islands are famous for, laboriously woven from the bleached and pounded spine of the coconut leaf. I made do with my one rather crumpled skirt and a borrowed ordinary straw hat. The service in Maori, didn't sound particularly inspiring. The vicar droned on disappointingly, fuzzily amplified by a poor public address system. People fidgeted and fanned themselves but just as I was wondering what was so special, the congregation burst into song and the effect was electrifying. A spirit of pure joy filled the room and poured out through the open windows like honey from the comb.

One old woman, Mama Moe, stood up and in a strong, confident soprano threw down the opening phrase like a gauntlet. Then everyone joined in, lifting their voices to the rafters, weaving strands of melody into complex patterns of counterpoint, improvising gorgeous polyphonic cathedrals of sound. Everybody sang: the women soaring above in flying buttresses, the men shoring up the structure with rich basso profound load-bearing columns. No sheet music, no hymn books, no conductor, just a spontaneous, superb natural musicality which must pre-date by a long way the coming of Europeans and Christianity.

Apparently when the missionaries arrived they simply put Christian words to the existing songs. The rhythms, harmonies and basic contrapuntal structure are pure Maori. I was spellbound. I knew that I wanted to meet Mama Moe. In the late afternoon I walked up the road, past the little church, past a pen of pigs, past a *taro* plantation (the dense, fibrous root that is the staple food of the islands), past Dorice's family land with its sacred stone *marae* or temple, to the little house on the beach where Mama Moe lives.

All around the breadfruit that brought Captain Bligh to the Pacific hangs not in the loaves of childhood imagination but in the shape of spiky green footballs. Sadly, the beautiful indigenous dwellings, the open-walled, airy, thatched houses that used to be scattered about the islands in the dappled shade of the coconut groves, are practically non-existent days. Missionaries insisted on gathering the people into more condensed settlements within reach of the tolling Sunday bells and now almost everyone lives in cement boxes which keep the heat in and the ocean breezes out. Mama was sitting inside by her open door stitching a colourful appliquéd quilt – a skill introduced by the missionaries' wives and made their own by the local women. She invited me to come in and brought orange juice to drink.

Mama Moe epitomises the traditional Maori grandmother. Pure Cook Islander, born on the island of Aitutaki, she lived for a while in New Zealand where all Cook Islanders have citizenship and residency rights. But she never really liked it and is very happy to be home again.

In New Zealand the islanders find themselves at the bottom of the social pile where they struggle against poverty, inferior education, prejudiced attitudes and the way the 'good life' shimmers, tantalizingly, just out of reach. Mama Moe has raised six children and now looks after two of her nine grandchildren. The eldest she took when he was only a week old. It is the grandmother's prerogative to claim the first grandchild to bring up and this is rarely disputed. 'It's nice,' she said simply. 'I love the babies, it helps the parents, it stops me being lonely.' She once took the child to Australia to visit his parents and left him there awhile but had to go back to collect him as she missed him so terribly.

Mama Moe has been a widow for four years. Her husband was a farmer, a good, loving man, she says, who helped her, did a lot of the cooking, never argued, never hit the children. It's hard with him gone but one of her sons who is a chef at a hotel gives her money and she doesn't want for anything. Mama is well known and well respected by everyone for her singing and for her skills as a traditional cook, making an *umu* or underground oven, burying the food with hot stones. Her husband taught her to fish when they were young. She used to be afraid of slimy octopus tentacles sucking hold of her arm and dragging her down but now catching them is her specialty and she can make $4 a kilo selling to tourist hotels. Popping them in the freezer, she says, does away with the tedious task of bashing them on a rock to tenderise them. Then you boil them up, add onions and coconut sauce and you have one of the island specialities. She goes out on the reef fishing whenever she can – line fishing net fishing, poking about in holes for octopus, gathering shellfish and edible seaweed. She promised to take me with her one day.

Mama says to her grandchildren; 'Learn what I'm telling you while I'm still alive. Look after your life, stay home, learn the ways of your grandfather – planting, fishing – it's a good life to stay here. Don't leave your land, there's a living in the earth if you're not lazy.' She lamented the fact that so many of the young folk go abroad, never to return. Over the past couple of decades, 23,000 Cook Islanders had gone to live in New Zealand while only 17,000 remained on the islands.

This is the way things fall apart. In Cook Island tradition, for example, when an elderly woman dies, her grandchildren are called in to help bury her in her front garden. The villagers bring food and sing her praises. Upon her death, she will be wrapped in a comfortable cloth to be kissed, sung to, cuddled, massaged. Death is no reason to shun a person. Her family would not leave her alone cold in the earth in some faraway burial ground. They will ease her into death. They will sleep next to her tomb for as long as they feel she might need the comfort. As time passes her grandchildren and great-grandchildren will come to sit and play on her grave as if it were her lap – the continuity unbroken. But what if the world has changed? 'The young don't always grow up with their grandparents any more', said Mama Moe. 'Sometimes they don't even know them. It's very sad. The respect isn't there so when they get old they might put them in a sanatorium and that is what we fear'. The fragile thread of tradition broken.

Antony Alpers in his book *Legends of the South Sea*, makes a beautiful point about the difficulty outsiders have in understanding the Polynesian concept of time. For example old Polynesian epics and narrations never seem to have endings. Stories stand outside time, as we believe we understand it. We can't see the point. We want a conclusion. According to Alpers:

> *We like tick tock rather than tick tick …We need years, decades, eras for the reassuring sense of order they provide. In Polynesian storytelling the seasons play no part. They had no word for 'years'. Life just 'goes on' … Polynesians had never heard of tick tock until Captain Cook arrived with his chronometers and the whole sad ending was begun.*

Mama Moe had been shy about meeting me initially, claiming she didn't speak English well enough and, it's true, we couldn't exchange philosophical ideas as such, but the timeless heart language flowed. She showed me the fine pandanus mats she had woven out of the leaves sent by relatives on another island. She sang me the opening phrase with which she had initiated the singing in the church that morning. Mama had always loved to sing ever since she was a little girl. She stood close to the old women who led the singing in her church and learned all the hymns. Now it is she who chooses what is to be sung. 'If you sing with your heart, you know the Holy Spirit will lead you', she said.

Mama Moe is first cousin to Dorice's mother but called Mama or Tutu (grandmother) by many who aren't even in her family. She has the *mana* of age without holding any elevated position such as chief. *Mana*, as Dorice was later to explain to me, is a complex cluster of ideas which includes personal, spiritual and supernatural power. It is a mixture of karma, charisma and the life force itself which flows from a great universal source. This sense of a higher power flowing through all living things, a force which could be harnessed, was the basic concept underlying all religious thought in pre-Christian Polynesia. Prayer consisted of planting a seed of thought and nourishing it daily with the gift of *mana*. Sad how the missionaries often failed to see that the existing symbols and metaphors, such as sowing and reaping, were so extraordinarily similar to their own. Their literal minds were unable to see another finger pointing to the moon or conceive of merging another path to enlightenment with their own. Christian colonization was total but although Cook islanders today vehemently disclaim their pagan past, the concept of *mana* is alive and well.

Perhaps mana is what I am looking for – a mysterious substance with which to nourish my little seed prayers for wisdom and spiritual growth. Perhaps this is why I have come to the South Seas. A Pacific poet, Vaine Rasmussen, wrote this:

> ' …*When I grew old they gave me …a legend and a song. And a language to master a dying culture I had lost in my search. And I grew up at last …*'

Avarua is the biggest town on Rarotonga and therefore in the Cook Islands – comparatively untouched by the destructive aspects of modern tourism. (*NB: I am recalling this thirty years later and sadly doubt if it still holds true.*) But for now the pace is languid and no building is legally permitted to be taller than a coconut palm. It is a main street with a few shops, bars, cafes, a bank where I pick up some colourful money depicting a bare-breasted goddess riding on a shark, and a police station where I collected a Cook Island Driving Licence so I could hire a scooter.

I had been feeling overdressed in my sensible Rohan travelling clothes ever since I arrived. The local style is a length of tie-dyed gauze called a *pareu* knotted about the chest and a flower behind one ear. As little as £3.50 bought me a lovely one. A bloom from a handy hibiscus bush and I was all set. Absolutely the coolest, most comfortable apparel and flattering to all ages and figures. I felt pretty and feminine and the carapace of Western guardedness began to flake away. I went to the University of the Cook Islands' bookshop and bought two little volumes of poetry and took out temporary membership of the library in order to make use of the excellent Pacific section.

I plucked up the courage to rent a little motorbike. I had never ridden one before so the man gave me a lesson. ('This one brmmm brmmm, this one brake. OK?'). I more or less got the hang of it and careered off home in bare feet to practice a bit before launching myself on the open road. It may not have been a Harley Davidson but I felt like pretty hot stuff on my Yamaha 50cc.

I remember when I was about fourteen years old, feeling buffeted by the contradictory currents of adolescence which both held me in the childhood I didn't want to relinquish and a propelled me towards the freedoms and adult responsibilities I longed for. Middle-age (certainly grannyhood) has many similarities – a backward pull to whooping it up and a simultaneous yearning for for the higher ground of wisdom and serenity. On my motorbike, I rode the tightrope.

It only takes about an hour to drive right round Rarotonga but I took my time and stopped along the way to daydream. At Black Rock, a jagged outcrop facing the place where the sun sets, I scanned the horizon. It is from here that the souls of the dead are said to depart for the homeward journey to Avaike – the source. 'Where is Avaike?' I asked Dorice later. 'Aha!' she answered. 'The $64,000 question. 'Perhaps on the island of Raiatea near Tahiti. Legend has it that this is the place from which the original Polynesians sailed forth to explore the Pacific.' Once upon a time, against enormous odds, courageous sailors and their womenfolk came here in a couple of canoes with dogs, pigs and plants. Why? How? Was it chance or did they know where to come?

On a map of the South Seas the Cooks appear as a sprinkling of tiny stars. Fifteen little islands (with a combined land mass smaller than that of Luxembourg) spread out over 850,000 square miles of ocean, halfway between Tahiti and Samoa. Unity would seem to be hard to achieve but they have strong ties and the 'coconut wireless' spreads news and information at the speed of rumour. What connects them to other Polynesians is the generous and benevolent mother, Moana Moa – the Pacific Ocean – and the ancient plaited rope of history that takes them back to a common ancestry, common gods. I sat on the shore and read *Island Boy* by Tom Davis, the ex-Prime Minister. It is the story of Polynesian navigation, boat-building and seamanship told by a Polynesian, himself a world class sailor, who feels passionately that the real truth has been suppressed.

European history books and European anthropologists with their Eurocentric myopia, he maintains, have always assumed that the original inhabitants arrived here accidentally after having drifted aimlessly about the South Pacific. Not so. He believes they knew exactly where they were going and had a good idea of how to get there. The people would have been very familiar with the sea, with the tides the currents and weather patterns. Fishing expeditions would have taken them on long offshore adventures and, like the nomads of the desert, these nomads of the winds would have developed great skill in travelling huge, featureless expanses of ocean.

The marathon journeys, probably taken in order to reduce population pressures, would have been meticulously planned and skilfully carried out in well-designed, fast, seaworthy craft. Men and women travelled together, their skills complimenting one another's. They brought livestock, tools, fire and plant seedlings. They navigated by the sun and by the stars and had invented a kind of sextant. Their huge ocean-going double-hulled sailing canoes where as sophisticated and manoeuvrable as anything ever built by Europeans. But this didn't fit in with the Western view of Polynesians as primitive savages and heathen cannibals who had to be civilised, so the evidence was deliberately overlooked, and biased accounts geared towards imperial supremacy replaced the true story of their breathtaking achievements.

Tom Davis' view is that the Polynesians were the greatest sailors and navigators of the ancient world. Before the birth of Christ and long before the Vikings crossed the Atlantic Polynesians were sailing across the largest, emptiest stretch of water on the globe, Nowhere else had one people occupied so great an area. Along with the tools and the fire they also brought their mythology. They came from the legendary homeland of Avaike – the source, the world below, the south lands, a darker place of origin. Not necessarily an actual geographical place but somewhere other than the upper world, the world of light, the world of being. Like the Dreamtime of the Australian Aborigines, it is their creation myth. When you hear the blazing polyphony of their singing it doesn't matter what the words say. The music comes straight from the source.

I contemplated the reef. On a calm day it foams and hums gently in the background but its presence is what keeps this tiny dot of land from being entirely submerged by the crushing power of the sea. And when the wind gets up, as it began to that afternoon, and the noise of the surf becomes more and more thunderous, the sense of vulnerability and insignificance becomes acute. When a cyclone passes anywhere within 1000 miles, the waters surge over the living coral barrier and the benevolent lagoon arrives in your living room like a furious monster. When a hurricane strikes – as it did not long ago – the devastation is terrible.

By evening the coconut palms were doubled over and the noise of the wind howled through the louvres of Dorice's house. I walked alone along the beach with my pareu and my hair whipping about dramatically as I thought about the fragility of existence. I am a mere speck of life, a vital spark incarnate, existing in the universe by only the most incredible fluke and yet somehow part of the whole with a place in the scheme of things and a feeling of destiny. I felt close to the mystery. Einstein once said, 'The most beautiful thing we can experience is the mystery.' I feel that more and more. The sense of wonder carries us forward as it did in childhood. We are healed by what we turn towards, not what we turn from. Dorice thought I was mad to go out.

That night I lay in bed with the roaring, crashing reef and the screaming wind pounding in my ears. Nobody else seemed in the least perturbed. There is an assumption that the reef always has and always will keep the Pacific Ocean at arm's length but I am very conscious of perching on the rim of the crater of a submerged volcano in the middle of a million square miles of water. A tiny dot of earth, if earth these fairy rings of foaming coral can be called.

Here in paradise it's important to remember that terrible things went on in these islands. In the late nineteenth century Peruvian slave ships raided the outer islands and the London Missionary Society turned a blind eye to the true nature of their activities, accepting $5 a head for helping to organise 'volunteers' – the proceeds going towards building their church. Robert Dean Frisbie, an American trader on Puka Puka, wrote in 1928:

> *Clothes, clothes, clothes! The missionaries are obsessed by the thought of clothes …longer skirts, longer sleeves, higher necks for women's dresses. 'Cover up the sinful body' is the text of most of their sermons.*

All this has left a legacy of confusion – almost schizophrenia – in the minds of the Cook Islanders. I want to hear somebody say, 'We had a rich culture before we were brainwashed and made to feel ashamed of it.'

Dorice took me one morning to meet Her Excellency Mrs Maui Short, wife of the Queen's Representative here in the Cook Islands and one of the elders whom Dorice most admires. She has fourteen children including two sets of twins and forty-nine grandchildren and great-grandchildren. Like Dorice, she is a hereditary chief and for twenty years was president of the Council of Chiefs. We sat on her deep, cool verandah with embroidered cushions plumped on wicker chairs. As a tribal chief she is worried about the law courts erosion of the traditional arbitrator role. 'Formerly if there was a dispute in the district – marital or land related, for example, – people would go to the paramount chief who was very knowledgeable about tribal law, ancestry and inheritance. A meeting would be called in the family *marae* or sacred temple ground and the matter sorted out. Now people go to lawyers.'

Of course there is a basic conflict between a democratic system of government and the old autocratic tribal system but Mama Maui believes they could coexist harmoniously if the chiefs were seen in the role of ombudsmen. 'When things are taken to courts and handled by lawyers who are outsiders, they argue the pros and cons without knowing the people involved. We have given our power away and once it's gone you never get it back.' Historically, the traditional chiefs had always controlled such situations at a family or tribal level and settled disputes without recourse to law books. 'Rich and poor were treated equally,' said Mama Maui. 'Nowadays it takes a lot of money for our people to take a matter to court and those who can afford to hire lawyers will win the case.'

The Council of Chiefs at Takitumu (Dorice's and Mama Maui's district) is named after the pandanus tree. 'A strong tree with deep roots that grows by the sea and resists adverse conditions,' said Mama Maui. 'A good symbol of what we are striving for.'

Maui Short has a stone temple in her garden. Her home is part of her *marae*. Her relatives are buried there. The *marae* and the tribal chief system are the last remaining things from a once proud culture. 'Even though our religion is Christian, this is our connection with our most ancient past, to the land, to the sea, to our myths and legends,' she said. 'If you don't have something like that in your life you don't know where you have come from.'

The islands, particularly Rarotonga, sit pretty much in the centre of the Polynesian triangle and have been the source of some of the most beautiful art – particularly sculpture – in the Pacific. Christian missionaries tore down the temples and burned the images of their gods but the spirits still lurk here and many supernatural manifestations have been experienced by traditionalists who are also devout Christians and don't appear to be bothered by the contradictions.

There are conundrums concerning the whole issue of tourism too. A great deal of controversy, for instance, surrounds the building of a 300-bed Sheraton hotel on land sold by one of the chiefs against the wishes of the people. The reason tourists come to the Cook Islands in the first place is because there is nothing to do. Unlike Tahiti and Fiji which are already ruined by discos and traffic jams, there is no nightlife here, no TV. Yachties don't come here because you can't sail past the reef. There's one road that goes round the island and that's that. You can hike in the mountains, swim in the lagoon or lie in a hammock. It's wonderful. Nobody locks their doors at night and people leave their car keys in the ignition. The Cook Islanders themselves are friendly and easy-going. Even more importantly, they are in the majority. They own all the land. There are few nice crafts to buy and good places to eat so whoever comes here will leave their dollars behind them. Whatever revenue comes in from tourism stays in local pockets. The infrastructure is efficient enough but amiably amateurish so that you feel like a visitor, a traveller, rather than a portion-controlled unit.

Being the Marketing Manager for the Tourist Authority, Dorice is understandably keen to attract as many tourists as possible but she is also concerned that the growth in tourism shouldn't exceed the ability of the people to cope with the changes. 'Our people and our way of life *are* our national treasures,' she has said. Her husband, who grows vegetables in his small market garden would rather see the ladder pulled up and the character of the place fiercely protected.

As an outsider, I'm inclined to agree with him. I hate being a tourist. I want to be an 'insider' seeing the 'real thing'. But of course I am part of the rot and the real thing hardly exists anymore because we wiped it out. Take the fate of the god Tangaroa for example. Missionaries destroyed all the statues of Tangaroa proudly displaying his knee-length manhood (except for the ones they pinched which now live in the British Museum). For ages poor old local Tangaroas were neutered. Now the penis has been reinstated, though not in its original role as a symbol of power and virility but as a crude joke. In the souvenir shops you can purchase repellent plastic replicas of Tangaroa with pop-up willies, Tangaroa bottle openers, Tangaroa keyrings. He's no longer a god, he's a prostitute.

It was the arrival of European sailing ships 150 years ago that began the inevitable destruction of these fragile homogenous cultures. Now the jumbo jets and cameras *(NB: and more recently, in the 21st century, the gigantic cruise ships)* are finishing the job. Increasingly, tourism seems like a dreadful form of pollution. There's practically nowhere left that hasn't been damaged by its impact and I hate the fact that I am a part of it. The dilemma is that the tourism industry is the source of most employment on the island. Without it an even greater percentage of the population would go away forever to New Zealand. They are damned with it and damned without it.

Dorice respects and admires Maui Short. 'People like her are the keepers of the ancient traditions. I look up to her. She knows how to be fair, how to be persuasive and how to speak straight. She can interpret signs. She knows the history and remembers the stories told to her by the old chiefs before her. She knows the correct way of doing things. I am learning from her so that I, too, can pass it on to the next generation when it's my turn. Old women can best use their influence by keeping the culture alive. It is people like her who hold together the traditional chiefs and ensure that the *mana* is not eroded by other influences.

Mama Maui had prepared a wonderful feast for us with all the traditional delicacies I had come to like so much: marinaded raw fish in lime juice, baked mashed plantains with arrowroot and coconut cream, roast chicken, sweet potatoes and vegetables. We were totally stuffed and merry. The question I came away with was: 'How can we help the "differentness" in different societies to withstand the intrusions?' I don't know the answer but the sharing and goodwill between us as older women felt so lovely and important. The last thing I would want is for my presence to contribute to the erosion.

Tropical rain drummed all night on the corrugated roof and on the banana leaves – perfect sound effects for a scene of steamy embraces and rapturous passion. A curtain of water streamed from the eaves of the verandah. In the morning the sky was gunmetal grey, the sea a peridot green. Hundreds of delirious squawking birds had invaded the garden enjoying the rainwater pools and the fat worms on the lawn. A hot, still, overcast day and I walked along the beach at low tide watching the small figures of the fishermen out on the reef. Illusions and images formed and reformed in my mind. In the end things are what we imagine them to be. Reality is clouded by our search for paradise – an actual perfect place, a perfect love, a mythical destination, a haven over the rainbow where the heart finds meaning, clarity and contentment. I was yearning so deeply for this place to be perfect that I was in danger of inventing it. Somewhere out there is my fantasy island life. I don't know what it is. It may not exist. It may never have existed. Probably Mama Moe, with her singing and her quilting and her octopus- catching, comes closest to that image. Just then, out on the lagoon, an outrigger canoe full of children paddled by. It was the definitive Cook Island image that I wanted to take away with me. Little slippery bodies with sleek, wet hair laughing and splashing. A dog in the prow, a fishing line dangling, their radiant smiles as they waved. My first thought was 'Where's my camera?!' But then I said to myself, 'No. Just remember this. Don't try to capture it. It's a gift. It's yours and no one can ever take it away.' Perhaps some things should remain only as fleeting visions.

It was another Sunday and I decided to go to church again. I had loved the singing so much I wanted to hear it again. At the door, a beautiful child pinned a spray of flowers on my dress and kissed me 'because it's Mother's Day'. Mother's Day! and so far from all my babies! A rush of tears filled my eyes and I sat in the pew thinking about love, missing the physicality of holding my beloved ones. This is part of the challenge of my long journey. All the people I love are on the other side of the world. What if I was never to see them again? Can I really cope with the notion of impermanence? Can I just rest lightly in the as-it-isness of life? Of being in the moment? Can I allow myself to be warmed and filled with the richness of love without needing to possess and hold on? Getting old can be so arid. Touch-starved we shrivel and shrink. I yearned to fill my arms again. And then the singing began. I closed my eyes and was transported. The whole church reverberated like a struck tuning-fork. If I were God, I would tune in to the Cook Islands every Sunday. The sweetness of the harmonies opened a direct line to heaven. I filled myself up with it. Like drinking from a mountain stream or smelling a rose, it was pure nourishment and the knowledge came into my heart of hearts: 'Love is within me. It doesn't depend on the proximity of the love object. When I am alone I am not diminished.' I felt the impact of those words in my innermost being and my sad mood evaporated. I have always been afraid to be alone. If I'm not somebody's partner, somebody's mother, somebody's daughter, somebody's healer, who am I? But of course I am all those things and always will be. Like the untaken photographs they remain part of the sum total of my life. When I am alone I am not diminished.

I was invited to join some of the ladies for a special Mother's Day lunch at the best hotel on the island. I hadn't realised what a big deal they make of Mother's Day. It seems as if every mother in Rarotonga was there to be honoured by her family. From the richest to the poorest, all dressed in flowing muumuus with leis of gorgeous flowers in their hair. There was a great feast and a band but by far the most enjoyable thing was the presence of two tables full of old ladies who had come on their own. Maybe their children had gone abroad, maybe they didn't have any, but they were there to have a good time and to celebrate the abstract quality of motherhood. They had a ukulele, a guitar and several bottles of sparkling wine and sang non-stop the most wonderful songs with inventive harmonies with, according to Dorice, saucy Maori words. They got merrier and more risqué as the afternoon wore on. Occasionally one elderly gran would spring to her feet and undulate her hips in true Polynesian style to whoops of glee and applause from the others. Eventually the legitimate band admitted defeat and the old ladies became the centre of attention. They were still going strong when we left. Crone power *par excellence*!

Dorice and I called in to see Mama Maura, a traditional healer of much renown. Mama Maura, aged seventy four, is a skinny little woman who lives in a house by a papaya plantation down an unpaved back road. She was resting on her bed when we arrived. The bed entirely fills the tiny cabin-like room and is piled high on three sides by all the marvellous quilts she has made. There is a torn curtain on a string, and a shelf with a Bible and an ashtray. She was resting because she had already been to the 6 am and 10 am services at the church and was just about to go to the evening one. Mama lit up a dog end and coughed furiously until she'd managed to kickstart her lungs, then she settled back on her pillows. 'Nowhere in the Bible does it say you can't smoke,' she informed us, wheezing and gasping.

Mama Maura was born on Penrhyn, the most northerly of the northern group of the Cook Islands and the most remote. Her grandmother delivered babies and made medicines from local plants. The skills have been passed down through Mama Maura's mother to her, and she, in turn, is training a granddaughter to carry on the tradition. Herbalism is a very ancient family craft stretching back through many generations to long before the coming of the missionaries. Locals will vouch that Mama Maura has been party to many wonderful healings – a boy who was paralysed; another who was possessed … She helps people with whom the hospital can find nothing wrong and yet are experiencing pain – particularly pregnant women with backache. Mama massages them with special herbs. She makes many of her medicines from the ubiquitous coconut – the inner jelly of the unripe nut, the milk, the water. At one point I asked her is she had any medicine for women who were going through a hard time with the menopause. A blank look came over her face. Dorice tried again with different words. 'What did I mean "hard time"?' she answered puzzled. 'Why would there be any problems? It's not an illness, it's just the end of the reproductive period. A time to celebrate!'

I sensed that in this society women have no need to fear growing old. Being fat, being wrinkled or being old does not detract from your attractiveness, sexuality or worth. Don't have any children of your own? Bring up one of your brother's. This is what Mama Maura has done. A lovely plump little three year old boy with long black curls climbed onto her bed. She kissed him and stroked his hair and he toddled off again. The place is full of youngsters whom she calls her grandchildren but she never actually had any children herself. Her brother died while quite young and she took in some of his children, bringing them up as her own. Watching this and the joyful way in which the old grandmothers celebrated Mother's Day made me conscious of how much we have lost in comparison with a way of life in which family and community ties are still so strong. No one is shunted off to a 'care home' here.

Mama is a deeply believing Christian and yet she feels the presence of traditional island spirits around helping her. The ancient spirits of the land are alive and well, and like any earth spirits, they will abide. Pagan religions were all about respecting the nature spirits; caring for the land; honouring the creatures which give us food. They understood about balance and harmony. Tangaroa is only another name for God. The god of creation, the god of the sea, the god of fishing, of planting, of fertility.

Having heard she was quite a specialist in the field I hoped Mama Maura might be able to suggest something to help my chronic back pain. She knew just what to do and told me to come back the following day when she would make me some special medicine and give me a massage. She kissed me and hugged me, her little old crone face smiling so sweetly, a frangipani flower tucked into her silver hair. She lives in what, in an urban ghetto, would be considered appalling poverty – a concrete hovel with practically no furniture – but here on an island in the South Pacific, on her own piece of land with breadfruit, coconuts, mangoes, bananas, flowers, herbs, a few chickens and a houseful of 'grandchildren' she is rich. She sells a few hats and a few quilts, She is strong, confident, loved, loving, spiritually fulfilled and useful. I asked myself if we have lost the capacity to live such harmonious lives. No, it's a *choice*. I can create – *invent* – a powerful, effective old age for myself whatever my outward circumstances may be. The secret is an inward balance.

When I turned up next day at the appointed hour, Mama Maura was sitting on her kitchen floor with a fag in her mouth stitching a yellow and purple appliqué quilt, bony fingers flying while she watched *Death Wish II* on the video. My medicine was already prepared and waiting on the table. After the massage I was to drink a quarter of a tumblerful of pure coconut oil. I made a face. 'Then you eat this,' she said, handing me a pint-sized yogurt carton filled with what looked like snot, or maybe squid entrails. 'Dear God! What it is?' I quailed, surveying the grey slime with horror. Teach me to dabble with native medicines! Mama laughed, the granddaughter laughed, the baby laughed. 'Taste it, it's good,' she urged. I stuck my finger in it tentatively. It was sweet and not nearly as terrible as it looked. 'Green coconut cooked with arrowroot powder and raw brown sugar mixed with coconut oil,' said Mama, smiling encouragingly. I was to eat as much of it as caused me to have a good clear out. Mama offered a lengthy prayer in Maori of which the only words I recognised were 'good shit'. I managed to force down about half of it and felt things were definitely on the move.

I bought one of her straw hats and gave her my red silk scarf from England not knowing what sort of gift would be appropriate but she seemed very happy with it and we kissed each other goodbye. I certainly felt the benefit and my back ache eased considerably.

In my own quest on this journey I have been constantly asking myself, 'What sort of old woman do I want to be?'. Coming to the Cook Islands was a good choice. Older women here have always been treated with a good deal of respect. It's a matrilineal society. Women are chiefs. It's as good a place as you could find to learn how to age with confidence and grace. The plusses of ageing are the increased courage to be yourself; an increasingly strong sense of the power of the universe and that we can be conduits for that power when we open ourselves. As I see it, this is the only way to avoid the *fear* of ageing. Getting older is not without its pain but if you're growing outwards you're expanding into whatever comes next, you're welcoming the change rather than trying to hang on to the past.

The business of letting go has to be confronted every minute of one's life; children growing up, relationships ending, death, the loss of one's looks, one's health. Gradually everything will go from you until you die. This is a fact of life. Learning to be with what is is the only choice we have and in the meantime we can love. I can try to be a kinder, nicer, more tolerant person; more generous of heart, more useful.

On my last morning I did my t'ai-chi practice as usual on the edge of the lagoon and a heron came to keep me company. He stood in the surf a few feet away and watched until the very end when I'd carried the tiger to the mountain, bowed, and said the prayer I always say: 'Divine Spirit, Creator of all things, Abide with me.' Then he lifted off on his huge wings and flapped away into the dawn. I wrote a little haiku for him:

> *Heron on one leg*
> *Wings enfold the rising sun*
> *And my heart stands still*

Later that evening *I* flew away draped in enough flowers to open a shop – exquisite leis made of pandanus fruits, single gardenias, flame-tree blooms and yellow chrysanthemums. I felt like Titania from *A Midsummer Night's Dream* with two garlands around my neck and another on my head. Each one would have taken ages to make and would have been done, not for profit, but just for its own sake. This is an art form so transitory it only lasts a day – just to say, 'be safe, come back, you are loved'.

CHAPTER NINE

Growing up in California, for as long as I can remember I had been drawn to the stories, the romance, the legendary spirituality, the wisdom of the American Indians. The desert landscape of rocks and sand, canyons and cactus formed the imaginary background to so many of our childhood games. When 'playing cowboys and Indians' I always wanted to be an Indian. Knowing how to walk silently through a forest without the giveaway crack of a twig, knowing how to track animals, make arrowheads, ride bareback, send smoke-signals: these were impressive skills indeed. My best friend at school was one-eighth Cherokee and I longed to be her. (She thought it was cool to be Jewish like me and that matzos, 'big crackers', were the most delicious food in the world.)

So, why not start there? In a sudden burst of determination to finally do something about it, I flew to Tucson, Arizona and began by spending a couple of days with my cousin Peter.

Coming here to the South-West was the fulfilment of a long-held dream. The reality, however, was rather sobering. All around the edges of Tucson you can see 'Indian neighbourhoods'. They look pretty broken-hearted places. The level of good relationships to the white community is in inverse proportion to proximity and class. Local working-class people see the Indians as drunks, work-shy and trashy. They are jealous of the government handouts they get. The further removed they are, the more they are romanticised as 'noble' and spiritual'. There doesn't seem to be a middle way where people are just people.

Also there is no homogenous 'Indian culture', no kind of shared endeavour on the part of 'Native Americans' to improve their lot. They are as varied and uncoordinated as any other bunch of people trying to find their place in the sun. After several initial failures to find any leads or make any contact, a friend of Peter's gave me the name of an old Navajo basket maker and I made an appointment to visit her. I rented a car and drove the eighty miles to the reservation where she lived. A bleak, arid stretch of dirt road led to a cluster of concrete box houses and a mission church. I saw smoke coming out of a chimney and knocked on the door. A woman directed me to the basket-maker's house and I waited for over an hour but no one came. Being stood up had become a fairly regular *leitmotif* on the wisdom trail so far. I never got used to it, though, and it always hurt. Back to square one. 'Remember, whatever happens is the story,' I told myself.

Then an old trucker to whom I was telling my woes at a gas station suggested I try the Apache Tribal Office at San Carlos. 'They can be more approachable than the Navajos,' he said. I decided to try my luck and just turn up.

Everything in Arizona is a long way off. The reservations themselves are bigger than some states. I took the Oracle Road that goes north-east through the desert. On and on through the Coronado National Forest, over the El Capitano Pass where Kit Carson took his troops through the mountains, through more forest and more desert to the town of Globe which seemed as good a place as any to stop for the night.

A sleepy little town that was once the heart of the copper mining industry, Globe now dozes in the sun and life has passed it by. I chose the Willow Motel from a few straggled along the highway. They all looked like the Bates Motel from *Psycho* and I found myself checking the lock on the shower door and looking to see if there were any peepholes in the wall.

I read this in Larry Cheek's book, *Arizona*:

> No ethnic tribe on the planet has bounced so far from utter vilification to romantic glorification as have the Apache ... they were 'blood drunk and beast hot ... fetid breathed and shrieking ... lecherous and without honour or mercy ... the Apaches hate life and they are

139

the enemy of mankind.' (All this from the 1950's novels of James Warner Bellah). Or alternatively, from another novel of the time: 'There is no cheating, no private hoarding. Whatever they have is divided equally ...there is no caste system, and no aristocrats and commoners ... I wonder by what standards we have arrogated to ourselves the right to call Indians savages.'

The next day started with breakfast at the Blue Ribbon Cafe where enormous men in cowboy hats, exaggerated high-heeled pointy boots and bellies set like shopping baskets on their laps shovelled in mountains of eggs, fries, burritos, beans, chilli and cornbread. I never got over being astonished by the sheer quantities of food in American diners – a 'short stack' of pancakes was ten pancakes and a 'tall-stack' twenty all smothered in melted butter, maple syrup and rashers of crispy bacon.

It didn't take long from Globe to drive to the Apache Reservation at San Carlos and there were the dilapidated motor homes, the concrete box houses, the down-at-heel general store, the chain-link fencing, the rusting broken-down cars. I went to the tribal office feeling extremely intimidated by my lack of knowledge about Apache tribal culture. I knew minus nothing, I'd barely spoken to an Indian person and never met an Apache. One of my favourite films as a child had been *Taza Son of Cochise* – starring a white actor, Rock Hudson, – of course, but at least it showed the Indians in a dignified, heroic light. So different from most of the stuff we saw at the drive-in, dollar-a-car-load, movie theatre – films featuring savage redskins, renegades and murderous raiders.

So I was embarrassingly naive. Also I was both curious and slightly apprehensive about meeting them because of their largely negative reputation. Everybody loves the artistic Navajo and the spiritual Hopi – the peaceful pueblo dwellers, pottery-makers and blanket weavers but the fierce Apache were never sentimentalised in the same way. The Director, Ernie Vincent, a striking-looking man with wide, high cheekbones, shoulder length black hair parted in the middle and a red bandana tied around his head, kindly made time for me and invited me in. Ernie's office is plastered with posters urging 'Apache Pride' and advertising Alcoholics Anonymous meetings. Apache pride was pretty non-existent, Ernie admitted, but even so, after 500 years of continual oppression, they were miraculously still here. Their language which was forbidden, still exists and their oral history still remembered. The Apache fought longest and hardest against the 'White Eyes' who usurped their homelands, broke the treaties and tricked and massacred their people. It is a dolorous tale.

Ernie was perfectly friendly but doubted if any of the old ladies would want to talk. He felt they would probably be too timid but, nevertheless, he took me across to the seniors' centre where a woman named Elizabeth Classay runs a nutrition programme, providing a hot lunch for the elderly people of the reservation and busses them in from their homes every day so that, whatever their circumstances, they always eat at least one decent meal.

'What a pity you're not going to be here in two weeks,' said Elizabeth, and told me about the Sunrise Dance which was going to be taking place. This is the most famous of all Apache ceremonies – a young girl's puberty initiation. The godmother who guides her through it is an older woman chosen by the girl's parents as the person they most want her to be like when she grows up. Elizabeth was to be the godmother. I was so excited by this bit of amazing good luck that I instantly decided to alter my plans and come back for the ceremony. It was too good an opportunity to miss.

In the meantime it was lunch hour and suddenly the place started to fill up. A bus-load of wizened old ladies with faces like polished walnuts came waddling in, swathed in the attractive long cotton skirts and high-necked smocks that constitute traditional dress for older women (the young wear the ubiquitous jeans, of course). They collected their trays and sat at the tables. Ernie introduced me to an old cattle rancher named Frances Cutter, who said, 'Sure! Sit down. Have some lunch with us,' and never stopped talking. More good luck. The beginning of a timely friendship.

Frances, aged seventy-two, was one of five daughters and because there were no sons her father taught her to be a rancher so she could follow in his footsteps. She could ride like a man, mend fences, lassoo, brand and castrate (she called it 'castrasize') calves. When her father died, Frances took over the running of the place but her own children, in turn, who were all educated, married out and moved away. So many of the young people, she said, are not interested in carrying on with traditional ways and once gone, they never come back.

An excellent linguist, Frances speaks fluent Spanish, English, Apache, Navajo and Yavapai and it is a great source of pride to her that none of her children have succumbed to the dreaded plague of alcoholism which stalks the Indians more mercilessly than the US Cavalry ever did.

Frances is fiercely independent. Her cattle business is still a going concern. She is the only woman member of the Cattle Association and says the men respect her. She doesn't wait for the transport to bring her to town, she drives her own pick-up. She tries to keep herself strong and healthy and likes to go off into the hills looking for peridots (one of only three places in the world where they are found). The hills here are radiant with gemstones and crystals of every type. Arizona has immense mineral wealth.

I went home with Frances to meet her husband John. A retired miner he now makes jewellery to sell – and got out all his stuff to show me when I told him my son, Tim, was also a jeweller. John made me try on a little silver and turquoise ring which he then altered to fit me. When I asked the price he said, 'You can have it for a souvenir.' He loaded me up with chunks of fire agate, amethyst, peridot and tiger's eye that he had found while digging about in the hills. I felt bad about not buying anything but giving gifts is a sacred part of Apache culture, he said, and put a lovely little necklace of opal, turquoise and rattle-snake bones around my neck.

Frances cooked supper and invited me to stay the night. She wanted to get an early start in the morning to take me way out to the Apache reservation wilderness area about seventy miles across country towards the White Mountains to a place called Point of Pines and Ash Creek. 'Look at this land! Isn't that beautiful?' exclaimed Frances whistling under her breath. 'Gol-*ly*! Boy! God sure thought of everything! You name it!' All day long she kept up a running commentary on everything we saw and told stories of going out with her father when she was a child to catch wild horses, sleeping under the stars rolled up like a tamale in a blanket; how they would often meet a bear or a mountain lion and how her father taught her what to do. ('They won't bother you none so long as you don't scare 'em.') She told me which bushes her grandma used to collect leaves from to dry and powder for use as a poultice dressing for wounds and boils. 'I was raised on the land, raised to be a cowgirl and I'm happiest when I'm outdoors doing something physical.'

The surrounding meadows were a glorious carpet of orange poppies and purple spiky flowers like bluebells with the noble saguaro cacti standing guard. 'Oh boy, will you look at that!' said Frances, visibly moved. 'Ain't that pretty!' We took photos on her old Polaroid of each other sitting in the poppies. Frances had been driving all day with no sign of flagging while I was struggling to keep my eyes open. Back at her home, I managed to stay awake long enough to make us a tuna salad for dinner then we all fell into bed by 9 pm.

The next day I decided to travel on and see something of Arizona until it was time to come back for the Sunrise Dance. Inviting me to stay with them again on my return, Frances hugged me and wished me luck. It is humbling that it is so often the people with very little who are the most generous.

By the time I left San Carlos it was getting late and I wanted to try and make the town of Show Low, named after a card game, eighty miles away, before dark. A huge wind got up as I set off on the lonely road north through the high country. It became quite cold as the road climbed into the mountains. 'Watch out for Animals' for the next seventy-seven miles said a sign but all I saw was a squashed coyote and a flattened jackrabbit. I stayed the night at the Deuce of Clubs Motel and it was so cold I had to put my socks on and shivered under two blankets.

In the morning I was longing for a walk so I decided to do the Mogollon Rim loop. I was the only person there – my little Dodge parked all alone in the Apache-Sitgreaves National Forest car park. From the sublime escarpment of the rim overlook there are trees as far as the eye can see. Huge stands of tall ponderosa pines, piñon pines, alligator pines and juniper trees. Quite surprising when the popular image of Arizona is a desert. This is Arizona's least-known high country scenery and (back then at least) there wasn't one town along the eighty-seven-mile Route 666. Of course it wasn't really a wilderness – too tamed for that – but for a townie like me it felt pretty wild. Most of the quest journeys I've read about involve some sort of search for the traveller's connection to the sacred. Mine didn't feel quite like that. The sacred seems to be already in and around me. It is in my body and the trees and the land. I needed to leave home for other things – to learn to trust myself, to learn to be open to whatever comes next. To turn towards the unknown, not the familiar. I lay face down on a carpet of sweet, pungent pine needles and embraced the earth.

I carried on to the little town of Chinle which is at the mouth of the beautiful Canyon de Chelly – one of the loveliest natural wonders in a state filled with them. It is forbidden to enter the canyon without a Navajo guide. It is their land and many people live there, have farms and grazing land and ceremonial summer camping grounds so I asked one of the waiting hopefuls to take me on an all-day horseback expedition.

We rode between the steep, sheer, 1,000 ft high sandstone walls which look like slabs of Norwegian caramel cheese cut with a wire. We rode through the soft sand and shallow water for miles and miles to visit the ruined cliff-dwellings of the Navajo, the Hopi and the Anasazi people – the earliest Indians – known as The Ancient Ones. Human beings have lived in the canyon for 2,000 years and have left over 400 ruins throughout the centuries. Handprints and paintings of antelopes, horsemen, snakes, suns and moons adorn the rock face where overhangs protect it from the rain.

The canyon, like so many of the mute witnesses to the atrocities of the past, has a melancholy history. One branch of it, the Canyon des Muertos, testifies to the terrible massacre in 1805 of more than 100 Navajos – mostly women and children – by a Spanish expedition seeking gold. They refused to believe there really was no gold hidden there and slaughtered everyone in their path.

My guide wasn't exactly taciturn but he was not very talkative either. 'The old people told us to take care of the land,' he said. 'Take care of it and it will take care of you,' they said. 'Land still here,

144

Navajo still here, Spaniards gone.' He rode on with his hat pulled down over his eyes. I, not much of a rider, foolishly didn't have one and in addition to my saddle sores I got a frightful headache from the blinding sun. I felt parched and desiccated, my nose and throat prickled, my eyes stung but I was glad I had come.

Chinle, the little town where I stayed the night, perfectly encapsulates the paradoxes of modern Indian life and only served to strengthen my feelings of frustration and alienation. Everyone in the town of 3360 people is a Navajo but I had no way of knowing to what extent they still feel connected to the old Navajo ways which have been eroded as inexorably as the sandstone rock formations which dominate the Great Basin Desert. The values and influences of white culture have seeped across the reservation borders to eat away at the traditional customs. Videos, pop-music and liquor, fast-food and pushbutton living make the hard life of their fore-mothers unattractive to modern kids who just want out as fast as possible. There was a big supermarket in Chinle where I stopped to buy some fruit. There, pushing their trollies and loading up with washing-powder and microwave dinners were nut-brown, crinkley-faced old ladies laden with turquoise jewellery, carrying hand-woven bags in brilliant colours. I longed to stop one and say, 'Please stop and talk. Tell me something about your beautiful traditions. How can I learn to be a wise old woman? What can you teach me? But I'm already well aware that writers and 'seekers' like me are just seen as the latest manifestation of the genus 'Colonialist' – a line that descends from soldiers and missionaries, through settlers and traders to anthropologists and folklorists who sweep through, help themselves to the riches and leave the Indians somehow the poorer. They have stolen the land and the crops, they have murdered the buffalo, they have looted the very bones of the ancestors and now they're after the spiritual and aesthetic treasures.

I can understand the suspicion but I think it is a great shame. Spiritual treasures are not diminished when shared, they are multiplied and many ears are ready to hear the teachings. We need each other, we need to identify with each other's sorrow and ultimately we must trust each other. Naomi Shihab Nye, a Palestinian-American poet expresses this in her beautiful poem – 'Kindness'

' … You must travel where the Indian in a white poncho
lies dead by the side of the road.
You must see how this could be you,
how he, too, was someone who journeyed
through the night with plans.'

Next morning I carried on up to the Utah border where Monument Valley straddles the two states. It is still Navajo land although it is designated a national park. I decided to walk the trail on foot as I was aching and stiff from so much driving and riding. Again, visitors were supposed to be accompanied by a guide but it wasn't worth anyone's while to go with just one person, they said, so I could go on my own as long as I stayed on the dirt road.

But I didn't. Once out of sight, no one would know where I went. I hiked around in the desert all day carrying a rucksack with water and suncream. Everywhere were tracks saying 'PRIVATE KEEP OUT! and pick-ups full of Indians would roar past on their way to distant farms dotted about the valley. I felt as cut off from them as they probably would if they visited an English stately home. It was like being in an enchanted nursery where the toys only come alive after dark. By one of the most picturesque spots, I came upon a woman selling jewellery. It was dreadful old tourist tat although what she, herself, was wearing was gorgeous – old silver and enormous chunks of turquoise glowing with the patina of age. 'How's business?' I asked and she shrugged. 'Not much. Still early in the season.'

Just then a tour jeep drove up. Several men in baseball caps got out. 'This is Suzy,' said the tour guide.

'Well hello Suzy!' boomed a very fat man with lots of photographic equipment dangling in front him. 'Can I take your picture?'

'Sure,' said Suzy. 'One dollar'.

'Oh boy! This is what I been wanting to get ever since I got here!' said the man and he took his photo of a real Indian in Monument Valley. As soon as they'd driven off Suzy went and sat back in her pick-up and closed her eyes.

Monument Valley certainly reinforces any sense of insignificance a person might have. It is a bizarre, haunting landscape – the Navajo

Badlands – a jagged forbidding country with a geology like nowhere else. It's like being at the bottom of vast ocean, 1,000 feet deep, from which all the water has been drained. It stretches as far as the eye can see in every direction with snowy mountains on the distant northern horizon.

It was a rare gift to be able to hike there alone all day. I kept on rounding a bend in the trail and gasping, 'Oh my God!' This time I saw a live jackrabbit who ran like the wind, his perfectly evolved huge sensitive ears translucent in the sun. I shared the vastness with a solitary hawk and a tiny lizard and lots of rattle snakes who turned out to be pieces of bleached desert driftwood. I also saw beer cans and condoms but I'll erase them from my memory.

As the local residents whizzed along the road going about their business I could see how important it was for them to keep us at arm's length. Our culture is so dominant, our reputation so tarnished, our tongues so forked that they are better off behind their 'Keep Out!' signs. Much as I hate to admit it, I'm no different from the guy with the camera, wanting to find my real Indian too. I want to shout, 'Let me in!' I want to fit in everywhere, to be a chameleon, to be a bridge, to be trusted, to be accepted. Maybe becoming wise isn't about finding out how everyone else does it but in discovering my own inner way. I'm sure no Navajo elder feels the need to be accepted by me.

The following day I saw the Grand Canyon. What must the first humans who set eyes on it have thought? How did anyone find their way across it or even down into it? As you drive the 160 miles from Kayenta the land looks innocent enough. Nothing prepares you for it except a few ominous cracks that begin to appear around the Little Colorado river. It is dinosaur country – primitive, arid, prehistoric-looking – with a few fissures and crevasses in the flat, featureless sandy scrub. Then you round the last bend and there it is! Aaaaaargh! Yikes!

The trouble with trying to describe the Grand Canyon is that the brain really has no precedent for processing visual information on this scale. All human endeavour is dwarfed by comparison except perhaps Bach's or Mozart's.

You can trek to the bottom of the Bright Angel Trail or ride on a mule. You can fly over it in a helicopter, you can raft the waters. What would be ten miles across to the other side if you were an eagle is 215 if you go round by the only road. It gets the adrenalin racing to walk along even the tamest of trails. I brought a hat this time and scared myself silly hiking along the precipice for about four hours. My whole body twitched and lurched with mixture of vertigo and emotion. At least those who named the various peaks and buttes understood that this was the landscape of the Gods. They are called Isis's Temple, Jupiter's Temple, Osiris, Shiva, Brahma, Venus, Vishnu, Solomon …

I had slept in the car so as to be there at dawn. In the perfect stillness of that moment when the sun rose turning the rock golden, pink and orange I wanted to fly. I wanted to cry. I wanted to sing and shout. Instead I sat on a rock and watched the panorama of changing colours, marvelling at my good fortune in being here, in being alive, in being a child of this Earth. I wrote in my journal:

'All my life I will remember that beautiful day. Thank you Great Spirit.'

CHAPTER TEN

'Their eyes mid many wrinkles, their eyes,
Their ancient glittering eyes, are gay'

W. B. Yeats, 'Lapis Lazuli'

The sound was thrilling, primal, electrifying. It seemed to reach right back to our most ancient connection to the nameless sacred mystery. Somehow we have all known this – the fire, the night, the stories, the drums. I didn't feel I was eavesdropping on something exotic and alien, rather that I was remembering something I had always known. I marvelled to think that all this had *survived* in spite of the prohibitions, forced exile, brainwashing, slaughter. Here in 1992 another generation of young Apaches were singing their hearts out in the ancient language, bringing tears to their grandmother's eyes.

As advised by Frances, I had purchased some suitable offerings – tobacco, a case of Coke, a large tin of coffee, a few pounds of biscuits and some bags of tortilla chips. It was nightfall by the time I got back to San Carlos and Elizabeth Classy was already out at the Beaver Springs Camp Ground making preparations. Someone drew me a map of how to get there – off the highway, under a bridge, over the railway tracks, a couple of miles down a dirt road to a grove of cottonwood trees. I'd know it was her by the maroon and grey truck.

It was pitch dark and everything on the reservation looked different. I had felt quite nervous heading off alone into the night with only my headlights and the eerie sound of distant Apache drums to guide me. I got myself horribly lost going down at least three wrong dirt roads and nearly stuck in a soft, sandy river bed but I finally made it to the right place. Now *this* was more like it. This was the scene I had imagined.

Elizabeth Classay came forward to greet me. She had changed into her traditional camp dress with feathers in her hair and looked wonderful. In the middle of their camp ground a fire was blazing and my gift joined the mountain of food they had been collecting. Many guests would be coming and everyone had to be fed. Elizabeth, her sisters and several of her women friends had been cooking up great vats of stew and fixing tortillas all day. The men had been building the wickiup – a beautiful sweet-smelling structure of leaves and branches – in which the godparents would sleep for the whole week. People had set up tents, motor homes and brush lean-tos. Way across on the other side of the enormous clearing the girl's family were making their own preparations.

About a dozen men sat in the middle of the enclosure drumming and singing the ancient chants. Elizabeth explained that the words were blessings, prayers for peace and prayers of thanksgiving. 'The words are so beautiful I get quite emotional every time I hear them,' she said. 'So much wisdom and poetry. So much deep meaning.' Then she laughed, 'Come on, let's dance,' and showed me what to do. A group of women link arms and stamp rhythmically from foot to foot – six steps forward, six steps back – while travelling in a clockwise circle. The structure is very informal. People join in and leave as the spirit moves them, dancing for as long or as short a time as they like. The whole spontaneous choreography was so peaceful, graceful and harmonious – each dancer unique and yet part of the whole, in step with the rhythm of their ageless, eternal story. It was everything that the wretched reservation towns are not. The sense of sisterhood and belonging with women from such a different culture was so comfortable. I fell into a hypnotic, meditative reverie and hardly noticed the two hours go by.

The ceremony itself was scheduled to begin at sunrise the following morning and I hardly slept because I didn't want to miss anything. Frances and I got up just as the sky was lightening to the east and raced over to the camp ground by 5 am. The men were building the fires, splitting logs, carrying heavy cast-iron pans. The women were peeling, chopping, frying chicken, making tortillas, a big breakfast of 'fry bread', fried potatoes, bacon, eggs and coffee was dished up to the workers.

As the sun rose, the godmother's party walked across to the girl's camp to dress her in her symbolic accoutrements. Frances had lent me one of her camp dresses so I could meld in. Reynelda Cassador, the young girl, was waiting demurely in her wickiup arrayed in a lustrous purple and gold camp dress and beautiful beaded moccasins and necklace. Planted on the ground outside her doorway was a staff adorned with eagle feathers and ribbon streamers. Elizabeth circled around the staff and entered the wickiup. She then tied a thong with an abalone shell disc on Reynelda's forehead. By this she will be identified as 'White Shell Woman' or 'Changing Woman'. Another strip of rawhide with a drinking tube and a scratching stick hanging on it was fastened round her neck. During the four days she must only drink through the tube and scratch herself with the stick.

A white eagle feather – the colour her hair will be when she is old – is fastened to the back of her head to symbolise long life and the eagle down feathers on her shoulders will enable her to walk as lightly as feathers on the wind. The staff is placed in her hand, reminding her of the cane she will need in old age and thereby symbolising the many years she will live as a wise old woman. Elizabeth, her godmother, has been specially chosen as the older woman of ideal character whom the parents most want their daughter to emulate.

The Medicine Man then made a long speech in Apache translated for me by Elizabeth. He told us that this four-day ceremony called 'The Gift of Changing Woman' or 'The Sunrise Ceremony', is the single most important event in an Apache girl's life. Each time the ceremony is held, the Apache world is created anew – nothing is more meaningful in the Apache world view.

In their language the ritual is known simply as 'Nai'ez' or 'It is Happening'. Changing Woman was the first woman on earth (created before man). Longing for children, she made love with the sun and gave birth to twins. The twins grew up to clear the world of evil and make it good for humankind. During the 'Changing Woman' ceremony, Reynelda will become the embodiment of the deity's spirit and be prepared for her role as an Apache mother and life-giver. The ceremony also ensures that she will have strength, an even temperament, prosperity and longevity – all qualities associated with Changing Woman. It is a re-enactment of the creation of the world and the coming of the Apache people – a celebration of life.

The Medicine Man then called on the assembled company to henceforth respect the young girl as a fully-fledged woman. Then we all departed and returned to our cooking. Mid-morning the great gift exchange began. All the vast cauldrons of food – stews, cakes, roast meat, salads, punch – were to be taken over to the other camp and they would do the same. This symbolises the willingness to give away everything you have and the special bond that now unites the two families.

First a modest quantity was taken across the camp ground to the men's sweat lodge on the banks of the river. Men had been going over there on an off all night long to purify themselves and there were still several men inside chanting and praying. The drummers in our camp began the beat and all the women in their colourful dresses initiated the dance. Men, in their finest embroidered shirts and white stetsons, linked arms with us and joined in. After about five songs we could hear a terrific cacophony as the food-bringing procession from the other camp, led by Reynelda and her parents, arrived dancing and drumming, singing and beeping their truck horns. We ignored them and carried on dancing to our own rhythm while they circled around us and set all their offerings out on a long table.

Then they joined our circle and we all danced together. After a while they returned to their camp again and we formed into a procession of our own led by Elizabeth and her husband. Someone put a cake in my arms to dance across with and off we went – heavy cauldrons in the trucks, lighter things carried by the woman, men chanting and drumming.

It was exhilarating to be in the middle of it. The heat, the swirling dust from everybody's feet, the blowing, drifting seeds from the cottonwood trees creating a dreamlike silvery haze. It was hard to believe I was really there. 'English Traveller Dances With Apaches!' Colours whirling, moccasins stamping, people laughing, tiny children joining in, fat old women reliving their youth. Magical. We set our food down on their table in the same way while they pretended nothing was happening. Then we synchronised our footsteps with theirs and all danced together again. By this time everyone was famished. We returned to our camp and tucked in to the feast – everyone piling my plate with things I had to try: acorn soup, roast corn, Indian tacos, squash and lima bean stew – and then relaxed in the shade for a siesta during the heat of the afternoon.

I asked a young girl of seventeen how it had felt when she had been the focus of all the attention. She said it was both wonderful and embarrassing, 'Like everyone's looking at you and knows you've just got your period – but you feel so proud to be a woman.'

Apache society is matrilineal. This was the first time I had ever been in a culture where it actually felt more important to be a woman, a culture where the whole tribe celebrated the onset of the life-giving menstrual blood; the only blood shed without violence. An occasion for joy, not a 'curse'. The men, though, have suffered terribly. As someone said to me, 'Women always have their role as mothers and nurturers whatever happens to them but the warriors, the defenders and hunters of the conquered, defeated society have nothing. Only their shame.' It's true and it was wonderful on this day to hear the powerful, virile sound of the men's singing and drumming, reclaiming their manhood and their dignity.

There were quite a few jokes at my expense – 'Aren't you afraid to be here with us wild Indians?' 'Hasn't anyone told you we scalp people?' – but after the initial banter the mood became more serious. 'Don't let anyone tell you we were a bloodthirsty people,' said one man. 'We're all so tired of hearing that. It just wasn't true. It was US Army propaganda to paint us as subhuman.'

'We had a reputation as fierce raiders,' said another, 'but the terrible bloodletting never really happened until the white invaders threatened our homelands.' Personally, I find it hard to imagine that any culture with such a poetic and female-based creation myth could have been so cruel and savage as they were portrayed.

They called themselves simply, 'The People' but to nearly everyone else they were known as 'The Enemy', perhaps because few people ever fought harder to hang on to their territory and their way of life. They were one of the last to be defeated. Their famous vitality and tenacity have served them well even though they finally lost their battle against the usurpers of their land and were confined on reservations. Their spiritual view, which treats each day as a sacred path to be walked with concern for all created things, can have new life breathed into it with every ceremony such as this. Although alcohol and drugs lie ever in wait to push them into the abyss.

Frances never gave her own daughters a Sunrise Dance because these rituals were illegal forty years ago and people were still mightily crushed by missionary efforts to change their religious beliefs. They have only recently begun to reclaim their history and salvage their identity. It is a terrible story.

By evening a huge bonfire had been lit in the middle of the central clearing. Drummers from both camps were drumming and strings of dancers were stamping about. Tradition demands that sixteen songs be played (each one can last up to twenty minutes). Reynelda, accompanied by her godmother must dance from beginning to end to display her stamina. For everyone else this session was mostly a social dance with much whooping and hollering and snogging in cars and over-excited children running about chasing each other in the dust. Frances and I lasted till about 10.30 then snuck off to bed.

The next day was another dawn start so we returned to the camp ground at 5.30 to help make the tortillas for breakfast. Six or seven women each with their own cooking fire sat around companionably slapping and stretching the balls of dough to the right thinness. Nothing has ever tasted more delicious than those tortillas freshly baked on bits of old sheet metal bent over little piles of hot embers!

Just after first light, both camps formed into one huge circle in the big clearing. Down the middle had been laid a line of crates of oranges, cases of Coke and burden baskets filled with sweets, Facing the east stood the drummers in full voice with a pile of blankets and buckskins in front of them. While the rest of us kept time with our feet, Reynelda knelt on the buckskins with her hands raised in the air and her eyes closed. She began to sway from side to side, her beautiful little face illuminated by the rays of the rising sun. Elizabeth, as her godmother, stayed beside her throughout, giving instruction and moral support, wiping her face and giving her sips of water through the tube. By re-enacting the posture in which Changing Woman underwent her first menstrual period the initiate opens herself to the spirit of the deity which now enters her body. She did, indeed, look quite possessed.

All the time this was going on, little raiding parties of three or four ladies would detach themselves from the circle, dance over to capture a man from the other side and dance him back over to their side. The old grandmothers were tireless. Two of them linked arms with me and off we went, stomping our way across. 'Come on, let's go and get him before someone else does,' they cackled. Although the underlying theme of the dance was serious, it was tremendous fun and everyone was laughing and joking. Very young girls captured old men, children danced with each other and with their fathers. At the end of each set, the men would return only to get grabbed again by the next chain of marauding ladies.

The next part of the ceremony required the girl to lie face down on the buckskin and to be massaged all over quite roughly by the godmother. This is to symbolically mould her into a woman – to give her straightness, beauty and strength. The staff with the feathers is set out in four positions, each a little further away, signifying the four stages of childhood, adolescence, maturity and old age that she will pass through. She then has to run, while everyone chases her, to the four directions, showing that, like Changing Woman, she can run swiftly and never get tired.

A man stood holding a basket of sacred yellow cat-tail pollen and we all lined up to file past Reynelda, taking a pinch to sprinkle on her. Another basket filled with candy, corn kernels and coins was poured over her by the Medicine Man. The crates of oranges and Coke were flung in the air and everyone scrambled to take something. By now all the food had become blessed and holy so the people were assured of abundance.

Reynelda's last action of the day was to throw the buckskin to the east and the blankets to each of the other three directions. This ensured that there would always be deer meat, plenty of blankets and good hunting or everyone in her camp.

By this time there had been over four hours of continuous dancing in the hot sun and everyone was wilting. We went back to our camp for the great lunch-cooking marathon. More tortillas were flap-flapped in deft hands and cooked over hot coals on pieces of bent tin, more lumps of dough fried in hot oil. Corn and acorn soup, beans and bacon, pig's trotters and salad ... . It was all wolfed down and people sat around in the shade talking.

'I'm glad you've come to see the truth for yourself,' said one old lady. 'A lot of white people have no idea of who we really are and believe the terrible things that have been said about us for so long.' I was feeling quite overwhelmed by what I'd seen – by the beauty and importance of a ceremony which gives a young woman on the threshold of adulthood such a wonderful sense of self-worth and a role which will continue right through into old age. It is the miracle of a woman's life-giving womb which its being celebrated, bringing happiness and plenty to the whole tribe. It links the present to the ancient past, giving a sense of continuity and cultural richness.

I also learned some more about the Western Apache creation myth: Changing Woman never became old. When she got to a certain age she went walking to the East and saw herself coming toward her. When they came together there was only one – the young one, So Changing Woman has the power of perpetual renewal.

At dusk another enormous fire was lit in the central clearing. Reynelda and four young female companions stood together, all dressed in the most gorgeous, fringed and beaded buckskin dresses and moccasins. The rest of us formed a giant circle around them. Suddenly, in a great hullaballoo of stamping and bells and the ghostly moan of a bull-roarer, into the firelight leapt the Crown Dancers who impersonate the Mountain Spirits – four benevolent ones and a trickster/clown who represents the whirlwind, the mischief-maker, the unpredictable aspect of nature. They had come to bless the new incarnation of Changing Woman and to ensure her well-being through life.

The musicians drummed and chanted and the Mountain Spirits

with their painted bodies, elaborate head-dresses and carved wands, danced in the firelight casting grotesque shadows. It was a spectacular sight and it really felt as if a magical transformation was taking place. The spirits led Reynelda and her companions in a dance weaving in and out of the circle and finally ending up in an open-sided wigwam made out of four saplings with the musicians inside. Again they danced wildly to the four directions, yelping and hollering – clouds of dust almost obscuring them from view. Little Reynelda bore it all with great dignity and fortitude.

On the last day the Mountain Spirits came again. They arrived at sunrise as the girl stood waiting under the four saplings facing east. While we linked arms and danced on the spot they painted her all over with a preparation of white clay until she was transformed into White Painted Lady with the power to bestow blessings which she did by dancing round the circle flicking the clay on all of us. Finally everyone followed her and the Mountain Spirits as they danced four times through the saplings to the four directions, honouring the unifying qualities that reside there. And that was it.

There would be another feast, time for the old men to tell again the teaching stories and myths; then in the evening, the final gift exchange. All the remaining food, some blankets, camp dresses, turquoise jewellery would be danced across to the other side. Nothing is hoarded, Everything is given away. What a tragedy we didn't learn all this while we had the chance. Maybe it's not too late.

Elizabeth handed me some of the sacred yellow pollen to take with me on my journey as a blessing. Frances gave me a bag oranges. I also took away with me an indelible vision of renewal – vital to the continued life of the Apache people – of older women handing on their wisdom and experience to the next generation and of men as potent guardians and protectors.

CHAPTER ELEVEN

I've always been a bit disturbed by the phenomenon of the International Date Line. 'You lose a day,' people say blithely, but I felt weird when Monday the 18th of May disappeared. It vanished into the hole in the mysteries of time. It's like that moment when a digital clock reads 00.00 at midnight. What if I fell into that nowhere, nothing, non-existent minute? The ice floes of time would close over my head and I wouldn't be able to find the crack to get out again. A bottomless crevasse lies in wait for unwary travellers who don't ski fast enough across the international date line.

Once, years ago, when I was on an Outward Bound course with Matt, I had to swing on a rope over a slimy bog. All the others who did it first managed effortlessly and sailed across to the waiting nets on the far side – especially Matt who was as nimble as a flying squirrel. I didn't make it. I fell in and the horrid ooze engulfed me. This is how I felt when I arrived in Australia. I had been in an altered state when I boarded my flight leaving the Cook Islands, wearing my fairy crown that Dorice made me, my head full of images of my last walk in the enchanted forest of the interior and of my last naked full-moon swim in the phosphorescent waters of the lagoon where my limbs shed droplets of light as I moved and a shoal of flying fish exploded through the surface like submarine-launched missiles I possibly wasn't in a state to defend myself against the perils of the crack in time waiting to swallow me up. I languished in limbo for quite a few days waiting for my soul to catch up with my body again.

In Perth I met up with my beautiful daughter Femi whom I hadn't seen for three years, during which time she had established a singing career for herself in Australia. I went with a crowd of her friends to hear her solo gig at a nightclub. It was the first time I had heard her new sound and I was so touched and impressed and proud I could hardly stop myself bawling. She had gained much strength and confidence and looked completely at home on the stage. Femi's friends all welcomed me and I felt happy to fit in so comfortably with the young people. In fact most of the time I don't feel any different in age to them. That's one of the reasons ageing is such a challenge. The ageless, eternal child in me – the youthful spirit – has remained unchanged but the body gets creaky and the humours get cranky.

Western women have a hard time experiencing the pain of invisibility. One day you're an attractive, alluring woman with men buzzing around and the next you become one of the faceless group of old ladies who sit alone in cafes and on park benches. One of the wrinklies, shrinklies, crumblies, old bags, old bats – bewildered at the speed of descent – dismissed as irrelevant, dying of loneliness. With no recognised rites of passage, haunted by the legacy of horrid images of witches and crones, we grope unsteadily through the period of transition, unsure of what lies ahead, afraid to relinquish what has gone before. We lie about our age, have liposuction and face lifts. The Cook Island women showed me another way.

This journey has given me time for reflection, time to try and distil the wisdom from experience. I want to hold hands with the child I was and the old woman I will become.

Femi and I went away for a few days to get to know each other again. She drove us in her little jeep down to the south-western tip of Western Australia where she had booked us into a lovely old 1920s' country hotel in beautiful grounds near the sea. Late autumn weather and we walked down through the valley to dip our toes in the Indian ocean and watch the brave sleek lads, like young seal pups, ride the crashing surf on fibreglass boards. We walked in the towering forest and breathed in the woody smell. The trees of this land of my birth bring back my happiest, earliest, primary coloured memories. The blue skies through eucalyptus trees, the kindly, wrinkly, old skin of the white ghost gums, the fragrant flowering yellow mimosas, the generous ti-trees with their healing oils, the comical bottlebrushes full of screaming clouds of green parakeets – all flashbacks to my babyhood when I was born in passing in this far-away country. I was happy to be with Femi and to know the blessed closeness of love with a daughter. I was aware that there had been a gradual shift in our relationship since she'd been living abroad. Now she was all grown up. Assuming more of the parental role. We were on her territory here and she had made all the arrangements. I thank God for my children – they make it so much easier to grow old and to move on.

My Femi. What a miracle it was, that 'appointment' in the mission hospital in Nigeria where I first met her and her twin brother Tim. People have often asked me, 'But do you feel the same about your adopted children as your natural children?' It's a question impossible to answer. I don't feel the same about any of my children. Each one is so completely unique and calls forth from me the different things that they need. Yes, there is an umbilical tie with the babies I gave birth to but the adopted ones fill me with so much pride and awe at their strength and determination, their beauty and their capacity to love after such a terrible start to life. We were lucky to find each other and the twins being part of our family has immeasurably added to the blessings we all feel.

The story, years later, of the discovery of their birth family is another miracle: in 1981 Richard returned to Nigeria for the first time since we left to make a film for the BBC about a famous Yoruba travelling theatre group' 'Ogunde: Man of the Theatre'. While in the area he decided to do a bit of detective work and, with the help of his translator, they toured the villages around the mission hospital at Oke-Ofa, put a notice in the local paper and an announcement on the radio asking if anyone remembered an incident twenty years before when a mother had died giving birth to twins because they were alive and well and anxious to trace any living relatives. Listening to his transistor radio in the barbershop a young man leapt to his feet. 'My god!' he cried. 'It sounds like my long-lost baby brother and sister.' He went running to the rendezvous that Richard had set up and the moment he arrived, Richard knew he must be their brother. The family resemblance was so strong. Through him, the old father was traced also the two other brothers and the elder sister. Juliana, their sister, who had been twelve at the time of their mother's death had tried to find the babies after she got married. She would have taken them to live with her but, alas, by then staff at the mission had changed and no one knew what had happened to them.

So, excited messages went back and forth between England and Nigeria. In those pre-internet days we sent photos and tape recorded messages and I was determined to try and take them there in time for their twenty-first birthday.

The cost of the flights was prohibitive but I had the idea of selling the exclusive story to *Woman Magazine* – UK's best-selling women's weekly and after they accepted, going next to British Caledonian Airways and offering to give them a mention in my article in exchange for three free flights. They agreed! So in April 1982 we arrived at Lagos airport. Communications with the family had been a bit haphazard and I had no idea if anyone would actually be there to meet us. I needn't have worried. Not only the immediate family but the entire extended family all wearing matching clothes of the same fabric, singing and praising were in the airport building. The TV cameras were there. The *Lagos Sunday Times* had been alerted and we were on the front page: 'THE TWINS FLY HOME'.

Juliana and Femi fell into each other's arms weeping, the old father had tears in his eyes and we were swept off in a motorcade of hooting cars. We were offered the choice of staying in a hotel or, their preference, staying with Juliana. Naturally we chose the latter. Juliana's business is selling Coca Cola at a little roadside stand. She, her husband Jide and their six children live in a small shack with an outside privy and chickens in the yard. The generosity was extraordinary. There was one bed. They made us take it and they slept on the floor. One fan, they insisted we had it, they went without. Every morning neighbours would leave something on the doorstep knowing they were feeding extra mouths: a few potatoes, a chicken, a little pile of maize. Villagers would press coins into Tim and Femi's palms as they passed. These are people who have NOTHING. Yet never before had I experienced such hospitality and kindness.

During our weeks there we learned more of the story: the reason Joseph, their father, had abandoned the twins was because, in the first place, he was in shock. He and the other children had all witnessed the death of Felicia, his wife, who had gone into labour trying to reach the mission hospital but had given birth on the bush path and haemorrhaged uncontrollably. The best thing he could think to do was to take the tiny premature bundles to the mission and say, 'For God's sake, take care of these babies!' and then disappear leaving a false name and address. There was no way he could have managed on his own. Usually, in such circumstances, a grandmother or aunt would step in and look after the children but, as we learned later, in this case, the family were far from home. Joseph had come to Ibadan to find work as a trader selling watches in the market place so he had no nearby relatives to call on.

Now he was fearful that we might blame him but, of course, there was no question of that. He did the best he could and we were just so overjoyed to have found him. During our month in Nigeria, with Juliana's help, we took Tim and Femi to visit all the sacred sites of their babyhood: the village where the family had been living; their mother's grave; the Oke-Ofa mission hospital (now called the Babies' Home) where we delivered a large bag of baby clothes collected from friends in London; and best of all, a visit to their parents' home village near Abeokuta where their elderly grandmother still lived. A beautiful, white haired old woman who looked so like Femi with her fine features and high cheekbones, it was uncanny. She had been bathing in the river when we arrived and somebody was sent to fetch her. She came running, half naked, holding her arms to heaven and fell on her knees praising God and crying. Femi raised her up and they kissed and hugged. Not a word could we say to each other but the joy on everyone's faces told the story.

In the following days we did the rounds of relatives homes, we spent time with Tim and Femi's three brothers Sunday, Simon and Dayo, we got to know Juliana's six beautiful children for whom she had unlimited ambition. They would be doctors, lawyers, professors … .The youngest; six-year-old twins Taiwo and Kahinde studied their schoolbooks every evening by candlelight.

A celebration was organised with wonderful dancing and Femi was hauled on stage to join in which she gamely did. And on the final Sunday which was Tim and Femi's twenty-first birthday a special service at the Catholic church was arranged. Juliana was really the star as she led the procession dancing down the aisle dressed in her most exuberant outfit followed by the three of us. It felt like a perfect circle had been achieved as I had been twenty-one when first Tim and Femi came into our lives.

There was quite a lot of pressure, especially from Juliana, trying to persuade them to stay in Nigeria and marry locals but they have made their lives elsewhere and feel most at home in England.

As a lovely postscript: Dayo, the brother closest in age to them who was only two when their mother died, eventually came to live in London with his wife Nicky. Their three daughters; Ayo, Buki and Damilola were bridesmaids at Femi's wedding and many years later Femi was maid of honour at Ayo's wedding and I was honorary grandmother.

Femi married David, a Scotsman with whom she has two sons Jack seventeen and Zen nineteen. She is now married to Claus, a Dane and lives in Denmark. Tim married Jeannine, a Dutch woman, lives in Holland and has three children in their twenties. Sean, Zoe and Lisa.

So back in Australia: I had been corresponding with Diane McCudden whose deadpan tales of life in the Outback were a continuous delight and had now brought me to Laverton, a remote gold-mining town in the middle of the Great Victoria Desert of Western Australia. She was there waiting for Femi and me on the airstrip with Sarah, her four year old adopted Aboriginal daughter, and we all squeezed into the front seat of a truck she had borrowed to drive us around while we were there. This is a harsh place to live. Dry as a bone and hot as hell most of the year. People come here to make money working in the mines and the population is strikingly young. There are rows of pre-fab houses, a school, a supermarket and a pub. Scattered across thousands of square miles of desert are a few homesteads – sheep stations and cattle stations. Woven into this social fabric, although never exactly a part of it, are the original occupants of this land, the Aborigines. Quite a few live in the town and many more in the surrounding reserves. The relationship between them and the white mining community is one of barely concealed animosity.

I had come to stay with Di in the hope that she could introduce me to an Aboriginal grandmother or two. They have endured so long and witnessed so much. Were the elders still connected, I wondered, to the thread of dreams, imaginings and deep collective memories of the oldest known human culture? Di, an ex-nurse, is a singularly unprejudiced, open and enlightened person who has lived in the area most of her life. The Aborigines, or Wongai as they call themselves in this part of Australia, have suffered a lot in their collision with white fence-building, time-keeping, land-owning values. I wanted to ask the old women what kept them going. I also wanted to journey to the most distant memory of our human race. I had a felt a stirring in the recesses of my own memory, a sense of affinity with a people who melded so well with their world; a people to whom body and land were one. An Aboriginal woman recently interviewed on television said, 'With your vision you might see me sitting on a rock, but I am sitting on the body of my ancestor. The earth, his body and my body are identical.' This speaks directly to that part of me which comes from my own pagan past, the part of me descended from the healers, herbalists and witches of pre-Christian Europe; the part that knows we are all part of the whole of nature.

Just before leaving on my round-the-world journey I went to Stonehenge on a cold day in winter. I felt terrible for the stones imprisoned now behind the wire fence which keeps people from touching them. It was like visiting elephants in the zoo. They looked so lonely and bereft. Then I read in Robert Lawlor's book, *Voices of the First Day*, where he tells of the time he visited a huge standing rock formation in Arizona with a Cherokee man who sat down and played his flute to the stones. 'They are like lonely old people standing and waiting to be sung to,' he said. 'Our people have always sung songs of admiration to the qualities of strength and beauty and endurance that stones bring to the world …they are tired and lonely now because the world has become blind and selfish. They live in a hollow, unsung world.'

Aboriginal, Polynesian, Native American, Hawaiian, European

pagan perceptions all contain the seeds of archaic awareness that I feel lie dormant within me I want to connect with my own dreaming where my inner vision and outer perception are woven in a dance of energy with the natural world and with all of creation.

'You should talk to Dimple Sullivan,' said Di. The great-grandmother of Sarah, the child she has adopted. 'She's a lovely old thing and she knows a lot.'

At seventy, Dimple Sullivan is one of the most senior ladies in this part of the world and quite a matriarch, with five sons, one daughter, twenty grandchildren and ten great-grandchildren. Dimple, a big woman, wearing a vast floral dress and a crocheted hat came round to meet me, parked herself at Di's kitchen table and held out her hand. It was to be the first of several conversations where I gained some valuable insight into an all but vanished way of life. She is head of her household and lives in the town with several members of her family including a five-year-old great-granddaughter, Azaria, whom she looks after. Nana Dimple has trouble with asthma these days but otherwise she is in pretty good health which is rare. Very few Wongai live past the age of fifty. 'White man's tucker, easy money and grog,' says Dimple. The grog's certainly taken its toll here, as their finely tuned metabolisms which have withstood 40,000 (latest archeological evidence suggests it may be as much as 150,000) years of hardships in this inhospitable land apparently cannot tolerate the toxic effects of alcohol.

We talked about the past. Nana Dimple said she remembered, when she was eight years old, going walkabout with her mother and a few other family members. Incredibly, for a little child, they walked over 620 miles across the border into South Australia. They carried practically nothing with them – only the basic Aboriginal tool kit of digging stick, shallow wooden bowl, string bag for the women, spear and *woomera* (spear thrower) for the men. Lightweight, portable and easily replaceable. They made stone cutting tools as and when they needed them. The purpose of the journey was to meet up with other family group members.

The thing that Aborigines most need and love to do, said Dimple, is to travel up and down the length and breadth of their country weaving a web of kinship and affirming it with ceremony. If ever you meet one when you are out and about and ask them what they are doing they say, 'Oh just having a look round.' They are forever in motion in a huge join-the-dots game. They are the caretakers who, through their wanderings continually recreate the world. Bruce Chatwin wrote about this most beautifully in his book *Songlines*. Relationships are everything. Relationships with each other and with the land. In none of the many Aboriginal languages is there a word for ownership.

But as the Europeans began to explore, and later to settle and farm, they dismissed the Aborigines as being simply isolated bands of barbarians and ignored the fact that they possessed an intimate relationship and ultimate mastery over their land. The two cultures had totally different perceptions of the world and man's place in the scheme of things. And now the old patterns are gone and will never be recaptured. The in-comers built cities and roads on the sacred sites. The ancient Dreaming pathways were severed and the web of interdependency broken.

The Aborigines had evolved a pattern of life which was well-suited to their environment. They had a story for every aspect of the natural world – their great and beautiful epic called the Dreamtime. The Dreamtime myths portrayed the physical world as a language to be learned – part of the education of every child. Reading the seasons, talking to trees, listening to the emanations of plants, feeling the energy of rocks, being in communication with the elements and with the spirits. The world was a language to be read and interpreted only by those with their ear to the ground, and continual education was a feature of Aboriginal life. Ritual and religious knowledge involved patient learning throughout a lifetime. Continued observation – 'having a look round' – supplemented the survival skills that all children were taught.

The Aborigines lived in harmony with their environment because they had developed a capacity to integrate their inner and outer worlds, their waking and dreaming states, their conscious and unconscious minds. They had a sense of common consciousness very difficult for us to comprehend. The visible and the invisible were one.

Money has somehow fatally damaged this fragile equation. Out of guilt for past brutalities and acts of land theft, large amounts of compensation money are now doled out every two weeks by the government and the mining companies in the form of welfare cheques or mining rights. But his has only tended to exacerbate the problem. The spirit of the Wongai is at an all-time low. There is no incentive to work or to hunt their own food. They buy huge Landcruisers, television sets, booze and junk food with the money. Their health has been irreparably damaged. The young people, said Dimple, don't want to listen to their elders any more. Young men have even been known to beat their mothers up. Perhaps further out, in some of the bush communities, something of the traditional respect survives, but not in the towns.

In the Aboriginal world view, everything that happens leaves behind a vibrational residue. They believe that the spirit of their consciousness and way of life exists like a seed buried in the earth – a seed of knowledge and awareness that will sprout into life when the right fertile conditions come about. I long to believe that somebody carries the flame and that the Dreamtime stories live on deep in the DNA of the old ones, or in the cells of the not-yet-born, memories of the origins of life on earth.

As one tribal elder put it, 'They say we have been here for 40,000 years but it is much longer. We have been here since time began. We have come directly out of the Dreamtime of the creative ancestors. We have lived and kept the earth as it was on the first day.' The ancestors came from the direction of the rising sun, they walked the pathways of a flat featureless plain and sang the landscape, the elements, the plants into being. These epic journeys were depicted in the stories, the paintings, the ceremonies and the patterns of life that have been maintained for millennia. But the missionaries told them their sacred sites were devil-worshipping places and discouraged their use. They banned the manhood circumcision rites, they took half-caste children away from their mothers by force and put in them in homes, and little by little their self-esteem seemed to dwindle. The earth is no longer as it was on the first day and most of the Wongai you see today are pretty broken.

Dimple's son Gary and his wife Lois do not come in this category.

Neither of them drink and they both work and love to go off looking for bush food. While we were talking, they arrived in their Toyota Landcruiser with about eight kids. They had seen emu tracks out in the bush and were going to hunt for eggs. They said we could follow them if we wanted to. I was very excited to get this chance to experience a taste of the hunter/gatherer life of our earliest ancestors – the oldest race of people on earth.

Di, Femi and I tailed their four-wheel drive, jouncing out across the red sand and spinifex vastness miles off the road until we came to a place that, to me, looked exactly like everywhere else. Mulga scrub all around as far as the eye could see. We stopped and got out of the vehicles. There were the tell-tale, giant, three-toed emu tracks and immediately the family dispersed in different directions. We tagged along behind two of the women. They walked fast and kept their eyes unerringly on the bird tracks. I really had to search to spot the higgledy-piggledy marks in the dust but they saw them as easily as if they had been picked out in fluorescent paint. They can tell if the emu is coming or going from its water source by the pattern of the prints. They know that this is the time of year to find eggs because, 'The emu has appeared in the Milky Way in the night sky.'

Try as we might it was impossible to keep up with them. After two hours walking, when they had completely disappeared from view, we acknowledged defeat and retraced our own steps back to the truck to find the Toyota had gone. Luckily Di is at home in this country and managed to follow their tyre tracks. It was beginning to get dark. All we spotted were three rotten last year's eggs which had obviously been rejected by the others – their footprints were all around the place. Eventually we caught up with them, calmly waiting for us under a tree. They's had a good haul and were in excellent spirits. They blow out the egg contents to eat and then carve delicate pictures on the dark green shells which sell to tourists for up to $500 if the quality is high enough.

It was lovely to see these ancient people of the land in their true setting. By and large they are not at ease in houses in towns. They love to camp, to hunt and to sit around under the trees. They are brilliant at tracking, at finding their way across this wasteland, at knowing where the water is, at attuning themselves to the landscape and the creatures. We started back towards Laverton when suddenly a large kangaroo appeared up ahead, caught in the headlights of their vehicle. In a flash they had a spotlight on him and gave chase. A shot from Gary wounded the poor creature and everyone else jumped out of the truck and clubbed it to death with crowbars. I was both horrified by this bloody bit of reality and impressed with the speed of their reactions in catching their dinner. I got out of the truck and walked over. Lois severed the thin skin between the tendons of the powerful back legs and threaded a rope through. They strung the unfortunate animal up to the luggage rack and bounced back to town where Dimple would skin him and make him into a stew.

During my time in Laverton I met quite a few of the older women. Women like Gladys who are still just about managing to hold their broken families together against tremendous odds but who have so little sense of their own self-worth. Generations of abuse and victim consciousness have taken their toll. Gladys turned up on Di's doorstep one day. Her son had just been sent to prison. He was picked up by the police with some bad company, drinking and driving around in a stolen car. She had come to appeal to the local constabulary to get him transferred to a nearer jail where she could visit and keep an eye on him. He knows nobody where he is and is pining terribly. The aborigines cannot bear to be separated from their kinfolk. In a culture where family cooperation has always meant everything and survival on one's own would have been impossible, ostracism is the worst possible punishment.

I felt so sad for Gladys, a woman of about my age with classical Aboriginal features – round, flat and broad with very deep-set eyes and unruly curly hair. She was patient, enduring and matter of fact but the pain in her eyes was immense. The changes have come so quickly and the dislocation has been enormous. The stark contrast between the simple harmonious life of the past and this wretched present is almost unbearably poignant. For a woman like Gladys, coping with the twentieth century must sometimes seem an impossible task. So easy to fall into the time warp and find oneself spinning out of reach, misunderstood, unheard.

A couple of days later, on the road to Cosmo Newberry where the sky was huge and the bush was endless, we stopped at the site of an old Aboriginal camp ground. Di hunted around and picked up several small rocks which were unremarkable to an untrained eye but were actually stone tools. As soon as she showed me what to look for, I could see where they had been chipped away to make sharp-edged cutting tools for skinning animals. This was a graphic reminder of how recent the Stone Age was in these people's lives. Visiting their camp site which was probably only fifty years old was a jump back in time of thousands of years. Dimple also showed us the flat grindstones which the women would have used for making flour out of seeds. She told me about the time her mother, who was skilled in the art of native medicines, boiled a special kind of rock for hours in water and gave it to a sickly newborn to drink and how the baby recovered and thrived.

Dimple showed us a bush whose twigs you could boil for two hours to make an effective remedy for sore throats, a couple of grasses whose seeds could be ground to make a kind of bread, a low, ground-creeper plant with succulent leaves that can be eaten raw or cooked. She pointed to a tree whose roots contain water so that you will never go thirsty in the desert. We also saw the remains of a bivouac-style shelter or humpy made of bent-over branches. We saw where a mulga tree had been split with a stone hand axe and a piece removed to fashion a woomera. Dimple is a frail old lady and breathless with asthma but she got really enthusiastic about sharing some of her bush knowledge with us. It was lovely to see her in her element. She would never be lost in the outback. I would feel perfectly safe if I were with her, no matter how harsh the conditions.

Often in the white community you hear, 'They're lazy, they don't want to work, we're killing them with kindness, they're dirty, quarrelsome, drunk.' And it has to be said that what you often see on the surface are a lot of derelict no-hopers on social security with no pride in themselves and a woeful lack of purpose. But they have been treated so dismissively and with such a total lack of sensitivity that it's not surprising.

This is from a book called *In Darkest Western Australia*, written in

1909. Its author, H. G. B. Mason, proposes castration of 'bucks' as a solution to 'the Native Problem':

> *Castration has a wonderfully soothing and beneficial effect on all creatures with a wild and vicious blood ...it seems to quieten and cow them once and forever ...The more a nigger is educated the bigger scoundrel he becomes. If one happens to have bush natives doing fairly well, and one of these educated 'gentlemen' appears on the scene – goodbye to all further control over them ...Since the advent of the whites, nothing that mortal man can do will prevent the passing of the Australian black within a few decades. Niggers are cut out for the wild and free life ...thousands of pounds will be frittered away in experimenting [with solutions] ...and in the end they will remain the same filthy, troublesome, thriftless race.*

Many people's opinions were coloured by this sort of appalling propaganda and the scene was set for a fatal collision between the strong, dominant invading culture and the fragile, dreamy, defenceless one. I thought about the 'survival of the fittest' and how we've all been taught that 'natural selection' and inevitable evolution is the way of the world. But even watching the Olympic Games that year I found myself uneasy with the constant parade of winners and losers, flag waving, national pride and chauvinism. 'It's just a healthy outlet for mankind's naturally competitive nature', is the received wisdom. But is it so natural? Isn't it more natural to be cooperative? Our energy can just as easily be channelled into dance, music, ceremony, carnival, acts of initiation, courage, endurance. There don't have to be winners and losers. Have we been conned for too long by Darwinian excuses for a deadly mutant strain of humans who have led us to the brink of destruction. The fittest but also the cruellest, the most devious, the greediest. In a finite world they can only survive so long.

Is our great 'advanced', technological, competitive Western, white, male-dominated civilisation necessarily the peak of human achievement? And has it brought us happiness? A recent advertisement for a brand of beer shows three men (commodity brokers? lawyers? military strategists?) dressed in rugged outdoor gear, enjoying a weekend fishing by a quiet, unspoilt lake. What do they do for the other fifty-two weeks of the year? Work at stressful jobs in polluted cities, achieve 'success' in the rat race, fail to have a relationship with their children because they're too busy earning pots of money so they can buy a holiday in one of the few places that haven't been ruined by 'progress' and the survival of the fittest.

Perhaps the real measure of the success of a culture is not achievement but relative affluence measured in actual free time and in personal satisfaction. This is from Captain Cook's journal, on his first sighting of the Aborigines:

> *They appear to be in reality far happier than we Europeans, being wholly unacquainted not only with superfluous but 'necessary' conveniences so much sought after in Europe, they are happy in not knowing the use of them. They live in tranquillity which is not disturbed by the inequality of condition: The earth and sea of their own accord furnish them with all the things necessary for life. They covet not Magnificent Houses, Household Stuff etc., they live in warm and fine Climate and enjoy very wholesome Air, so that they have very little need of clothing ... in short they seemed to set no value upon anything we gave them ...they hunted for food, and when they had enough for their meals they devoted their time to social and ceremonial pursuits.*

An Aboriginal man quoted in Robert Lawlor's important book, *Voices of the First Day*, remembers his grandmother saying to him:

> *The white men say terrible things about the Aborigines only because we are not farmers, builders, merchants and soldiers. The Aborigines are something else – they are dancers, hunters, wanderers and mystics and because of that they call us ignorant and lazy. Someday you will see the beauty and power of our people.*

The Aborigines still love to hunt and to sit with their families around a fire and to travel freely about the country. Possessions have little value, clothes only get dirty. As well as having no word for ownership, Aboriginal languages also have no word for times. All our thoughts are expressed in past, present and future tenses, whereas Aborigines conceive time as a passage from dream to reality.

The missed opportunities, mistakes and blunders are a tragedy too huge to grasp. The loss of an entire way of knowing. There is so much we should have learned from these people. Sometimes I wish I could step for a while into the Dreamtime, for a glimpse into a vision of humanity reintegrated with nature, to acknowledge once again the feeling, the intelligence and consciousness of other aspects of creation apart from our own, to grasp the seed of wisdom that lies dormant. But it seems there is nobody left to take me there. And why would they? Why would they trust me not to betray them? People are struggling vainly and I am reminded of those terrible images from the Gulf War of sea birds drowning and suffocating in the spilled black oil; bewildered, washed up on the shores of 'civilization'. We put liquor stores where their wilderness once was; multi-storey car parks where the rainbow serpent sleeps.

It is in the same way that I want to reclaim my own ancient pagan inheritance of magic, power and witchcraft from the fear and shame that engulfed it. I feel that just underneath the arrogant cultural subjugation, brainwashing and domination of ancient peoples lies an indigenous mysticism of great beauty and profundity that is also waiting patiently to be reclaimed – the seed of which the Aborigines speak – waiting to take root when the time is right; when there are ears to hear.

Dimple took us on to a hill where we could 'spec' for gold. Gary had once found several nuggets in the area. Dimple walked about the stony terrain peering around for the tell-tale glint of yellow metal but we found nothing that day. We decided instead to pay a visit to the shell of an abandoned homestead. You can't walk two steps out of the truck in these parts without being covered in those awful outback flies who, desperate for moisture, seem determined to fly up your nostrils and aim for the corners of your eyes. I wandered around the old place where you could still see the initials of the last family who had lived there carved into the fence post. I imagined coming here to this heat, this inhospitable land, this loneliness. Trying to raise kids and maintain remembered suburban standards of cleanliness in the relentless dust. Women arrived here in their long skirts with their little upright pianos and their Staffordshire bone china tea sets and made homes for the rugged pioneer men. They battled the flies, the snakes, the spiders, the drought, the bush fires. But often the bush won, as it had here, and the people gave up the struggle. The price of wool fell, the cost of living rose and the mining towns beckoned.

We drove on to Minnie Creek, a blessed oasis in this arid emptiness, a rock hole where we refilled the water bottles and washed our dusty faces. Dimple remembered the death of her stepfather at Minnie Creek when she went on that great Walkabout as a child. Two days later her mother gave birth to a baby boy down by the water's edge. Dimple found her next morning lying next to the newborn infant which was covered with ants. She ran and fetched the other women who cleaned the ants off the baby and helped the mother. The child survived and grew up to be the father of Rhys, a nice man who I met in the settlement at Cosmo Newberry and who showed us how to spot the emu in the Milky Way. (Just beneath the Southern Cross is a black shape among the whiteness. It only appears in winter when the Seven Sisters go below the horizon. This is the period of time permitted to hunt for emu eggs.)

On the road home in the failing light a mother kangaroo with a joey in her pouch sprang across the track with a young one hopping behind. A very large emu broke cover and ran alongside the road for maybe half a mile or more going as fast as the truck. Magical! I was glad that this time nobody was trying to catch their supper. We got home tired and dusty after 150 miles of being squashed in the cab of the truck with a wiggly four year old. But I loved the day. It's not often you go out for a picnic and come home with a handful of stone-age cutting tools and two shooting stars which had fallen to earth on the desert.

We were all exhausted the next day and nobody was keen to travel so we made a big plate of ham sandwiches and sat around talking. 'After my husband died I never want no other man,' said Dimple. 'They no good, the lot of them.' Then she added as an afterthought, 'Not that the doctor didn't try to have me. I thought about it for a while and said to myself, "Naaaah!" so since I been a widow I ain't had no sex!' she roared with laughter. Although it was a shocking example of the unprofessional and abusive way women get taken advantage of in consulting rooms I couldn't help seeing the funny side – all twenty stone of her, no front teeth, whiskers on her chin and the crocheted hat pulled down over her forehead, considering the proposition and taking her time to turn him down!

She showed me a book called *A Drop in the Bucket* about the early days of the Mount Margaret Mission. Dimple was forcibly taken from her mother and sent there. She remembers the terror of running away into the bush and the Principal chasing after her in the truck. She was finally caught and dragged off crying and hollering while her mother was given compensation in the form of some stores. To a little child it seemed as if they had sold her. And she remembered being taken once on an outing to Perth where the Aboriginal children were not allowed to ride on the elephant at the zoo …So many stories. Dimple is full of information on kinship ties, bush lore and bits of local history. Di has offered to spend some regular time getting some of the stories on tape.

When Dimple came round to say goodbye on our last day she brought me a carved emu egg as a present. I was very touched knowing how hard it is to find them and how difficult they are to carve without breaking.

It was a stormy afternoon with a perfect rainbow vaulting the airstrip, splashing the greyness with colour. The Aborigines have a profound perception of the rainbow as the symbol of the edge of the unconscious, the place where invisible potential begins to become visible – their fundamental guiding narrative. I thought about the Bible telling us that the meek shall inherit the earth and what an unlikely prospect that seems. Our popular culture seems to be preparing us for annihilation. At the little video rental shop in Laverton, as everywhere else, the shelves are stacked with films like *Die Hard, Lethal Weapon, Terminator* – orgies of killing, explosions and smashed vehicles. These days the word meek is used to mean 'submissive', 'spineless', 'long-suffering'. The original, now obsolete, definition was 'gentle', 'cooperative' 'amenable'. Surely Jesus meant, 'Those who can live in gentle harmony and cooperation with nature shall inherit the earth'

Femi and I flew away in our little Skyways plane back to the city where we went our separate ways not knowing how long it would be before we saw each other again. I gave her the emu egg and boarded my flight to India.

In 'Little Gidding' T. S. Eliot wrote:

We shall not cease from exploration
And the end of all our exploring
will be to arrive where we started
And know the place for the first time.

CHAPTER TWELVE

After six weeks travelling in India meeting women for my book 'Older Than Time', I finally boarded the train from Delhi to Bombay. The Rajdhani Express, billed as 'India's Most Prestigious Train', left promptly on time. A miracle. A pearl of efficiency in a sea of muddle, and we were served with cheese straws and dear little individual thermos flasks of tea. Trains are the way to see India. It was like watching a film and being in it at the same time. Hindi music piped into the carriage, a cross section of friendly chatty fellow travellers all accompanied by a diorama of white-hot, biscuit-fired landscape that slid past the train windows for hour after hour until, gradually, the fading paprika sunset seen through the dusty haze turned to night. There is an arid beauty in the spice-coloured plains, in the throbbing vistas of saffron and cinnamon, but I don't know how anyone can wrest a living from such a harsh environment.

Seventeen hours after leaving Delhi we arrived in Bombay Central. All along the tracks as you approach, cheerfully smiling folk, dhotis gathered up, are squatting down for a companionable morning crap. This phenomenon has been noted by other travellers to India and, as James Cameron remarked, 'One would not have to be especially fastidious to feel that this, as a public relations gesture, is whimsical indeed.' It is certainly not the most salubrious view to accompany one's breakfast.

My generous hosts, Rasheeda and Anees, friends of friends whom I had never met before, greeted me with the news that, alas, they had to leave that very morning for London but I would be welcome to use their apartment. They had enlisted various friends and relations to show me around and their four servants would look after me! I was wafted into another world.

And what a contrast ... From the heat and dust of the parched desert landscape to the air-con comfort of a private apartment along the seafront in the wealthiest part of Bombay – a city of extremes. Up to this point, from my conversations with Indian women, I had gained an impression of the mother-in-law as a dominant and frequently forbidding figure. After a lifetime of powerlessness she eventually comes into her own when she can terrorise her own daughters-in-law. Now one of Rasheeda's friends was keen for me to meet an exception to this stereotype, the matriarch of a top-drawer, multi generational family living under one roof.

A Gujerati of the Mafatlal family ('one of the ten largest industrial families in the country'), Mrs Mahadevia reigns over her extended family in a luxurious complex of two adjoining apartments in one of Bombay's most exclusive residential areas.

Mrs Mahadevia greeted us cordially. A handsome, elegant woman in her sixties, she was dressed in a gorgeous shot-silk sari of purple and peacock hues with gold thread embroidery. I felt a frightful frump in my cotton jersey parachute pants and a cheap *kurta* from a Delhi street bazaar. We sat in her cool, spacious drawing room overlooking the bay. An enormous St Bernard lolled by the air-conditioning unit. Eight servants live in the place. ('Not all at once, of course,' she laughed. 'Sometimes one or two of them are on leave.') One of then brought delicious buttermilk to drink and freshly made tasty, savoury puffs and bowls of home-made mango ice cream. The daughters-in-law came in and kissed her on the cheek, the three grandchildren came in to be stroked and tousled and they all plainly adore her. One son came in from playing golf, the other was a polo ace away on a tournament.

Her own mother-in-law had lived with them for forty years until her recent death making it a four-generation household. 'I wouldn't say it was easy,' said Mrs Mahadevia, remembering the days. 'We used to have a lot of conflicts, mainly about the servants. She was much less tolerant than I but then I had been spoiled rotten since childhood. We had servants to tie our shoe laces, brush our hair, put out our clothes. We never had to do a thing.' In the end she and her husband's mother always made up their disagreements and made a pact 'never to tell tales – we never involved the males!'

She, herself, had a patchy education and left school before matriculation. She married in what would have been her final year but feels she made up for any shortfall in formal education with voracious reading. I asked her if she had ever had a desire for a career outside the home and she told a rather wistful story: Her brother was a social worker who conducted eye camps in rural areas. For six weeks every year she used to join him and help out. She became so competent at assisting doctors that one of them, incredibly, asked her if she would like to try her hand at doing a cataract removal operation as she had watched so many of them. 'I said I would love to and actually performed a few before this was discovered by a higher authority who put a stop to it.' Her hands fluttered gracefully, describing the vanished possibilities. 'I never missed my education,' she said, 'because I always felt I could hold my own but when they stopped me from operating because I was not qualified, then I was sorry.'

Mrs Mahadevia had been brought up in a very sheltered environment. 'It was strict and traditional,' she said. 'I thought marriage would mean freedom, but it was right from the frying pan into the fire! I tried to grow wings but I decided it was not worth it. Too many people to fight. Anyway I loved my husband. I was brought up not to cause trouble or hurt people and there are so many people involved in an Indian family. The pressures are too much. Ultimately you either stay in the family set-up and abide by the rules or you leave. I stayed and have not regretted my decision for one single moment.' Now, as matriarch, she presides over the family with firmness and diplomacy. 'There is no coercion,' she says, smiling sweetly, 'but I generally get my own way.' She had three sons, the eldest of whom tragically died at the age of thirty-four from a mysterious illness. His widow and children live nearby. In her immediate household are her two other married sons, her two daughters-in-law and three grandchildren. I asked if the young wives had been her choices or her sons' choices. 'Their choice but, naturally, with my complete approval,' she answered emphatically, eyes flashing.

The elder daughter-in-law, Mona, is a stunning, languid beauty with waist-length glossy hair and a flawless complexion of golden honey who used to be a model for Helena Rubenstein. Mona had confessed to her mother-in-law after the wedding that her new husband had given her an ultimatum – if she wanted him to propose to her she would have to give up her modelling career. He did not want a working wife. 'What if I give up my career and you don't propose?' she asked him. 'That's a chance you will have to take,' he answered. They all found that very amusing. 'You see! My boys are such chauvinists,' laughed Mrs Mahadevia indulgently, adding with a shrug, 'although I, myself, was proud of the girls and would have liked them to go out in the world.' I asked Mona if she missed the fashion world. 'Not at all' she answered, popping a date into her mouth. 'I grew out of that a long time ago.'

In the joint household there is only one kitchen. Everyone is vegetarian (except the dog whose food is prepared out on the balcony and his mouth rinsed out before he is allowed to breathe his carnivorous, doggy breath all over people) but mealtimes are very flexible. Mrs M. always waits and has lunch with her small grand-daughter who tends not to eat properly and needs a little companionship and encouragement. Her life, she says, is completely full. She prays for an hour and a half each day at her special little shrine. She visits people in hospital. She plays bridge every day and, twice a week, all day. She writes poetry, paints and sculpts.

Mrs Mahadevia lives a life that has all but disappeared in England but would have been quite common before the Second World War. 'My interests are aesthetic rather than political. I'm not interested in what's happening in the world if it doesn't directly affect me.' She laughed merrily. 'You'll be amused to hear I was briefly very interested in Marxism in my youth until I realised I would have to give everything up!'

Without a doubt there was a most attractive warmth and stability in their home and a real lynchpin role for the grandmother. An ambience of charm and tranquillity, cohesion and loyalty that we have all but lost in the West. I must say it's a lovely fantasy – to be surrounded by my family where each member has their own space and we all live with love, tolerance and respect and I am queen. It must be one of the nicest ways to live. I am also aware that having eight servants helps considerably to oil the domestic wheels. Meals appear at the ping of a little bell, clean laundry arrives in your room the same evening (when you left it strewn on the bedroom floor that morning), the driver smooths your shopping trips and visits to the bridge club by depositing you from your air-conditioned car to the door of your destination. When Mrs M. says, 'I would not trade my life for anything in this world,' who can blame her?

When we left the lap of luxury and descended to earth, Disha, my companion for the day, took me to visit some of her favourite little shops selling textiles and suchlike. The monsoon had arrived that morning with a vengeance bringing a welcome drop in temperature but also streets awash with unsavoury bilge, dead furry things and muddy puddles. Disha picked her way delicately in her pale yellow Swiss-embroidered *salwar kameez* and high-heeled sandals and I trudged along behind with my glasses steamed up, perspiring like a pig. My hair had gone totally out of control and resembled a bush. I really envy the classic elegance of Indian women and wish I knew how to achieve it.

I was whisked off to tea by some young friends of Rasheeda's daughter – this time a Parsee family. I was quite overwhelmed by the hospitality and kindness of everyone I met – aunties, cousins, friends. Somehow I can't imagine, if a total stranger came to stay in my house in London, that my friends, particularly my *children's* friends would take the slightest interest. This was another big, multi-generational family with a place for everyone. I am sure that like the archetypal Jewish or Irish family, there is suffocation, frustration, emotional blackmail and restriction, but the arid isolation and fragmentation of a large percentage of families in the West seems a very poor alternative. So many people I know have experimented with living in communes and ashrams, joined groups and residential workshops, searched for gurus. Longing to belong somewhere.

There is a very low divorce rate in India, not least because a couple have a lot of emotional support. It's not just a marriage between two people but between two families, between two grandmothers. And yet, sadly, the erosion of the family is taking place here too. Due to economic pressures and lack of housing, young people move into small flats on their own. They need two salaries to live on, there's no room for grandma, the kids go to a childminder …the hard-won freedoms ring hollow. I don't think human societies have come up with a better unit than the extended family.

In the evening, Rasheeda's elderly parents treated me to dinner at the famed Willingdon Club, named after Lord Willingdon, a late Viceroy of India, and frozen in an Edwardian time warp, with its huge airy verandah, card room and billiard table. The sahibs and memsahibs have gone now but their Indian impersonators dream on, caricatures down to the last detail, nursing little pegs of whisky in their leather club chairs, watching Wimbledon on the television and shouting, 'Oh jolly good *shot*!' Rasheeda's father was chivalry itself and must have been a devilish ladies' man in his youth. He told me of his days as a passionate ballroom dancer and of the time he won a competition on an ocean liner with an Australian girl for a partner. It must be agony for him to be so incapacitated now. He walks with a stick and takes a man-servant everywhere but he still dresses elegantly and his beautiful old eyes still shine at the memory of days on the polo field and nights of the Viennese waltz.

So there it was. A whole day of Bombay high society! Accident of birth is such an unfathomable mystery although, of course, if you believe in karmic rebirth you get no less than you deserve. No guilt if you get lucky next time round; resignation if you end up in the gutter.

I read in the paper that 45,000 millionaires live in Bombay and it's not hard to believe, though one does wonder why some of the money isn't channelled into building a drainage system, for example, which would prevent the city turning into a vast open sewer every time it rains. Enormous wealth and privilege coexist quite openly with wretched rock-bottom destitution. The slums are among the worst in Asia and whole families live in cardboard lean-tos right outside the posh apartment buildings. Tiny ragged children come and scratch on the windows of the air-conditioned cars that wait at traffic lights, a baby lies on the pavement with a plastic begging cup next to it and leprous beggars thrust their stumps at you as you pass.

Another newspaper story concerned the recent discovery by the authorities of a colony of about 1,000 people living like rats *underneath* the labyrinth of platforms at Calcutta railway station. Side by side with these horrifying aspects are all the paradoxes: they have some of the finest writers, mystics, poets, scientists, musicians, philosophers and entrepreneurs in the world, yet in the country where Mrs Gandhi ruled most women lead wretched lives and only ten percent can read and write. Like most foreigners who come here with romantic notions, longing to love India and penetrate its complex psyche, I can only scratch the surface and be overwhelmed by the enormity of its problems. The reality, loath as I am to admit it, is that coping with India is a bit beyond me; the contrasts are so confusing. Spirituality and heartlessness; idealism and fatalism; culture and corruption; beauty and squalor. How can I ignore the children's outstretched hands and pitiful little faces? How can I harden my heart and cross the road or shoo them away? But I know that if I stop a dozen more will appear out of the shadows.

And then another contrast ...

A few days later I had arranged an appointment at Mani Bhavan, Gandhi's old Bombay headquarters, now the museum and Research Institute for Gandhian Thought and Rural Development. I was to meet the Hon. President, Dr Usha Mehta. A tiny bird-like figure dressed in khadi, the plain cotton home-spun cloth that became a symbol of Gandhi's moral leadership, she received me in her little book-lined study surrounded by old polished-wood, glass-fronted shelves filled with volumes on Gandhi, Aurobindo, Vivekananda, political philosophy and religious thought. I was thrilled to meet her and again amazed at the way my footsteps had been guided to yet another life-enhancing encounter.

Usha Mehta was born in 1920 into a traditional but enlightened family. Her father was a judge and insisted from their childhood that his daughters should know what was going on in the world around them. 'During vacations, instead of taking us out to some posh places and hill-stations he insisted on our going to the villages,' she said. 'He wanted us to see the conditions for ourselves.' Her earliest and most profound influence, however, was her own grandmother who, along with hundreds and thousands of women, was transformed by the civil disobedience being preached by Gandhi at the time.

She remembers, at the age of eight, seeing her grandmother, a simple, uneducated Hindu woman, outside in her yard lighting a fire to boil seawater and make illegal salt in defiance of the unjust salt tax which Gandhi was exhorting people to oppose. 'Here was an old lady, completely traditional, completely protected, who had never gone outside her home doing something so uncharacteristic. "Grandma, what are you doing?" we asked in amazement. "Bapu [Gandhi] has asked us to do this so we shall cease to be slaves," she replied. You know, under Gandhi's leadership there was hardly any section of society that was not touched, from the poorest to the richest families, and since that time I also felt it was everyone's duty to do something for the country and for the freedom of the nation.'

From then on there was no stopping the young Usha. She got involved in the children's protest movement. 'Mostly it was boys but I felt the girls should not lag behind so we formed ourselves into the "Cat Corps"!' she remembers, smiling. 'We marched in processions, we sang songs, we demonstrated against the Simon Commission, we shouted "Up with the National Flag. Down with the Union Jack!" I don't know where my mother got her strength from but she said to me, "You must do whatever you feel compelled to do." She was an inspiration.'

Committed to non-violence, she and the other children were often beaten up by the police with sticks. One little girl carrying a flag was knocked to the ground unconscious and the flag fell in the dust. That night, with the help of their mothers and grandmothers, they stitched themselves costumes out of khadi cloth dyed in the colours of the flag. 'Now see if you can bring down the flag,' they said.

As a student, Usha became interested in constructive social reform, gave literacy classes, went into harijan ['untouchable'] colonies. She became deeply committed to the freedom struggle. During the Quit India movement in '42, when the free press was banned, it was she and a few friends who initiated and ran, at great risk to themselves, the clandestine radio station 'Congress Radio Calling' that transmitted news bulletins from a secret location in Bombay. Every few days they had to move headquarters to avoid detection. Eventually they were betrayed by their own technician. Usha was arrested and sentenced to four years in jail. She was still in prison when Independence came.

Having been a brilliant student and a Fulbright scholar with a degree in philosophy, she became attached to the Women's University where she taught for the rest of her working life. She never married and has pursued a celibate life the better to follow her chosen path. These days her energies are divided between administering the two memorial trusts at Mani Bhavan. 'One is concerned with preserving this building as it was and looking after visitors,' she said, 'and the other is the Research Institute into Gandhian Thought which is also preparing students by giving training in rural development leading to an MA degree recognised by Bombay University.'

I was humbled by such tireless strength in such a tiny, frail frame. It is a mammoth task. Did she ever feel discouraged? 'Peace is what Gandhiji lived for and died for so we mustn't lose heart but we do have to face the fact that what is happening in India is not on Gandhian lines,' she answered sadly. 'As a matter of fact, sometimes we feel that it is absolutely going in the reverse direction – that this, certainly, is not the freedom we fought for. Unfortunately our government is trying to imitate the West and our concept of "development" is completely topsy-turvy. Government, Gandhi taught us, does not mean merely material development. After all, unless the individual himself is changed, unless he has some compassion, some feelings for the downtrodden, this "development"will have no meaning at all and we will only descend into greater inequality and disparity of income.'

I asked her, as a wise older woman, what advice she would give to the younger women of today. 'You know we have become so crushed, in India, by the corruption of politicians and so *lost* along the way. We can no longer claim to be fit for spiritual leadership, we have forfeited the right. Women are still imprisoned and tortured in their own homes. After more than forty years there is still so much illiteracy. And the *poverty!* Walking miles just to fetch a small bucket of water. I have seen the trend for our young women to want to imitate the West. I say, "Let's develop our own personality as Indian women and use it for the good of society. Peace lovers of the world unite and do something to save the world. My advice is this: Understand the real meaning of the term development. We must not just go after consumer goods. We must put a limit to our greed. Secondly have some aim, some purpose in your life. See that the country progresses without losing the old values and, thirdly, do not look down on physical work.'

It was a real privilege to have met such an outstanding woman, using her experience and her knowledge, influencing the young, presenting such a quiet, sterling example of courage and devotion. Before I went on my way, Dr Usha Mehta, freedom fighter, showed me round the lovely old house – the place where Mahatma Gandhi used to stay whenever he was in Bombay: the very books he read in prison (Ruskin, Shakespeare, the Bible); his room with his plain white sleeping mat and the little spinning wheel; some beautiful photographs of him from childhood through to the shocking sight of the gun that killed him, the blood-stained clothes and the final funeral pyre.

I was proud to remember that my dad met him and walked with him in a London park when he came to England.

CHAPTER THIRTEEN

Grandmothers had been on my mind throughout my wanderings but what did I know of my own grandmother, My father's mother, my namesake; Sura Tennenbaum? Only one photograph of her exists – a round-faced Orthodox Jewish woman dressed in black with a stiff, ill-fitting wig covering her shaven head. As far as I knew she had died before my father left his home town of Tomaschov Mazowiecka to come to England and all the Jews who were left behind along with all the other members of my father's family were rounded up and sent to the death camp at Treblinka in October 1942. I hoped one day to make a pilgrimage to Poland as part of my attempt to find out more about her.

Based on the very few things Dad had told me about her, this is what I wrote in one of those 'grandparent' exercises I used to set for my writing class participants:

My name is Sura Tennenbaum. I am the proud mother of my little miracle son Rachmil, born when I was 45. I never thought God would grant me a child after so many years waiting and then this perfect tiny boy arrived. So small and thin, I feared I would never raise him but he survived and bloomed and became the cleverest child in the village. We had a Torah hand-written (a huge expense) in thanksgiving for this great gift. We live, my husband Elia, Rachmil and I with my mother and my grandmother (who can still thread a needle at the age of 90 without wearing glasses) in a typical small Polish shtetl. I wear the traditional long black dress of a good Jewish wife. Black lisle stockings and stout black lace-up shoes. Rather like the English Queen Victoria whose picture I once saw in a newspaper. At my throat and cuffs, on shabbas, a little concession to vanity – a beautiful piece of Belgian lace brought to me from Warsaw by a visiting friend. On my head I must wear the hated wig as is the custom in our culture. It itches and makes me hot and bothered on summer days. I was sad when all my waist-length, thick, black hair was shaved off after my wedding. But I love the traditional life of our people with its known and trusted rhythms. We live here in reasonable co-existence with our gentile neighbours but we don't mix at all and we live in dread and fear of the pogroms, the Cossacks galloping through the town, breaking windows, setting fire to people's homes, causing trouble and roughing people up. Once their horses trampled a child to death and as the mother screamed in the street, they laughed as they rode on. The authorities do nothing.

I supervise the household and run my small provisions shop which never makes any money. My husband is a good and pious man, a saint among men, but he is too generous. When he serves behind the counter he undercharges and gives too much change if he knows people are poor. He brings home beggars and gives away his clothes. How many mornings have I found a tramp asleep in my son's bed? Oy vey! He is impossible.

My little Rachmil goes to the schule. He is a brilliant, studious boy and so clever. Already he knows more than his teachers. Sometimes he frightens me with the questions he asks. I know he will make a great scholar one day – even a rabbi, please God.

I love the ritual of Friday night; Elia and Rachmil go to the synagogue and when they return I light the sabbath candles, bringing the light into my eyes; inviting the sabbath bride into our home. The soft gleam of silver, the white linen napkin covering the chola, the smell of chicken soup or borscht, the sense of peace and tradition and my deep happiness reflected in the love of my son ... ...but for how long? Why are our people singled out for persecution?

And now I fast forward to my death bed. I am dying of liver cancer. My skin is yellow and I haven't many days left to go. Terrible things have happened to destroy the peace of our home. That sabbath eve when ruffians burst in and murdered my dear

Elia. I will never be able to get that image out of my head of him falling almost soundlessly — just a sigh; "My God, My God," and the single round hole in his head and the blood spilling out in pool around him. Rachmil screaming, "Father, Father." A child should never see such a sight. The times have changed. No more walks by the blue pool in the woods, no more shop. People from our village are leaving for America or Palestine. What will become of my son in this fearful world. I foresee a time of even greater tragedy to come. I die an unquiet death. But maybe Rachmil will get away from here. This is my fervent prayer.

And to you, my granddaughter Allegra who will not be born for many years and whom I will never know, I want to say, 'Carry the flame and never forget your heritage'. May the old songs sing in you. May you remember the stories and tell them to your children. Then our people will survive as they always have.

I wish I could leave you my silver candlesticks but I fear there will be nothing left when the holocaust has done its worst. So I wish you a life of peace and joy and family and your own thick, lovely hair.

★

'Hello, is that Allegra?' said a deep, heavily accented woman's voice when I answered the telephone one day in 1993.

'Yes it is.'

'My name is Janka Hochland. Your grandmother was my great aunt which means you and I are second cousins. I have been trying to trace surviving relatives. Would you like to meet me while I am in London?'

I was so excited I could hardly speak as I rushed off to the rendezvous at her daughter's house not ten miles from where I lived. Janka's home was in Manchester and for the past few years she had begun to feel passionately about putting together a family archive before the time ran out and all the witnesses were dead. I had thought they *were* all dead. She had traced me through my brother's name in the London telephone directory. She told me that in Israel, still alive but in her late eighties and very frail, is the oldest surviving relative, also named Sara Tenenbaum! A first cousin of my father's and also of Janka's mother. I knew that, come what may, I must try to visit her – to physically touch the last remaining link with my grandmother. The problem was that she spoke no English so I would need to go with someone who spoke Yiddish or Hebrew.

A few months passed during which time I struggled to come to terms with my second bout of breast cancer, wondering what riddles I should be trying to solve, which voices I should be trying to listen to more acutely; wondering if I would be granted a life long enough to complete this quest. Then one day I heard that Levana, my dear Israeli friend was going to Tel Aviv, so I asked her to call the old people's home where Janka thought Sara Tenenbaum was living, having taken shelter there during the Gulf War. She was there and Levana managed to speak to her directly. Yes, of course, she remembered my father; yes, of course, she remembered my grandmother. Yes she would like to meet me. Her daughter, Malka, was arriving that very week from America so we would be able to converse through her. I knew this was one more journey I had to make.

I rang my travel agent who managed to book me on a flight the following day. Now for the next miracle … . That very evening I met Sari, an Israeli woman, at a dinner party. When I told her of my mission and she heard I had nowhere to stay she immediately offered me the use of her apartment right in the centre of Tel Aviv. A total stranger. On the eve of my departure. Thank you, guardians, angels, guides and spirits. I rang Janka. She was going to be in Tel Aviv too.

Everything went according to plan: the airport bus dropped me at the corner of my road, the key was there, the door opened, Sari's mother had left me some bread and some fruit. I was in Israel.

I had brought with me my father's manuscript of his unfinished memoirs, *The Wanderings of a Wondering Jew*, which I had skimmed through years before when I was too young and too preoccupied with the present to be interested in the past. This time I hoped it would fill in some of the missing bits of the jigsaw. I read for a bit, then walked down to the beach at sunset. I knew it was important to take things gently and let the story unfold of its own accord. I stood in the Mediterranean in the warm twilight air, marvelling at the way the wave of events had suddenly picked me up and brought me here.

I had a day to myself before the historic meeting so I walked around Tel Aviv. I found myself in Hacarmel, the street market; a feast for the senses. Piles of melons and almonds, coriander and olives, sticky Middle Eastern pastries and vats of creamy cheese. Biblical foods. I bought two mangoes, a pickled herring and some onion bagels using fractured Hebrew from my phrase book. I stopped spell-bound outside a stall selling music cassettes, mesmerised by a rich baritone voice singing those heart-rending Yiddish songs my father used to sing. I wandered down Nahlat Binyamin, a pedestrian street filled with cafes, craft sellers and street musicians, soaking up the heady mix of smells and sounds: a violinist and an oboe player making exquisite seventeenth century chamber music, a mournful sax and trombone playing 'Autumn Leaves', two fiery Romanians fiddling a passionate rhapsody fit to bust. So many places in the world have become synonymous with violence and hatred – Israel, Lebanon, Northern Ireland. It was good to be reminded that normal life also goes on, that artists still create beautiful things and that most people just want to be happy. I bought a little silver ring depicting a woman and a tree. The last time I had been in Israel – with Francesca – writing a children's book about life on a Kibbutz, we had planted two olive trees for my parents in the Jerusalem Peace Forest.

I sat at a cafe in the shade and read some more of my father's tragic manuscript – the bit where he witnessed his father's murder – the German police arriving and sealing off the house, leaving the body inside all alone – these images were to haunt him all his life.

I knew the story of course but I read it this time with more awareness and receptivity. I had always tried to protect myself from my father's pain. Its unspoken presence was so overwhelming in my childhood – in the sound of his terrible shouting nightmares echoing through the house and my mothers voice, 'It's alright darling, it's alright;' in the sight of him suddenly convulsed with weeping, sitting in his study when he didn't see me standing there – that I never wanted to hear about it. It was too enormous for a child to deal with. I wished he had lived until a time when I was mature enough to get him to talk. Now I want to know everything. I want to know what happened to all of them. It's my turn to be a witness.

I walked along the shore with a bag of plums. Couples strolled with their arms around each other. Gorgeous young women with mahogany tans and tiny bikinis kidded around with beefy lads on the sand. There were enormous Russian peasant women, white as lard, with skirts tucked into their bloomers standing in the surf. Ethiopians, American Jews with 'I Love Israel' hats and ridiculous nose-shields, Oriental families packed like sardines under one umbrella playing their radios and cooking huge feasts. The Baltic, the Middle East, North Africa – people of every conceivable ethnic origin come together to make one nation.

As I'd already discovered, a stark feature of being a middle aged woman is solitude. Not that I mind it but it's different. At any other time of my life from the age of eleven onwards, I would have had to deal with the attentions (welcome or unwelcome) of cruising Romeos. This time the only man who approached was a young gigolo. He was oiling around looking for a meal ticket and thought I might be grateful for the company. He was rather surprised when I declined his offer. It made me feel quite melancholy. I went back to the flat, changed for dinner and ate my herrings alone.

The next day I met up with Janka and we caught a taxi over to B'nai Brak, the ultra Orthodox Jewish suburb of Tel Aviv where Sara Tenenbaum lived. Her daughter Malka had just arrived from New York and immediately decided that her mother should leave the old people's home where she was desperately unhappy and come to live in America with her. If I'd left it another week she wouldn't have been there.

Malka, a warm, attractive woman of my age was waiting down on the street for us, feeling as emotional as Janka and I about all this new-found family. She took us upstairs to meet her mother and there she was, a tiny, bemused little woman with a headscarf tied under her chin in Eastern European style. My father's first cousin, daughter of my grandfather's sister Rachel. The only one left of that generation. I wept as we embraced each other. She hadn't quite understood who it was coming to see her but when she realised I was Rachmil's daughter she wept as well. I had brought her photos of my father as a small boy, of his father and mother, of him as a young man, a middle-aged man and an old man shortly before his death. Her eyes kept overflowing as she remembered the stories.

She remembered their great-grandmother Lipke, who lived to 106 and could thread a needle without glasses, their grandmother Chana, and Aunt Leah and her husband Moshe Aaron who took care of my father when he was orphaned. She remembered my dad had been a miracle child, born after eighteen years of marriage when his mother was 46. He was a brilliant child, she said, a *yeshiva hasid* – destined to be 'a spiritual leader of the Jewish people' by all accounts. She remembered how his parents, in gratitude and joy had commissioned a new Torah to be handwritten at his birth – a very expensive and rare event taking several years to complete. She recalled as if it were yesterday, the murder of my grandfather (her uncle) – a saintly and pious man.

When I told her that my father had finally turned his face against God and all the narrow repressive restrictions of Jewish ghetto life after the murder, Malka refused to translate. She wanted her mother to be left with her comforting memories and to tell her only things that would make her happy. She also didn't want her to know that I had married a non-Jew. Sara held my hand in hers and stroked my face shaking her head in disbelief and blotting her eyes. 'Rachmil's daughter, Rachmil's daughter,' she kept repeating.

I had never known for sure that my grandmother had not perished in the concentration camp but I was relieved to have it confirmed. Sara remembered her – Mimisura, as she was affectionately known – remarrying after her husband's murder and 'passing away' from 'natural causes' about two years later. [I suddenly remembered my father telling me once how, as a teenager, he identified with Hamlet. How could Shakespeare write so accurately about his own story? Hamlet's fury with his mother and sense of betrayal when she marries his uncle.]

Amongst Jews of the older generation words like 'death' and 'cancer' are too crude and cruel to be spoken out loud and the accepted euphemisms are used to soften the reality but cancer is what it seems to have been, possible liver cancer as I had surmised. She went completely yellow, 'as yellow as lemons', and died at the age of fifty-nine. At least she hadn't died in Treblinka as I'd always half feared. It seems awful to be glad she died of cancer. And only just in time. Within a few years the entire Jewish population of Tomaszow Mazowiecki died in the gas chambers.

My grandmother had been a sharp, shrewd woman who ran her own delicatessen and was clever and resourceful with money, enabling her husband and her only son to spend much of their time studying the holy scriptures. Learning and education (for men only, of course) were valued above all things, so much of the income had to be generated by women.

I had been fantasising about tapping into some ancient Jewish crone wisdom rich in folklore and tradition but what I found was a sweet, gentle old lady who had left Poland as a young bride in 1933 and never seen any of her family again, believing them all to be dead after the war. She had never spoken about it to her own children because they couldn't bear to hear any more than I could. If ever she tried she became hysterical with grief, so eventually her husband forbade her to speak of the past and the pain was locked away behind closed doors. But of course it didn't go away. It is etched in the lines of her face and the expression in her eyes to this day. Nobody thought there might be any survivors. Sara's three children were born in Israel and all of us second cousins grew up scattered to the four winds, not knowing of each other's existence.

Now, here we were, all grandmothers ourselves, weeping with joy at rediscovering each other. The power and the wisdom were not in the past where I had been looking but with us – building, networking, chronicling, travelling thousands of miles to repair the fragmentation and mend our family. We put our arms around each other in a bond of common blood and I felt a great sense of contentment and completion. I had bought with me a tape recorder to do an interview with old Sara and get it translated but it wasn't appropriate. Rehashing the pain of the past is not what she needs now. What matters is that the family lives on. We rose from the ashes of the Holocaust but there aren't just bones and ashes to look back on. There are new babies – our grandchildren – growing up and a future to look forward to.

Israel must be full of stories like ours; people looking for their kinfolk, piecing together splinters of broken lives. Janka and I, feeling very happy and pleased with ourselves went off to celebrate in the seedier part of town where the best Middle Eastern Jewish food is to be found. We had a wonderful meal in a popular, scruffy little Yemenite place – freshly baked pitta bread cooked by slapping the flattened dough inside the roof and sides of the little arched ovens, aubergine slices fried and marinated and dripping with fragrant olive oil and garlic, melt-in-the-mouth goose-liver kebabs and cool, sweet slices of watermelon to finish.

That night I read some more of my father's writings which gave me a very vivid picture of the little Polish *shtetl* in which he grew up and the narrow confines against which he rebelled. He describes an incident in his teens of a terrible fire at his home which started accidentally when a barrel of oil caught light. The Chassidim, who ran from the synagogue to help, began throwing his precious collection of books into the flames saying it was because of these godless, subversive, blasphemous volumes that the fire had struck. It made him hate them even more for their fanaticism, bigotry and closed minds. He resolved to flaunt his 'godlessness' and his 'epicureanism' more than ever. To dare to be a free thinker and a non-believer took a lot of courage. In an act of revenge against the Chassidim he stole back from the synagogue the Torah scroll his father had had written at the time of his birth and hid it in a cupboard. He was threatened with *hairem* (a combination of excommunication and ostracism), the ultimate punishment the Rabbinical Court could impose. In the end he argued his own case successfully, got a hefty sum in compensation for his destroyed library, replaced them with more 'godless' books and returned the hostage Torah.

He comes across in his writings, as a very precocious, disturbed youngster – brilliant, conceited and courageous. It was no wonder, given the peculiar mix of his upbringing. Total adoration followed by the catastrophic loss of his parents at a young age; the extreme religious orthodoxy of his community coupled with his own innate intellectual curiosity.

Convinced from an early age of his own specialness, he didn't have to bother to empathise with other people. The women and girls in the family indulged him and the men he exasperated and outsmarted with his sophistry and cleverness. He read voraciously all his life, collecting knowledge like ammunition. His relationships with people often consisted of firing this knowledge at them, scoring points, delighting in being able to tell them things they didn't know. I can see him setting forth, cockily, from this fish pond to conquer the world of letters outside, completely unprepared for real life. And as the flames engulfed the world he left behind there was literally nowhere he belonged.

In the manuscript he writes movingly about how, as he moved further and further away from religion and the 614 *tariag mitzvah's* ('do' and 'don't' commandments that governed their lives), the more devoted he became to an inexplicable feeling of Jewishness. It was not Zionism or Jewish nationalism, which to his mind was as bad as any other nationalism, but a kind of universalism, a cosmopolitanism, an intellectualism. I always felt he was the most Jewish of men in his gentleness, wit and love of learning and gefilte fish, but as with any other suffocating tradition, it was necessary to break away before he could chose what he wanted to keep.

On my last day in Tel Aviv, I walked along the shore to the old city of Jaffa which has been tastefully restored and looks like a cross between a Biblical film set and a shopping mall of boutiques and galleries. I watched the sun go down and read the last bit of my father's memoirs. He describes going, with his mother, to his favourite place – The Blue Sources – a local beauty spot on the outskirts of town. People used to come from miles around to marvel at it.

> *It was a walk through the woods to the River Pilica and its blue effervescent source … A place called Molieskie Zrodla where you could look to the bottom of the sky-blue water several metres down and see the very place, deep and mysterious, where the water bubbles up out of the sand.*

One day I would find it.

★

In the last chapter of my book *Ladder to the Moon – Women in Search of Spirituality* I describe in some detail my pilgrimage in 1997 to Auschwitz. I had come on a Bearing Witness interfaith meditation retreat organised by Roshi Bernie Glassman and the American Zen Peacemaker Order. We were a group of Buddhists, Sufis, Christians, Jews, Muslims, monks, imams, priests, nuns, rabbis, teachers and seekers coming together in communion and intention – to live with the big questions of life and death, love and evil, compassion and suffering, mystery and understanding – to sit together for a week inside the barbed wire, to talk, meditate, be with the fact of Auschwitz. The experience was not just a trail of tears but an unparalleled opportunity to go into the heart of the fire sharing the stories of the descendants of both survivors and perpetrators; a crucible of healing and learning; a rite of passage.

During my walking meditations in that dreadful place I thought constantly; 'Who am I now?' Auschwitz presents us with a challenge – to meet our own darkness, because only then is it possible to find another kind of ground in which to plant the tree of life. Also, if there is no compassion for the abusers and oppressors – for those who have no compassion – do I not become like them? Do I not, then, enter the darkness myself? A compassionate heart is the most effective way of challenging the power of evil. It can bring light where there was none. All this is in retrospect of course. No amount of compassion back then could have eliminated the evil in that hell on earth. But it helps me to understand that I must examine *my* choices each moment in terms of whether they move me toward the light or away from it. It shows me that the place to begin the task of eliminating evil is within myself.

★

At the end of the retreat, my head still full of it I decided to stay on in Poland for a few days in order to continue my pilgrimage and visit the little town of Tomaszchow-Mazowiecki – my father's birthplace. The Director of the Centre for Jewish Culture in Cracow kindly arranged a car and an interpreter to go with me.

Any romantic notions I may have had about a little Fiddler on the Roof *shtetl* were quickly dispelled. It is a straggly, unimpressive, strung-out town surrounded by blocks and blocks of concrete Soviet-style apartment buildings. We arrive at dusk – in the rain, driving past a few dismal and disconsolate – looking hookers plying their trade near the truck stops along the highway, and ask a local taxi-driver to recommend a nice hotel. He directs us to *the* hotel – the only one in town – the glum Mazowiecki Hotel. Vacancies are not a problem and a glance at the town map pinned on the wall shows us that Warszawska Street where my dad grew up is actually an extension of the very street the hotel is on.

We drive around in the dark peering through the windscreen wipers at any old building that might have been a shop on a corner but there is nothing to see – town completely dead – so we give up and spend the rest of the evening in the KLUB★PARADISE★ on the first floor of the hotel. We are the only customers. We sit on swivvley bar stools under the flashing UV lights, bombarded by high-volume, low grade disco tunes and watch the National Lottery on TV as our driver Pawel has bought a ticket. If he wins he is going to drive me all the way home to London free of charge. He doesn't win. Instead he has a beer. Robert my charming young interpreter, has a tequila and mint syrup with soda in a glass frosted with coconut and garnished with a paper toadstool. I knock back a couple of buffalo-grass vodkas. It is a surreal experience to be sitting in the ★PARADISE★ night club here in this ghost town where 14,000 Jews were transported to Treblinka on two terrible days in May 1942.

Next day, through a rusty iron gate, right on the far side of the town cemetery, we find an ancient, neglected burial ground overgrown with creepers and tree roots with hundreds of Jewish tombstones, all fallen down and broken, strewn about in the long grass. All the inscriptions are in Hebrew so no chance of identifying which graves might belong to my grandparents.

We pay a visit to the Kafkaesque Town Hall to make some enquiries about what happened to Warszawska Street but they only keep records going back fifty years. The Town Archive, however, on the other side of town were very helpful. They bring out some old leather-bound ledgers from the time of the Russian occupation. Records were kept up to date from the end of the eighteenth century until 1917 when the Russians left and, there, sure enough were the names Elia and Sura Honig (nee Tenenbaum) – my grandparents – and their only child Rachmil Yitzak, my father, born in 1905. My heart leaps. My fingers brush the spidery, faded, brown Russian copperplate and I think of the proud parents coming to register their miracle baby. The book, alas, does not record the family's exact address in Warszawska Street and the trail goes cold.

But, most importantly, the map on the wall of the hotel reception shows the little nature reserve called The Blue Sources. I've found it! We drive over there on the outskirts of the town and the lads leave me to be on my own. On this cold, overcast day it doesn't look very blue but it is a quiet, majestic place – really a series of interconnected ponds studded with mossy tree-covered islands. There is nobody about and I follow a winding path around the water's edge through a birch forest until I come to a particularly lovely spot. I know that my grandmother would have come here to this exact place – perhaps even when she, herself, was a girl. She certainly would have brought my father here for picnics with his cousins and friends. I imagine the sound of their childish laughter as I walk in their footsteps on the land of my ancestors – starkly beautiful on this grey day with black, leafless winter trees reflected in the still waters.

I had brought with me five red tulip bulbs from Francesca and I plant them in the rich, loamy soil under a silver birch by the river bank. I place acorns from Ben into the shallow silt with the hope that one day four English oak trees from Richmond Park may take root somewhere here. I throw a beautiful amethyst crystal onto the nearest island as a gift to my grandmother. I tell her I love her and that she will never be forgotten. I light my six floating candles – one for each of my children and send them off among the little islands carrying the light of life and remembrance. I stand and watch, in the darkening day, the miniature beacons, like fairies dancing, drifting silently out, carried by the gentlest of breezes, their tiny flames reflected in the water. 'L'Chaim,' I whisper. 'To life.'

★

In 2005 Zu and I decided to travel to Poland to celebrate our Dad's 100th birthday. We stayed in Krakow and explored the area of Kazimierz the old Jewish quarter now beautifully restored as a tourist destination after the huge popularity of Spielberg's film *Schindler's List*. There are no Jews living there. The restaurants serving Jewish food are run by non-Jews. The nice young guides offering their services are also non-Jews. Tasteless caricature figures of Klezmer musicians with long beards and hooked noses can be purchased at the souvenir shops. The place feels haunted.

We hired a vehicle and drove on to Tomaszow. We never managed to locate his house but we walked the length of Warszawska Street and visited the little nature reserve of The Blue Sources. This time we lit floating candles for each of *our* grandchildren – Dad's sixteen great-grandchildren and sent the flickering lights to twinkle amongst the islands. Another generation – reaffirming the continuity of the life of this Jewish family who once lived here.

We also went to the sad, desecrated, neglected Jewish cemetery, right at the far end of the Christian cemetery and through the rusty gate, where we spent quite a long time and found some beautiful old carved tombstones. Our guide Tomek explained that the carved images on each tombstone tell a story about the person buried there: A carving of books signifies a learned person; candlesticks – a woman; broken candles – she died young; a hand and a coin – a charitable person; a broken tree – a young man etc. Since my last visit some attempt had been made by Israeli groups to catalogue and raise up some of the stones and thanks to Tomek, plus the internet site he found, we were able to identify both our grandmother Sura Tenenbaum's and our great-grandmother Chana Honig's tombstones. The bottom line of the inscription reads: 'May her soul once again join the circle of the living.' And so it has. I was so happy to share the experience with my beloved sister and only wish our brother Yehudi could have been with us.

I asked Tomek why he, a non-Jew, has chosen to work at the Centre for Jewish Culture and he replied that he wants to help celebrate and revive the incalculable contribution that Jewish life brought to his country's history. To that end he has learned to read Hebrew. We could not have made our discovery without him.

CHAPTER FOURTEEN

Richard made a film for the BBC during the Vietnam War in 1969 *Assignment in Vietnam* and, some years after the war, he followed it up with a film of a series of interviews with American Vietnam veterans – many of whom had 'gone bush' and were living like hermits in remote locations in the hills and woods of America. A startling statistic emerged of the number of veterans who committed suicide after the war. A combination of the terrible things they had seen; terrible things they themselves had done; the tide of anti-war feeling that had greeted them when they returned home; being called 'baby killers' and murderers, not heroes, fuelled their despair. It had been a hopeless, stupid, misbegotten war that left nothing but carnage.

In 2019 I went to Vietnam and Cambodia; really to follow in Richard's footsteps, see the locations for myself. Richard, of course, never got to Hanoi back when the war was going on. His film is available on YouTube now and I watched it once more before coming here. So beautifully made and so tragic. And so *him*! My trip was kind of a pilgrimage to him five years after his death to acknowledge his passion for making meaningful films and for trying to tell the truth. He always felt it was essential to bear witness and to try to make a difference. He was thirty-six when he made it. The country was pounded to death, destroyed, razed, turned to rubble. The people killed and traumatised and betrayed. Then deserted. A David and Goliath struggle. But of course there were atrocities on all sides. War in what was called Indochina had been going on since the French occupation at the beginning of the century and after the Americans left the war was not over by any means and spilled over into Cambodia. In reality the North and the South had been goaded into combat by the communist and the capitalist worlds. The fighting continued until in July 1975 North and South Vietnam were finally unified under hardline Communist rule. And Cambodia became the unimaginably cruel vipers nest that was the Khmer Rouge under Pol Pot.

I was reading an excellent book called *The Sympathizer* by Viet Thanh Nguyen, giving a Vietnamese perspective.

'What reason had millions more died in our great war to unify our country and liberate ourselves?' asks Nguyen. 'What cause had they died for? What do those who struggle against power do when they seize power? What does the revolutionary do when the revolution triumphs? Why do those who call for independence and freedom take away the independence and freedom of others?'

My first glimpse of steamy, humid Hanoi was at 5.30 in the morning: My hotel room not going to be ready until noon so, flagging a bit after an eleven-hour flight, I went out for a walk in the pouring tropical rain then hailed a ride in a cycle rickshaw covered against the deluge by sheets of plastic pinned into place. I couldn't really see much apart from the ingenious way the totally chaotic traffic seems to weave organically. No one pays any attention to zebra crossings or red lights. You just head into the fray and hope for the best. The overhead spider's web of electricity cables is a marvel of lethal wiring.

A soon as it was open I paid a visit to the 'Women's Museum' celebrating the role of women in this society with the particular focus on the heroic sacrifices many women made during the Vietnam War (now called the American War over here). What a monstrous crime that was.

By the end of the war, more than 58,000 Americans lost their lives. Vietnam would later release estimates that 1.1 million North Vietnamese and Viet Cong fighters were killed, up to 250,000 South Vietnamese soldiers died and more than 2 million civilians were killed on both sides of the war.

That was such a short time ago and until 1990 the country was pretty much closed to outsiders but in the last twenty years tourism has become a big earner. I hate to think of myself as a tourist. I prefer 'traveller' or 'adventurer' or 'seeker' but tourist is what I am like it or not. Trying to distance myself from the tour groups and the selfie snappers I sat at a little table on the third floor balcony of my little hotel overlooking the lights of the city that has miraculously regenerated itself in the last forty years. Eight million people live here now (and eight million motorbikes). There is a Rolls Royce showroom and a super expensive new housing project financed by the man who made his billions by inventing pot noodles. House prices cost upwards of two million dollars on what used to be rice fields. I keep wondering how the Vietnamese square away all this rampant capitalism with their communist ideology.

Squeezed in amongst the soaring towers and groups of tourists there is still Hanoi's historic heart where quite a few of the lovely old French colonial houses survive, narrow streets and hundreds of street-food stalls crowding the pavements with their tiny miniature tables and chairs and a busy, bustling feel. I had to snigger at the Fanny Ice Cream parlour – most popular flavour, Cum (Vanilla). I went to see the site of Vietnam's first university (established in 1076) which is now the Temple of Literature dedicated to Confucius and to gaze into the 'Well of Heavenly Clarity' – a rather murky pond surrounded by garish statues of Confucius and postcards of the old revolutionary posters.

Then on to visit Ho Chi Minh's Mausoleum. Old Papa has been dead since 1969 but his embalmed body lies in state guarded by four impeccably uniformed men in white. A very long queue snaked round the whole complex but it moved along. Strict rules while queueing: no talking, no hands in pockets, no cameras, modest dress. Most of the people in the queue are Vietnamese. They come from all over the country to pay their respects. Uncle Ho is much revered. His story and that of his people is heroic. Within an hour it was my turn to file past his frail, pale, spotlit body on its catafalque. Once a year he is returned to Russia where they renew and refresh the chemicals keeping him from deteriorating. A bit gruesome but very respectfully and tastefully done. Outside two enormous banners flank the building: one says – in

Vietnamese – 'Long live the Socialist Republic of Vietnam', and the other 'Ho Chi Minh Forever in our Hearts'.

Afterwards I got chatting with a local guy at a cafe and plied him with questions about the country. He told me people love nothing better than singing karaoke. Their most favourite pastime is to book a private room for a party and just take turns singing all evening. He talked about how you can only get on in a government job if you are a member of the Communist party. (If kids fall behind at school and boys don't receive the privilege of wearing the coveted red tie, they are not eligible to join the party. A terrible disgrace for the whole family.) He said unemployment is very low at only 2½% and social services are fair but corruption is off the scale. Bribery just a fact of life. A friendly, helpful guy – (one of the great advantages of being an old woman. Nobody hassles you.) – he recommended an eating place down a little alley where I had fabulous Mekong river fish and scallops. That night Vietnam won a historic football victory over the Philippines and the city went mad. Most of the eight million motor bikes were roaring about – each with three or four people on them including babies in arms. Everyone waving flags of the yellow star on the red background and blowing bull horns. The din was phenomenal but very good natured and happy. It was quite hazardous for this seventy-eight-year-old granny trying to get back to her lodgings. Nobody stops when you are trying to cross the road. You just have to tough it out and plough on while the traffic swerves round you.

The next day I took a three-hour bus trip to Halong Bay through countryside where people are still afflicted by the effects of 'Agent Orange' – the evil toxic cancer-causing chemical defoliant dropped by the Americans to destroy the forest cover and food resources of the North Vietnamese guerrilla fighters. 'Strategic deforestation' they called it and sprayed the stuff on 4.5 million acres of land over the course of ten years. Although many American soldiers also suffered from the effects of exposure to Agent Orange it has left tangible, long-term impacts upon the Vietnamese people that live in Vietnam as well as those who fled in the mass exodus (the 'boat people') from 1978 to the early 1990s. Soil was contaminated, ecosystems disrupted, birth defects multiplied … . The International Union for the Conservation of Nature concluded that 'much of the damage can probably never be repaired'. At a rest stop on the journey there was a laudable women's craft cooperative raising money by selling their skilful embroidery to help families still suffering the effects.

At Halong Bay – the famous postcard-pretty geological marvel – I bought a ticket to board a junk for a trip sailing in the emerald waters among the extraordinary towering limestone islands topped by rain forest vegetation. More than 3,000 uninhabited tree-covered rock formations. It does get a lot of tourists but somehow the area was big enough and magical enough to lose yourself in a state of wonderment. I wished I'd planned to stay longer and wake up to the dawn in that ravishing place. So beautiful I could hardly breathe.

Da Nang was a disappointment. The bus was to take us over the picturesque High Cloud Pass but the weather was foggy and my seat was on the wrong side of the bus so I didn't see the famed view over the Bay where the first American ground force troops landed in 1965. The high spot on the trip was a couple of depressing concrete 'pill boxes' used first by the French then the Americans. Lots of fighting went on here. Now only some tatty souvenir stalls, filthy toilets and lots of litter. On to Hue, a nice, quiet city. A World Heritage site where I splashed out on a room in the Imperial Hotel – quite grand in an old-style imperial way with pagoda type entrance and carved wooden doors. Hue is the spiritual heart of Vietnam and the Imperial Enclosure the epicentre of Vietnamese royal life. The home of Kings for over 1,000 years.

The guidebooks hardly mention the war here in central Vietnam but there are memories everywhere amongst all the thrusting development: The 'Army Cafe' with the waiters and the band in military uniform and a crashed helicopter hanging from the ceiling; The 'Demilitarized Zone' Hostel; 'Healing the Wounded Heart' craft centre and the Ho Chi Minh Trail which runs through the jungly mountains but there's nothing to see there as it was meant to be invisible and undetectable. Dien Bien Phu not far from here is where the French were finally defeated. So much death and brutality and hardship in the history of this country and yet the entrepreneurship and indomitability of the people is quite phenomenal. I was reading

Norman Lewis's book *A Dragon Apparent* written in 1951 and republished in 1982 with a preface to the new edition by Lewis. It makes such poignant reading ...he describes a rare, peaceful, harmonious society on the brink of catastrophe. There were once hunter/gatherer tribespeople in the remote forests and mountain regions. They no longer exist. He writes, 'They were bombed to nothingness by the B52s in the Vietnam War and such of the population who survived were forced into the armies fighting the Nationalist Viet Cong, who were revenged on them in due course when the US abandonment of the country took place.' The loss of yet another unchronicled indigenous culture. Wiped out.

Ralph Metzner, a pioneer in studies of cross-cultural consciousness, who died last year, once wrote: 'Between 200 and 600 million of the earth's people belong to indigenous societies comprising as many as five thousand different languages and cultures. Environmentalist and conservationists have increasingly looked to indigenous societies as models for the sustainable stewardship of natural resources, These people are the miner's canary of the human family; in direct dependence on nature, they are the first to suffer the effects of pollution, degradation and exploitation.'

Most of the population of Vietnam, Cambodia and Laos were Buddhist – gentle and tolerant. Their ancient civilisations had already been eroded by the invasion and colonisation by the French but the 'American War' turned South Vietnam into a wasteland devastated by high-explosives, poisons and fire. Lewis writes; 'Mr Kissinger had said that the dominoes were falling so now it was the turn of Cambodia and Laos, delivered to the greatest holocaust ever to be visited on the East. It consumed not only the present, but the past; an obliteration of cultures and values as much as physical things. From the ashes that remained no phoenix would ever rise. Not enough survived even to recreate the memory of what the world had lost.'

But a different Vietnam has arisen – a country of commerce and tour groups and here I am trying to take it all in. It was a clear, beautiful day and I went up onto the hotel roof where there is a shrine to Kwan Yin, the goddess of compassion and a wonderful view over the city and the Perfume River where later I took a ride in a Dragon Boat seeing the local fishermen and water buffaloes along the way.

Thich Nhat Hahn, the influential Zen Buddhist monk, master and teacher, poet and activist now lives back in Hue after many years exile in France. He is much more loved and well-known in Europe than he ever was here in his home country. His interpretation of Buddhism annoyed the traditionalists and the Communists didn't want him around either. Sadly he has had a stroke and, at ninety-three years of age, is now quite frail and suffering from some memory loss. He is cared for in a facility near the Imperial Palace that was originally a home for retired eunuchs who, having no children, had no one to look after them in old age. I felt honoured to be near him and I left some flowers for him. The spiritual centre he created in France – Plum Village – is an ever-growing international community who come together for retreat and the practice of the living art of mindfulness. His monastic and lay students continue to offer retreats and keep his teachings alive. Thich Nhat Hahn wrote, 'We have to walk in a way that we only print peace and serenity on the Earth. Walk as if you are kissing the Earth with your feet.' His simple and elegant calligraphies convey his powerful teachings. Martin Luther King proposed him for the Nobel Peace Prize but he never won it. Kissinger did instead.

On display in the palace grounds is the blue Austin car which was driven by Quang Duc, a Buddhist monk, in June 1963 to a central location in the city where he proceeded to douse himself in petrol and set himself alight in protest at the persecution of Buddhists. A photographer caught the moment and the ghastly image was broadcast all over the world alerting people to the plight of monks in Vietnam. His last words were:

Before closing my eyes and moving towards the vision of the Buddha, I respectfully plead to President Ngo Dinh Diem to take a mind of compassion towards the people of the nation and implement religious equality to maintain the strength of the homeland eternally. I call the venerables, reverends, members of the sangha and the lay Buddhists to organize in solidarity to make sacrifices to protect Buddhism.

David Halberstam the journalist who was present wrote:

Flames were coming from a human being; his body was slowly withering and shrivelling up, his head blackening and charring. In the air was the smell of burning human flesh; human beings burn surprisingly quickly. Behind me I could hear the sobbing of the Vietnamese who were now gathering. I was too shocked to cry, too confused to take notes or ask questions, too bewildered to even think … .As he burned he never moved a muscle, never uttered a sound, his outward composure in sharp contrast to the wailing people around him.

The famous shocking photograph adorns the front cover of Thich Nhat Hahn's book *Vietnam: Lotus in a Sea of Fire*.

Quang Duc's body was re-cremated later during the funeral. His heart did not burn and remained intact. It was considered to be holy so they placed it in a glass chalice at Xa Loi Pagoda. The heart became a symbol of compassion.

The next morning I took an early flight to Saigon (or Ho Chi Minh City as it is now called) – a buzzing metropolis of commerce, tourist hotels, lovely trees planted by the French that have to be guarded from theft for firewood and hellish traffic. This where I catch up with Richard's time here in 1969. The North of Vietnam was not accessible to Westerners during the war and his film, *Assignment in Vietnam*, focussed on the experiences of three journalists reporting in the South: Peter Arnett with the American forces, Dick West in the Mekong Delta and Mark Frankland in Saigon.

Most tourists who come here today come for the lovely beaches, delicious food and good value shopping opportunities. There are many beautiful things to see and do and one doesn't have to be reminded of past history but the The War Remnants Museum was one of the places I most wanted to visit. Coming to Vietnam, for me was a sort of homage to Richard and others who risked their lives documenting the war. It was a way to acquaint myself with what happened here and to think about that young man on the night bus to Nashville all those years ago.

The museum was a good place for me to start although I had to take a deep breath before going in through the doors. One floor, called 'Requiem', is devoted to the courageous photojournalists (many of whom died on the job, such as Robert Capa and Larry Burrows) who brought the truth of what was happening here to the attention of the world. It was the first television war and turned the tide of public opinion. Tim Page collected many of these iconic images by photographers from America, UK, Japan and Vietnam that are on display here. I remember so many of them from *Life Magazine* and *The Sunday Times* and other publications at the time: the child running down the road with her clothes burned of by napalm; the American soldier weeping; another setting fire to a straw hut with his Zippo lighter; the dead bodies; execution; torture and misery on all sides. And then the room devoted to the horrors of phosphorous and Agent Orange and deformed foetuses in jars and reconstructions of the tiny cages in which prisoners were kept and the guillotine used by the French ... . All horrible, barely believable.

The museum filled me with despair for the human race once again, as with my visit to Auschwitz twenty years ago. I remained stunned and tearful. How can we do such things to each other? Why so much cruelty? What hope do we have? We've learned nothing at all and keep repeating this useless cycle of violence.

And to think this was such a short time ago – in the lifetime of my children – now this modern city risen from the ashes – clean, entrepreneurial, competitive, industrious, hard-working, creative – it's such an astonishing achievement. Back then Saigon's main industry was servicing the war. Today it is manufacturing clothes for fashion retailers such as Marks and Spencer and servicing the tourism industry. The resilience and indomitability of the Vietnamese is truly extraordinary. I was amazed and moved to be able to actually witness the miracle of regeneration from the horrors of the past and enjoyed reading Graham Greene's *The Quiet American* while sitting in the bar of the Hotel Continental where he wrote it. Saigon is not a pretty city – choked by traffic and wreathed in pollution. It's a strange place and I guess you'd have to live here and have some kind of purpose or job to love it. There are not many cultural attractions apart from The Art Museum housing a gallery containing ancient sculptures and a large collection of modern art – some good, some naf, some infused with the sadness of war – a mother breastfeeding her baby with a rifle slung over her shoulder; a one-legged soldier coming home to his wife; a bombed-out village.

A large part of Richard's film is set in the Mekong Delta, a watery world of rivers, canals, buffalo and rice paddies, so I wanted to go there and experience first hand being in a canoe in those same mangroves and backwaters where he had filmed. About one and a half hours in a bus. *Big mistake!* Little did I know that because there are so few things for tourists to see here, the Delta is on everyone's itinerary. Loads of tour groups emerged from a fleet of buses and converged at the quayside in My Linh. Large boats then herd everyone out to Coconut Island where there is a gauntlet to run of souvenir shops and ladies making coconut products. Then a long line of four-seater canoes draw up alongside paddled by nimble-footed boatwomen who stand precariously at the back and we are all popped in like on a Disneyland ride and get rowed for fifteen minutes through a muddy tributary and back to our boats. So *not* what I envisaged. I suppose one should be glad that local people are making money from processing these packaged tourists but I hated it. If you half-closed your eyes and used your imagination while being paddled along the watery conveyor belt you could think of what it must have been like during the war for troops from all sides fighting in this area – the mud, the jungle, the hostile enemy, wading through the mosquito infested swamps carrying your rifle above your head, not being able to tell friend from foe, being ambushed, destroying villages, killing innocent people. All for what? Madness. Dick West's commentary in Richard's film captures the reality of the time very well. I could only picture it in my mind.

I left early the next morning to catch a Cambodian Airways plane to Phnom Penh. I had a contact here – my sister-in-law's nephew Sam who is living here while his job is building a golf course for the very wealthy. According to Sam, the King comes to play golf once a week and whereas all the other players get one shot, the King can take as many as it takes to pot his ball. Then everyone claps. Also this is a two-party state but at the last election the leader of the opposition was arrested and put in jail until the incumbent president was re-elected. Gossip is rife. Corruption here knows no bounds. No one is surprised and people just keep their heads down.

By all accounts from the past, this place was paradise; Cambodians the most gentle, peace loving people and Phnom Penh the jewel of Asia. A pretty city with golden temples dotted about all over the place.

So what happened next is hard to believe. An entire country was put in thrall to a dystopian ideal that negated anything and everything that was human.

Philip Short in the prologue to his terrifying account of the Khmer Rouge: *Pol Pot: The History of a Nightmare* writes, 'What is it about Cambodian society that has allowed and continues to allow, people to turn their backs on all they know of gentleness and compassion, goodness and decency and to commit appalling cruelties seemingly without conscience of the enormity of their acts and certainly without remorse.' It is a question one can ask of the Germans during the time of the Nazis; the Rwandans; the Turks in Armenia; the Serbs in Bosnia; the terrorist groups inspired by Islamic fundamentalism; slave owners in the past and those who hunted down indigenous people without mercy in America, Tasmania and elsewhere … . It goes on and on. But we also need to ask ourselves, as we did when I went on that Bearing Witness Buddhist Retreat to Auschwitz, 'Where does the hatred live in me? Where the evil? Where the coward? Under what circumstances could I become the murderer, the torturer?'

As I have never been tested, I hope I will never know. Would I be able to retain some courage and humanity in the face of terrible fear?

Anyway, to meditate on these things I made myself go to the dreadful Genocide Museum – S-21 – the interrogation centre and prison at Tuol Sleng where Pol Pot's, Khmer Rouge thugs tortured and killed thousands of hapless people. Nearly a quarter of the population of the country was exterminated during those years from 1975 to 1979 – only forty years ago. A couple of the worst perpetrators of this hell were brought before a war crimes tribunal later but most were simply reabsorbed back into ordinary life and are still around now in government jobs.

The tortures must have been thought up by the most sick, sadistic psychopaths. Ever more fiendish and imaginative ways to cause maximum suffering and all for what? Why would anyone want to destroy families, culture, love, loyalty to create this 'Year Zero' madness of a peasant communist society? A radical egalitarianism, a utopian dream which had to be enforced by a reign of terror in which more than a million people perished. Like the Nazis, the Khmer Rouge carefully documented everything. Photographs of the victims line the walls. The genocide continued at the 'Killing Fields' a little way out of town. People clubbed on the head, suffocated by plastic bags, mass graves, mountains of skulls and bones, a tree where babies were smashed against the trunk in front of their mothers who were then raped and killed themselves. That tree has now become a shrine with thousands of tiny braided bracelets hung on it.

Speechless with sadness and dazed by the overwhelming weight of pain and sorrow my tears flowed. That tree was the worst thing I'd seen since the piles of baby clothes and human hair at Auschwitz. Unimaginable until you are brought face to face. I bought some flowers and spent some time in the memorial pagoda where all the rows and rows of skulls are housed. Excavations are still going on and in the rainy season human bones are still surfacing in the Killing Fields. You can see them poking up out of the mud.

But again, Philip Short's book makes clear that Pol Pot and his henchmen did not act alone. The West – and above all the US, through its role in the Vietnam War – must share some responsibility. After that sobering experience, back in the hotel room on my iPad, I watched Richard's final film for the BBC: *The Unleashing of Evil* which talks about the complicity of the CIA and other clandestine Western agencies in the training methods; secret 'extraordinary renditions', (the government-sponsored abduction and extrajudicial transfer of a person from one country to another with the purpose of circumventing the former country's laws on interrogation, detention and torture); manufacturing of leg irons and other things we'd rather not know about. I've bought a book called, *Why Did They Kill?: Cambodia in the Shadow of Genocide* by Alexander Laban Hilton. Maybe it will help me to understand.

People used to ask Richard, 'Why would you want that stuff in your head?' And the same could be asked of the war photographers such as Don McCullin but Richard's answer was always, 'How could I not want to do something – maybe make a difference, document the truth, bring this darkness to the attention of the world?' Maybe some darkness in their own psyche takes them to the brink of the abyss. And what of my own motivation? All my life I have had a recurring half-waking, half-dreaming vision of myself as a small child standing on the edge of a pit full of bodies holding the hand of a little boy. We are both shot and thrown in … . Then I wake up. Years later I came across some photos of Sobibor, the Nazi extermination camp and I recognised the landscape. What does this mean? Some psychic ability that 'sees' the fate I might have had? I'll never know but I am also drawn to confronting the abyss and bearing witness to suffering.

Next day I felt the need to get out of Phnom Penh. A strange, unidentifiable sense that just underneath the surface, behind the impassive faces is a darkness. Everyone here must know someone or something.

Hoping to have an uplifting experience, I took a short flight to Siem Riep – sadly (for me), this is the epicentre of tourism in Cambodia with three million visitors last year going to Angkor Wat and this year even more are projected. This has all happened in the last few years and is definitely helping the economy but the crowds are the price to pay. Angkor Wat! One of the places I've always wanted to see – the largest religious site in the world. World Heritage status. One of the great wonders of the world. Richard came here when he was a soldier during the Korean War doing his National Service over sixty years ago. He was astonished by what he saw. There was no one here. Not one tourist, he said, it was almost as if he had discovered it. Hey Ho! That's all gone now. Nowhere left to discover.

In spite of everything, it lived up to my expectations. A day of wonders. It is an absolutely enormous site with dozens of temples – some in ruins, some being carefully restored, some being swallowed up by the jungle. You need a guide and a special ticket to enter the compound which is surrounded by a huge moat. Once inside you can wander around at your own pace. It would take a lifetime to see everything. Alas, millions of Chinese tourists also want to take the iconic photos and endless stupid selfies but we got there early and went in by the back entrance at 6.00 am and had a bit of peace and solitude before the hoards arrived.

I chose three temples to visit – the big, high, triple temple in all the postcards with quite scary steep steps up to the third level. (This seventy-eight-year-old great-grandmother was pretty pleased with herself for tackling the steps but it was really worth it.); the second one was Bayon where 216 huge Faces of Buddha look down on the pilgrims. The beatific, serene heads facing in the four directions and a fantastic, miraculously preserved carved frieze of daily life along one wall. Intricate, detailed bas relief work of elephants, domestic scenes, animals, farmers, soldiers, trees and birds, fish and boats. Humorous and fresh as if it were carved yesterday. More clambering about on huge stones and uneven paths but I did manage it. Finally, the most famous image of Angkhor Wat – the temples with the tree roots gradually swallowing the ruins alive. Roots, like boa constrictors, that have probed and infiltrated, strangled and practically suffocated the buildings. Tomb Raider or Temple of Doom or some such movie was filmed here which started the great tourist boom about ten years ago, more's the pity. I think I saw it not a moment too soon. There are just too many of us but I still loved it and walked miles in the humid heat.

For my final day I wanted to visit Tonle Sap Lake and the floating villages for a glimpse of the timeless world of fishing and rice growing with communities of people living as they've always done for hundreds of years in ramshackle floating wooden houses which have to be towed up river in the dry season when the water becomes shallow. The people are very poor and have nothing much except a tiny floating garden moored alongside with a few vegetables growing in oil drums but every house has a mobile phone and a Sky television ariel. I asked my guide what happened to these people during the Khmer Rouge days. He said that because they are largely uneducated and illiterate they were easily manipulated to become the dehumanised killers of the intellectuals and middle-class city folk who were being exterminated. As are child soldiers – the most merciless of killers – as they have not yet had a chance to develop empathy. Even today, the government prefers to keep them ignorant so that they can be recruited into the army when needed. To the locals the President (quite likely ex-Khmer Rouge) is like a movie star and they love him.

So, farewell to this unfathomable country. Two weeks, of course is not enough to learn much but my purpose of pilgrimage and reflection was important to me and brought me closer to understanding and appreciating aspects of my long journey with Richard, that complex, darling man.

CHAPTER FIFTEEN

I have written at length about the coming of the twins, Femi and Tim, into our family but, as yet, nothing about the last addition to our multi-national tribe – Fauzia. So this chapter will be about Kenya and the great good fortune of meeting her there. But first an introductory tale which will have relevance later … . When Femi was about fifteen she had an unplanned pregnancy with a boy from school. ('We only did it once!' she wailed, as if it was a game of Russian roulette.) We talked through her choices with her: have the baby and we would help her care for it; have the baby and stay with the boyfriend; have the baby and have it adopted; have a termination. She had just won a place at the prestigious London School of Contemporary Dance and was set on a career as a dancer. She wasn't at all ready or willing to become a mother so she chose the latter. At the time a wise friend said to me, 'Just make a note of the date her baby would have been born as you may notice around that time a change of mood or a depression. Even if intellectually she didn't want the baby, physically her body did.' So I wrote it down – February 17th, 1977.

Femi went from strength to strength getting her first job in a West End theatre at the age of sixteen – *Bubbling Brown Sugar* – with an all-black cast, moving up rapidly from a swing dancer to a solo spot dancing to Duke Ellington's 'Sophisticated Lady'.

Years passed and my 'quest of a novice healer' continued with a trip to Kenya on the trail of a local medicine man, traditional or 'witch' doctor. I had written to a Kikuyu friend asking for his advice. 'No problem!' he said. 'Come! We will arrange everything.' Being broke, as usual, I went to see the manager of Kenya Airways who generously agreed to sponsor my trip.

'No problem!' That marvellous ubiquitous African phrase is the curse that haunts all achievement-oriented foreigners who challenge the rhythm of life on that mighty continent. I'd arrived in Nairobi and nothing, of course, had actually been arranged and I became anxious that I was wasting time. All my initial contacts led me nowhere and on top of everything else I was starting to feel ill. My temperature rocketed and my throat closed up. I was forced to admit temporary defeat and let myself be wrapped up, put to bed and surrendered to the tender loving care of an extended African household where I was never left alone. Someone continuously watched over me, sat by me, washed my sweaty clothes and brought me tea to drink while the virus raged.

On the fourth day I woke and knew the fever had passed. A little girl was sitting on the end of my bed with a damp flannel to wipe my face. Her first question in rudimentary English was, 'You like Jane Fonda?' I said I did indeed. Then she said, 'You dance Jane Fonda?' and pulled out from under the bed an old cassette player with the Jane Fonda exercise tapes. It was when I finally got up to have a go at some of the moves with her that I saw she was tiny for her age and had twisted little legs like corkscrews but the sweetest face and a personality as big as the Ritz. Fauzia, aged seven, had been left to look after me as everyone else had gone out either to work or to school. She was unable to walk to school so just stayed home.

Gradually, the gentle sound of women's voices murmuring as they returned from work and the appetising smell from the little charcoal braziers filtered through and I was able to get to know the other members of the family who had rescued me. The Twaha family represented a perfect microcosm of contemporary Africa, illustrating all the paradoxes and dilemmas facing a people with one foot in a timeless rural past and the other foot in a high speed technological future.

The father, Ali, my original contact, was a news cameraman for the Voice of Kenya television station with a wide experience of the outside world. He seemed to know everyone and acts as interpreter and fixer for visiting film crews. (He had worked with Richard on a film about a Kenyan long-distance runner made for a BBC sports series.) Maryam is Ali's wife and central pivot of the household. She works all day as a catering assistant at the police headquarters and spends the rest of the time cooking and caring for her family. They have six children of their own. Another son died tragically some years before and they have adopted a little girl whose mother is mentally ill and also Fauzia, my little carer, who was rejected by her own family because of her disability. Her biological mother is one of Maryam's sisters. Their language is Swahili and there are kinship links on her father's side with Oman.

Maryam's youngest sister, Tijara, also lives in the compound as do three teenage nieces who help with the chores. Apart from the permanent residents, any number of neighbours' kids, friends and relatives constantly throng in and out. The house consists of a comfortable sprawl of six small rooms around a central courtyard. This is the hub of all activity – everything goes on in the courtyard: cooking, washing, sitting around, visiting, talking, feeding babies, break-dance practicing, hair-plaiting.

Because of Ali's relatively secure job, the family are better off than most of their neighbours. They have a proper toilet and a shower, a television, a video player and a battered old Renault, but that's where the luxury ends. Their only indulgence is to hire two video films a week and watch them on a Saturday night. Everyone has to be fed every day, school fees found, shoes, books, school uniforms bought, bills paid, poorer relations helped, family obligations honoured. It's a hard life and yet they made room for me so cheerfully and open-heartedly.

The weekend begins at 6 am on Saturday when three little charcoal braziers are lit to heat the washing water. There is a mountain of washing to be done so everyone takes a little low wooden stool and a bucket of suds and we sit around in the courtyard in the fresh morning sunshine scrubbing away. Nobody seems to mind that the cooking and the washing take all day. In fact they are regarded more as social occasions to be enjoyed rather than dreary tasks. Pleasure is taken in the job itself rather than in its completion. There is actually an ancient twin-tub washing machine on the premises and I asked why they don't use it. 'Too lonely', they said. From about 3 pm the great cooking marathon starts. Everyone cooks, not just one poor harassed mother slaving away. Its very unhurried and companionable. Stirring, chopping, peeling, frying, talking, laughing.

At one point the boys gave us an impromptu demonstration of their latest body-popping and break-dance routine. The tinny tranny belted out Herbie Hancock's Rocket Man and the lads jerked into action. The older boys were sensational, flipping and roboting and spinning round on their heads while the little guys with their skinny, flailing legs looked more like stick insects or electrocuted spiders. It was very touching to watch but also sad to see the way in which this aggressive, pulsating, imported American culture creates a restless dissatisfaction with their own traditions and whispers promises of excitement and unfulfilled longing that can only bring in their wake the destruction of all that this timeless fireside circle stands for.

The cooking took four hours and the meal was eaten in five minutes. After dinner the men usually watch football on the television and then go out – nobody asks where. The women crowd into the video room, wrap themselves in their kangas and watch videos. This Saturday the programme consisted of two unspeakable video nasties that would almost certainly be censored in this country. Fortunately the quality of these fourth-hand pirate copies is so bad that its nearly impossible to tell what's going on. The women all chew leaves with a mild stimulant effect so that they can make the most of Saturday night, stay awake till dawn and sleep on Sunday. Everyone chatted away cheerfully while people were tortured and dismembered on the screen. I felt quite ashamed of this example of Western 'culture' and took the little children off to show them how to make a game of Snakes and Ladders.

When I finally felt well enough to get back on the trail again I went to the offices of *The Nation*, one of Kenya's daily newspapers, to ask if they had any library material on traditional doctors. I spoke to a young reporter who remembered an article on the work of Dr. John Muir Kalii, an Akamba man from the Machakos district in the Eastern region. He had many miraculous cures ascribed to him and was held in some awe by local people. The article described the successes he had had with mental illness and infertility.

Only an hour later I happened to be talking to a woman writer who had just published a book on heroic Kenyan women. When asked her if she knew of any healers she immediately spoke of 'a remarkable man near Machakos called Kalli'. He had cured her sister who for years had suffered from suicidal depressions.

That same evening at dinner, a Ugandan refugee paediatrician working at the Kenyatta Hospital told me, 'If you are researching traditional healing you must try to locate a certain Dr. Kalii. He has an extraordinary knowledge of plants and herbs and has become quite a legend in his own lifetime.' Three references in one day. Kalii was obviously the chap I was meant to see. He has established a little 'hospital' about seven miles off the main Nairobi-Mombasa highway where he treats patients for a wide variety of physical and mental disorders, many of which have been declared incurable by conventional doctors.

I left Nairobi for the two-hour bus journey through green undulating plains dotted with trees and the occasional giraffe or ostrich looking as if posed there by the Kenyan Tourist Board. In Machakos, a small provincial town I looked up the local office of *The Nation* and engaged a young correspondent, Calvin, to be my guide and interpreter. Then on to Salama where I rented a concrete cell with a barred window, a bed and a Gideon Bible and had a meal in the little downstairs cafe selling chicken stew and chapattis, very good value for eighteen shillings, and a cup of boiled tea. Salama – a one-horse, truck-stop town of dilapidated shop fronts; mostly bars, dance halls, eating places, and knocking shops with barefoot hookers in faded frocks hoping to earn the price of a bowl of stew. Frequented by long distance lorry drivers, the place is alive with activity at night. Marvellously evocative Congolese dance music coming from the juke-box and a great deal of squeaking bed springs in the cubicle next to mine carried on until the sound of fifty long-haul truck engines warming up in the dawn light heralded the departure of the men on their way from Mombasa to Uganda. Everyone washed and peed right outside my little cell window at about 5 am before the mass exodus of monstrous motors.

That day I would meet the formidable Mzee Daktari, the 'old man doctor'.

In my first book *I Fly Out With Bright Feathers*, I wrote about the time I spent in his company – a remarkable healer and a canny, sometimes infuriating, old fox. I witnessed many unexplainable things and left with many unanswered questions.

On my last day I wanted to see as much as possible and Kalii announced I could come with him on safari to a Masai village two hours drive away. As usual he kept me waiting – hanging about for hours – he was always testing me to see if I would revert to type and pull the impatient white-woman stereotype on him. Every African I have met both here and elsewhere on the continent has long memories of insufferable colonial high-handedness. It's very hard to be just a person and not a symbol. Finally after having virtually ignored me all day, we piled into the Land Rover with his Rastafarian nephew at the wheel and about eight others in the back with me. A few weeks before he had treated a couple of very sick children with, he said, diphtheria and although he was sure there was nothing requiring further treatment, he just wanted to visit the family and make sure everything was alright. We jounced along the spectacularly rutted dirt roads on spine-jolting metal seats, red dust swirling into our throats and eyes, Doc in front with his stethoscope around his neck. Wherever we went people ran up to the car shouting 'Daktari! Daktari!' Kalii caressed the children's heads, touched and held everyone who came near.

We stopped at a little round mud and straw hamlet where a very old man in rags came hobbling out, both arms raised in praise and happiness, to see his beloved doctor. He had been terribly injured in a bus crash which had crushed both his legs. Doc had treated him after he came out of hospital paralysed and he seemed remarkably spry considering his age and the seriousness of his injuries. Everyone, no matter how ragged or anonymous, is treated with dignity. Although the Daktari is a 'Big Man', in this context he is not overbearing or power greedy. He is the good father, benevolent, caring, shepherding, and he is obviously adored.

The next stop was a hillside full of goats and a few herdsmen.

Doc got out and a long discussion and appraisal took place. Suddenly one of the goats was pounced on, tied up, and shoved bleating into the back of the truck with us passengers, where it butted around frantically, fanned little turds with its tail and peed copiously on our feet. No explanation. We lurched on along the potholed road across the invisible border that divided the Masai lands from anyone else's. They had suffered dreadfully in the last year's drought and many of their cattle had died. We drove through one area littered with skeletons every few yards – a vivid reminder of the tenuousness of nomadic life. If the rains fail, you starve; it's as simple as that. The Masai are a noble people – nomadic pastoralist herdsmen who have always stubbornly refused to change or fit in with anyone. Successive rulers have singularly failed to make them soldiers, slaves or domestic servants. It's tempting to romanticise them – their knowledge of the wild, their understanding of animals, their elegance and bravery – and the fact is, they haven't sold out They understand the value of land and they haven't become a miserable degraded tourist spectacle. People acknowledge and respect their otherness and the integrity which defies intrusion. It's good to see them retaining their dignity, bringing their ancient ways steadfastly into the twentieth century city while people move over for them – a feat not many so called 'primitive' cultures have carried off. I heard later that the reason you are forbidden to photograph them in the National Parks is that they actually killed a tourist who ignored their request not to – threw a spear right through him!

The men look very glamorous – tall, fine-featured, with elaborate hairstyles enhanced with red clay. They wear the characteristic draped red cloth or blanket, beaded necklaces, headbands, bracelets and earrings. They carry spears to defend their cattle against attack by lions and seem to look graceful whatever they do – walking along single file or leaping straight into the air in one of their amazing dances.

As we drove along it became dark. African nights descend like a blackout and the Milky Way enfolded us. I'd never seen so many stars near enough to touch, hanging in the trees like diamonds. A last we came to a round fenced enclosure with compact little beehive mud houses, a swept compound and a few cows. Lots of delighted children streamed forth and some splendidly adorned Masai women festooned like Christmas trees with collar-like beaded necklaces and dozens of pairs of beaded hoop earrings hanging from their elongated, perforated earlobes. All clamouring to touch their adored Daktari. They mostly have shaved heads and wear colourful red or pink kangas. They look perfect – epic – in the landscape but I always found it quite a surprise to see one of them sitting in a bar with a Coke or speeding by in a taxi in Nairobi.

Kalii took my hand and led me doubled over through the spiralling entrance passage of one of the houses. In the absence of a chimney, all the smoke from the fire inside finds its way out through the same passage and I was choking to death by the time we reached the single room inside. An old granny and several others were sitting round in there cooking something that was sending up clouds of acrid smoke. I couldn't see much by the light of the single candle and the atmosphere was so intensely suffocating that I had to flee outside again. Everyone laughed at me, the women doubled up with merriment. Mzee Daktari stroked everyone and asked how they were. He 'read' the childrens' blood by putting an ear to the inside of an arm and pronounced them completely better. They certainly looked fine. The whole trip seemed more like an excuse for a sociable outing. Doc asked one of the women to go and milk a cow for us, explaining to me that etiquette demands that the visitor must ask – it's not up to the host to offer; then they are happy that your needs have been met. Ten minutes later I was handed an old Mateus Rose bottle corked with a pared down corn cob and filled with fresh foaming warm milk. We sat around in the firelight for a while and a plump, dusty baby climbed into my lap. The mother admired my earrings so I swapped them for a beaded wristband.

Mission accomplished, we piled back in the truck and finally returned to Kalii's little hospital around 10 pm, where we all solemnly sat around some more in the parlour. Doc then made an elaborate speech to the effect that since I was his honoured guest (he'd hardly spoken to me all day), he intended to throw a farewell party for me. 'There is beer, music and a goat,' he said with a flourish. My heart sank at the thought of the poor goat. So that was why Doc had acquired it. A party! I hadn't realised I was to be responsible for its execution. Everyone gasped with pleasure and awe at this magnanimous gesture of hospitality and generosity. I knew we'd be in for a long wait as the goat was still protesting in the yard. Ten minutes later when I strolled outside for a breath of fresh air I saw the unfortunate creature strung up by its legs from a tree, being skinned.

A rickety record player arrived and a handful of scratched 45s – 'Daddy Cool' and about six different Kakamba and Kikuyu songs. Terrific dancing music, and within seconds the room filled up with recuperating patients magnetised by the therapeutic properties of the beat. Crates of beer arrived, donated by some wealthy merchants who'd called earlier in the day. The Doc pulled me to my feet and we initiated the dancing. The old boy was surprisingly nimble and graceful for his bulk and danced like a cross between a potentate and a jelly. Shirt-tails awry, he clasped his considerable belly with both hands and shook it provocatively in my direction. Everyone else instantly joined in until the room, like a struck tuning fork began to shimmer and reverberate in the hot equatorial night air. The dancing was wonderful. I don't care if it is a cliché: nobody can dance like Africans. Their bodies set up an undulating wave pattern that just oscillates to the rhythm. It got very sexy and suggestive rather quickly, with everybody laughing and cheering on the ribald gestures of the others. Several of the patients were unstoppable once they got going. The elderly primigravida sitting serenely in the corner, knitting, mostly confined herself to dancing from the waist up, but every once in a while the temptation became too great and she leapt to her feet for a little wiggle. 'Good exercise for the baby!' laughed Doc indulgently. He is convinced that music, laughter and having a good time are an essential part of getting well so parties are a fairly regular feature of hospital life. No one was dressed for a party – they wore just the faded, dusty, raggedy clothes, plastic sandals and tennis shoes minus laces they always wear, but it was a great party. Gallons of beer were consumed and the floor was awash with foam.

At one point the good Daktari became alarmingly amorous, as I'd rather feared he might, and started making little speeches about his blood being attracted to my blood and how he'd known it from the first moment he saw me. 'How does it feel to be the guest of honour of our beloved Doctor?' asked one young man, implying that intense horizontal gratitude should be the appropriate response. 'How do you propose to thank the Doctor when he has killed a goat for you?' was another query. Some delicate negotiations were called for, invoking my jealous husband, my chaste nature, the obligations of hosts to protect lady guests far from home, my untold joy at the prospect of being able, some day, to return the generous hospitality in England … . The situation was reasonably successfully diffused but a watchful attitude was necessary thereafter, like not letting myself get cornered by the doctorial bulk on the sofa.

Everyone was delighted that I ventured to dance in the proper African way and we churned away until three in the morning when the dismembered goat was carried in, done to a turn, and piled on several trays. I spared him a guilty vote of thanks for his sacrifice and then tucked in. It was not a pretty sight – everyone grabbed handfuls of crunchy intestines, giant knuckle bones and ribs like a scene from Dante's *Inferno*. A mountain of ugali (maize porridge) was consumed and the entire goat, down to his poor little hooves, vanished. Thank goodness Doc's Rasta nephew was a non-drinker since he was the one I hoped would drive me home to my flea-pit. I was relieved that I could depend on him since everyone else was extremely drunk and the merrymaking looked fit to carry on for days. My erstwhile bodyguard and translator, Calvin, was well away entangled in what looked like an endless vertical copulation with a young lady so he was in no hurry to leave but it was time to make my excuses as a rosy glow suffused the sky. The good doctor gave me a warm embrace and I thanked him for my party and my goat and slipped away. It was 5 am by the time Rastaman Martin got me to Salama and the place was completely dead. We had to hammer on the corrugated-iron fence to get the nightwatchman out of bed to let me in. My head was spinning and my throat constricted with dust. I kept doing goat-flavoured burps and one arm was sunburned from leaning out of the truck all day, but I crashed out on my little wooden cot and slept like a log. Calvin staggered in a couple of hours later with two girls and I could hear them heaving about noisily in the next cell.

I'd arranged with Martin to be picked up at 9 am to go and bid a final farewell to Doc so I dragged myself up, washed in cold water, and, of course, waited for three hours before he turned up. Calvin looked very much the worse for wear and poor Martin hadn't been to bed at all. On the drive up to Doc's place for the last time we had a spirited, rather acrimonious argument about the role of women in society They both conceded that I am an exception (freak?) but they would never marry a 'town woman'; they are all bad. You should never educate an African woman, they said, because she won't stay home and look after her family. Men are superior to women – it says so in the Bible – and women should be able to carry heavy loads on their backs – otherwise it proves they are lazy. 'Why don't you just marry a donkey?' I asked. At least we were able to laugh at each other. They thought my husband must be an awful wimp to let me go gallivanting off by myself.

Mzee welcomed us into his consulting room. He sat himself behind his desk with the leather-bound volumes on it and folded his hands. He said that as a parting present he would like to give me five packets each of his Sex Power for Men and Sex Power for Women medicine to pep up my reunion with my husband. You mix a teaspoon at a time in half a glass of boiling water, cool, strain, and drink simultaneously (it's terribly important that one of you doesn't get a head start) before going to bed. 'You will fly!' he guaranteed. 'Your bed will sing, and in the morning you will have to collect your mattress from the other side of the room.' He laughed with bawdy delight at the prospect and I said I could hardly wait since I loved my husband so much. He solemnly told me that I could be a great healer but I must keep my eyes open, be careful not to be foolishly indiscreet before I am sure I can trust someone, and always have a loving heart. He marvelled that he'd felt this great empathy with me and had been prepared to tell me everything (I don't know how he came to that conclusion; he has refused to divulge even the simplest of his secret recipes). He mentioned that he would like me to arrange a tour of England so he can meet with his medical colleagues and stay with me for two weeks, also perhaps if I could pay his fare …

Of course Kalii is a crafty old fox. On one level he is autocratic, vain, pompous and capricious. At times he can be intolerably rude and insufferably arrogant. But in his role as healer, counsellor, father-figure, provider, saviour to the thousands of sick, poor, struggling people – mainly peasant farmers – who come to him in need, he is a saint and a miracle worker. A real doctor in a true God-given sense with an uncanny shamanic power, a genius for diagnosis and treatment and a loving heart. We hugged good-bye affectionately and I got a lift back to Salama.

As soon as I'd given him the agreed fee for his services, Calvin, the rat, jumped on a bus going in the opposite direction and abandoned me to my fate by the roadside. 'No problem!' said someone waiting under a tree, seeing my forlorn look. He flagged down a seven-seater Peugeot with twelve people inside. They all breathed in obligingly, made room for two more and we sped back to Nairobi.

Back in the Twaha household I was warmly welcomed – everyone agog to hear my adventures. Little Fauzia wouldn't leave my side and I started to think seriously about anything I might be able to do to help her. As a baby, she had seemed perfectly normal but as soon as she began to stand her legs couldn't take the weight and gradually bent into little corkscrews. The family said that nothing could be done as she was a dwarf but it was obvious to me that she did not have achondroplasia as her arms were perfectly normal and so was the shape of her head.

'I do anything for straight legs,' she said one day. 'OK kid,' I thought. If you will do anything for straight legs, so will I.'

First of all I took several photographs of her then I made an appointment to take her to the radiology department at the Nairobi hospital for some X-Rays of her legs. My idea was to show these to various experts in London and to ask if there was some medicine I could send or treatment that could be suggested. That turned out to be rather a naive thought as the story unfolded … .

I returned home shortly after and contacted an endocrinologist friend, a cardiology consultant friend and a GP friend. 'Definitely not dwarfism,' they all concurred. 'It looks more like some sort of rickets but a paediatric orthopaedic surgeon would need to see the actual child in order to make a proper diagnosis. Any chance of bringing her over?'

I got in touch with Ali. 'No problem!' he said. 'I will get money for her fare and living expenses while she is in England if she can stay with you.' He subsequently tapped into his connections in the Lions Club or Rotary Club or some such and collected a small fortune – *none* of which I ever saw. However a few months later I got a call from Immigration at London Heathrow saying, 'There's a little child here with no passport or luggage and a note with your phone number on.' 'I'll be right there!' Why does nothing surprise me about Africa. And there she was, dressed in a little pink nylon party frock and broken plastic sandals carrying a huge bunch of flowers that she'd insisted on buying for me at Nairobi airport. I assured the immigration guys that I would take full responsibility for her and brought her home.

By this time, all our children had left and moved on with the exception of Francesca who was eighteen and hardly ever at home anyway. I fixed up Femi's old room for Fauzia and added a few old toys from the attic but her little face fell and she cried in dismay, 'I must sleep alone?? Where you other children?' I realised that she had never slept alone in her entire life but always in a great pile of siblings and cousins like a litter of puppies. She tearfully clung to our old dog and only agreed to go to bed if I let the dog sleep with her.

That was the first day. I was to learn so much about her. And so much from her. I have never met a more selfless, generous person. Having been brought up in a communal household it was unthinkable for her not to share everything. If anyone gave her a bag of crisps or a bar of chocolate she would spontaneously offer it to everyone in the room before taking any for herself; if I was cooking she'd drag a chair to the sink and immediately start washing up or laying the table without being asked. Her favourite food was a sliced unripe mango with salt and chilli and she was adamant right from the start that we respect her Muslim faith and dietary laws (at eight years old!)

As soon as we could we started the round of visits to doctors and hospital appointments, tests and scans. The diagnosis turned out to be a relatively rare condition: *hypophosphataemic rickets* where the body fails to metabolise phosphate and calcium which just gets peed away leaving the bones soft and bendy. Taking a daily supplement for life was the only reliable course of action and dramatic surgery the only way to straighten the deformed legs.

All of these treatments would be prohibitively expensive and would take years to accomplish. She would not be eligible to receive NHS treatment. Then, the first miracle: 'Look, this is why I became a doctor in the first place,' said the consultant and agreed to see her for free. Nobody I took her to charged me a penny.

And what about her education? Fauzia had never been to school. She couldn't tell the time; didn't know the days of the week or how to read. I took her to the local primary school where I knew the head teacher, who said, 'Well, this is why I became a teacher in the first place,' and agreed, off the record, to let her come to classes. I rode her there on the back of my bike every day and she insisted on wearing the pink party dress to school.

It was obvious that Fauzia would need to stay in England if there was to be any chance of really helping her. And for her to be eligible for NHS treatment she would need to become a British citizen – i.e we would need to adopt her.

So we looked into it. First stumbling block: Richard and I were too old to become adoptive parents. Secondly where were her papers? Where was the permission from her birth family? She had entered the country illegally? I went to visit a lovely barrister I knew: There turned out to be a wonderful loophole called *'The best interest of the child'*. Ali agreed to send a letter saying that they were unable to have Fauzia back and giving us permission to adopt her. Also promising to send all the money he had collected on her behalf (which never materialised). We wanted to make sure that Fauzia's birth mother would be happy with this so Richard and I invited Ali to bring her over to England so she could see where her child would be living and to reassure her that we would take great care of her.

They duly arrived to stay for a week and the poor woman was completely shell-shocked never having travelled anywhere before. She could hardly speak to Fauzia and lay on the bed with her face to the wall. I made a little speech which I asked Ali to translate saying that we would love her daughter as one of our own but that she would always be her mother. What followed was horrifying and sad: Her mother shouted to Fauzia, 'You are no longer my daughter. You belong to these people. You can forget me.' Then she said she wanted to go home so they left the next day. It's hard to imagine what that felt like for Fauzia. I told her I was sure her mother hadn't meant it and was just probably a bit confused.

Anyway the adoption went ahead with Fauzia, who always knew her own mind even at the age of eight, stating that she wanted to keep her own last name, 'Said', and her own religion, Muslim. So now she was able to legitimately receive free education and NHS treatment. [I realise, of course, how lucky we were. All this took place in kinder times – the mid-1980s. In today's anti-immigration climate and post-terrorist airport restrictions, none of it would have been possible in 2020.]

When it came to filling out the details for her adoption I asked her for her actual birthdate. 'February 17th 1977,' she said. My heart stood still. The very same date Femi's baby would have been born. Maybe that little spirit whose time was not then had found a way to become a part of our family after all. Meeting Fauzia in Kenya had always felt like an appointment with destiny.

The paediatric endocrinologist advised starting her on growth hormone injections as there was still a window of opportunity for her body to continue growing before puberty. (It gave her a couple of inches but she is till tiny.) The orthopaedic surgeon told us that if Fauzia didn't have the corrective surgery to her misshapen legs she would end up permanently in a wheelchair. The surgery, starkly nicknamed *The Shish Kebab*, was a painful and gruesome procedure where each leg was literally cut into chunks and reassembled on a metal skewer. This was to take years – first one leg then the other, then the first one again then the second then redoing a knee where the metal rod was sticking into her – and most of her teenage years were spent in and out of hospital. But it all gave her some sort of a better life than she would have had. As a result she was eventually able to walk, to run, to dance, to ride a bike, to drive a car and, ultimately, to have a baby – her beautiful son Raphael Xango Said Olivera (Raffi).

During all the difficult hospitalisations and long periods of convalescence I arranged for Ali to send over one of Fauzia's cousins from home so that she would always have someone with whom to speak Swahili if she was feeling homesick and so Zuhura (known as Zum) aged sixteen, arrived to stay with us for an indefinite period. She was and has remained a great boon and part of the family. She always made the most of any opportunity she was given to make a better life for herself, became a qualified bank employee, eventually married and had two lovely children, Alan and Meg.

Fauzia showed herself to be very talented in art and design and had a long term ambition to study to become a play therapist in a children's hospital having admired the work of those who helped her through her own many periods of hospitalisation. Young children always adored her and identified with someone small who got right down to their level. She was also the life and soul of any party and a little dynamo on the dance floor. She has managed to bring up her son alone and lives in a Housing Association flat with some disability benefits.

Alas, a few years ago following a whiplash injury while accidentally driving into the back of a stationary car at the traffic lights, she began to experience a huge amount of pain in her neck, clavicle and arms. A round of appointments with various neurosurgeons brought only frustration as one after another, none of them seemed to offer a real solution. She even underwent a dangerous brain operation to remove a *syrinx* – a fluid-filled cyst which had formed within her spinal cord. That only seemed to make things worse.

Eventually a diagnosis of a *Chiari malformation* was made. (CM) is a structural abnormality in the relationship of the skull and the brain. This means that the skull is small or misshapen, causing it to press on the brain at the base of the skull. It can cause brain tissue from the cerebellum to extend into the spinal canal. It might have possibly been there all her life undetected and become accelerated by the whiplash and to date she is still suffering constant pain, exhaustion and dramatic mood swings while undergoing a constant round of medical appointments hoping for an operation that could possibly give her back her life. This miserable experience has made her quite reclusive and all thoughts of study have been put on hold. It makes me very sad to see such a dynamic person so subdued. One of the hardest things about being a mother is the ultimate powerlessness. The knowledge that you cannot save your children from anything. You can only love them.

In the early '90s, Some years before the *Chiari Malformation* diagnosis, during a gap between her surgeries when Richard was at home and I could leave Fauzia in the care of Zum, I travelled to the United States as part of my research for Ladder To the Moon. The way that deep spiritual traditions live on, even buried under centuries of exile was a subject dear to my heart. How Tibetans had carried their Buddhist teachings far and wide; how the Jewish people had preserved their faith and now I wanted to talk with some of the African Americans of Yoruba descent living in New York to ask if they also felt a desire to connect with their ancient lineage.

And so, another flight, another city.

CHAPTER SIXTEEN

A bumper sticker spotted on Broadway proclaimed, 'There is no substitute for being totally unprepared.' A good motto for the Big Apple. No matter how much I think I'm ready, it always takes me by surprise. The urban craziness is only one aspect of New York and I was lucky enough to be staying in astonishing luxury with my friend Sue out of town in upper state New York. After a lifetime of Bohemian poverty, Sue unexpectedly came into some money and bought for herself and her two teenage children a gorgeous house in six acres of garden with a swimming pool, an orchard, a tea house and a canopied patio for alfresco dining. Last time I saw her she was pregnant, living in a basement flat in London and trying to scratch a living as a journalist. This time she sent a stretch limo to fetch me at the airport and I basked in the brief fantasy of being a star.

My visit was timed to coincide with my Femi who was currently living in New York training with the Alvin Ailey Dance Company. Together, as mother and daughter, we wanted to share the experience of meeting other women who had found their own way to come home to their spiritual roots. And there she was under the clock at Grand Central station.

We managed to get ourselves on the right train (Duke Ellington's famous 'A' Train) out to Brooklyn – not the most deprived neighbourhood by any means but very down-at-heel and neglected – such a stark contrast to the opulence of of the Hudson River Valley that morning. All the clichés were right there as we stepped out of the subway station. It looked like a war zone – garbage cans overflowing, an abandoned chain-link fenced basketball court strewn with broken glass, a posse of disaffected ten-year-olds sitting on a wall smoking. Confidence was not restored as we passed a young man lounging against a lamp post on a street corner cleaning his fingernails with a bowie knife. His tattered T-shirt proclaimed 'Fuck the World'. A notice above a door leading into the gloomy, beer-smelling interior of the Domino Bar said, 'No Weapons, No Drugs'; a peeling church sign-board read 'Crack Kills, Jesus Saves' and spray-painted graffiti on a billboard billboard shouted 'Niggaz With Attitude'. I was the only white person to be seen.

Both Femi and I were grateful to be abroad in the menacing streets with each other rather than on our own while, at the same time, being aware that with all the scare-mongering about walking around New York in hostile neighbourhoods the real danger is to project something that isn't there and create a negative energy vortex which becomes self-fulfilling.

I said to myself, as I had said once before while visiting a 'sangoma' (a healer) in Soweto, a township in South Africa', 'either we turn around and get out of here, giving in to fear and prejudice or we remind ourselves that this is also a place where ordinary people live, where families grow up, kids play, old people sit on their steps and watch the world go by.' I do not want my life to be governed by fear. Neither does Femi. We walked on, arriving at an old brownstone on Jefferson Street at the appointed time.

Iyalu Opeodo's daughter Ayo let us in the front door and showed us upstairs to their small apartment. Iyalu, a dark complexioned African American woman of generous proportions wearing traditional Nigerian dress and an elaborate woven hair style, was guarded and non-communicative at first. With such a long history of suspicion and mistrust between black and white in America – maybe I was being naive to imagine that reserve could be swept away in a tide of goodwill and shared ideas. Once she warmed up, however, and realised our interest in her spiritual practices was sympathetic rather than hostile, Iyalu began to speak about the feelings of pride and identity gained through the re-discovery of the religion of her ancestors. It has been, for her, a lifetime search for a sense of 'home'.

Born and bred in Brooklyn, Iyalu has no real knowledge of where her original forbears came from but found herself drawn, from an early age, to African music, dancing, drumming. 'Myself and a few others were the pioneers although we never looked on ourselves as such,' she said. 'Once a week at school assembly when I was a kid they would show films on geography and so on. There would be movies about Africa and the other kids would laugh at the antics of the 'savages' but I never laughed. Here were people who looked like me in terms of skin colour, and I was curious to know more about them. Remember, this was the 50s, the days of Tarzan and Jane; King Kong, so you know what was being put out there – Africans were being portrayed as wild and naked with bones through their noses.

'The first time I saw a woman with natural afro hair, I remember thinking, "Oh my God! When I get big I'm gonna wear my hair just like that. That's so beautiful!" I think it must be part of my mission here on this earth because I've always felt very strongly about people of colour and how we were made to look funny – the whole Amos 'n' Andy thing and the blackface minstrels. They never appeared funny to me and when I saw pictures of Lena Horne or Billy Holiday I was spellbound. They were my heroines. I knew there was a connection, a relationship between me and them.' I loved music but at school the only choice was between the baton twirlers or the drum and bugle club. Then one day someone gave me a record of Olatunji's "Drums of Passion". I took it home and danced and danced until I could dance no more. I just knew it was my music. This was the culture where I belonged!. I found out about some African dance classes going on up in town and there I met someone who took me to the Yoruba Temple where I was introduced to the "Orisha" – the Yoruba deities. Up until then I had been searching, searching for a spirituality that spoke my language. I was originally baptised into the Baptist Church but that wasn't "it" for me. I always felt like a very important part of me was missing. I tried Episcopalian, Pentecostal, Methodist, even Catholic – going with my friends to their different churches – but I never felt "this is the place" until I was introduced to the Orisha. As soon as I came into the Yoruba Temple I knew I was home. It has truly been the thing which has given me my identity and strength.'

Iyalu's family history has been lost, particularly the connection to

Africa. Her mother's father was from one of the West Indian islands. Her maternal grandmother is 100% Cherokee and her father's side are from the Deep South. 'I only know that some time, several generations back we must have come from West Africa,' she said. 'One day I'd really like to do a past-life regression and find out where. In the meantime, whenever I'd meet anyone from the African continent I'd quiz them; "What is it like? What do you do? Tell me about your ancient traditions, your culture." I was amazed. So much was like how I was raised as a child – the folk tales, the customs, respect your elders, it is sacrilege to throw food out or not share it and so on. I was desperate to travel to Nigeria but I had to wait until the time was right and that wasn't until after I was married to Kabaisi who is a full-blooded Nigerian.'

Iyalu met her husband to be at the Yoruba Cultural Centre. He was over on a visit and dropped in to listen to a group of them singing in the Yoruba language which they were trying to learn but which nobody really knew. He said he could understand every word and was astonished at how well the language and ritual had been preserved. (I was encouraged to hear of yet another example of a vestigial memory, of remnants of things suppressed for centuries bearing fruit.)

'You know,' said Iyalu, 'When our forefathers and foremothers were first brought to the Caribbean and the Southern plantations as slaves, they were forbidden from speaking their own language. Tribal groups were broken up so that people were unable to communicate with each other but a lot of the Yoruba language, culture and religion was preserved in places like Brazil, or Cuba or Puerto Rico where it could be disguised as a mixture of Christianity, Santeria and Voodoo. The Orisha could double as Catholic saints – biding their time until it was safe to come out of hiding. We are very grateful to the Cubans especially because they were the ones who really gave us back our culture – most of the initiations until recently were done through them. The first lady who transplanted the Orisha in New York was Obanjoko, a Cuban priestess who initiated somebody here so people didn't have to keep going to Cuba. Over here there was a lot more freedom but Orisha worship still had to be hidden. You'd come into someone's house and see a cabinet filled with pretty soup tureens but inside were really the Orisha. Now it doesn't have to be like that and shrines can openly be wherever you want them.'

The Yorubas, as I came to appreciate during the years I spent in Nigeria, are an exceptionally creative people with a vigorous culture. Throughout the years of the wretched and dolorous slave trade the people, their music, art and religion were dispersed all over but the result was that, in spite of everything terrible that happened, many seeds fell on fertile soil. In Venezuela, in Haiti, in Jamaica, the worship of the Yoruba Gods and Goddesses flourished – covertly at first but a trickle became a torrent and in recent years has been gaining popularity throughout the United States. 'Most definitely,' said Iyalu. 'At one time it was basically just New York. Now you have Philadelphia, Miami, Washington DC, the West Coast. I even know someone in Oklahoma and it's there too.'

The Orisha are deities of which there are five or six principal ones: Olodumare, the Supreme Being; Obatala, the God of Creation; Oshun, the River Goddess; Osanyin, the God of Medicine; Orunmila, the God of wisdom; Sango, the God of Thunder; Ogun, the God of Metals and Creativity; Yemonja, the Goddess of the Sea and up to 400 subsidiary ones including Ibeji (the twins). Iyalu is a priestess of Yemonja. The very goddess whose ceremony I attended in Lagos with Bunmi. Iyalu described Yemonja's special characteristics: 'Yemonja is the Mother of all the Orisha, the Great Mother. Being the Mother, she is the giver of nourishment. She is the patron of children. When you think of Yemonja, you think of the ocean and its vastness. As her priestesses we are moody – changing like the ocean, with the moon and the tides. She is the epitome of womanhood at its fullest – mysterious and deep. Whereas Oshun, the River Goddess is Miss Pretty, feminine and beautiful, Yemonja is the creator who gives birth, out of whom flow the rivers and the streams. She is tough love – fierce and protective. She has the power to create and the power to destroy.'

I asked Iyalu why she chose Yemonja to be her particular Orisha. She explained, 'We don't choose the Orisha, the Orisha chooses you. You go to a Babalawo for a reading. [A Babalawo is a High Priest or Priestess and diviner of the sacred oracle], you put on the *aleke* (special beads), you serve a period of apprenticeship and when the time comes for your initiation they sit you down to find out exactly who is your Orisha. I wasn't surprised when it turned out to be Yemonja – my mother always dressed me in blue, I love blue and blue is Yemonja's colour.

'When I am serving her as a priestess I don't *exactly* become her but the energy just sort of comes over me and it isn't me any more. Other people can see it even if I'm not aware of what's happening. My duties might consist of being present at initiations, maybe washing the Orisha, maybe making the herb water or cooking the Orisha food for feast days or holidays. Someone might want a godmother ceremony with the *aleke* or a birthday celebration. Once you are initiated you go through several ceremonies to find out what your powers are. Some people are healers and they would study the herbs and medicines, others do the work of removing curses, changing bad luck, winning back a lover. Still others have the ability to deal with the dark side. It's part of your training to be responsible with those powers although of course people do abuse them. We all have the potential to use our powers for good or evil. You can't have one without the other and it's up to the individual to know the difference. Defending yourself is one thing, setting out deliberately to cause harm is another. You never get away with it. There will always be repercussions.'

Iyalu explained that the Yoruba religion is very earth-based and nature oriented. 'We are constantly aware of our connection to the elements, to Mother Nature and to the animals,' she said. 'Although animals are used in ceremony, it is always with great respect. You pray over them, you ask the animal to carry certain things symbolically and you thank the animal for its sacrifice.' Some priestesses can read smoke or water, ashes or coffee grinds, she told us. Some have visions or use crystal balls, others are mediums who actually become possessed by the spirit of the Orisha. 'A lot of things just come to me,' said Iyalu. 'Often through dreams or I might hear a female voice. I read and interpret the patterns in the cowrie shells. Each one of us has a duty to find out what our power is, how to tap into it, how to use it and how to value ourselves. It's partly intuition and partly being open to divine guidance.'

When romance blossomed between Iyalu and Kabaisi the issue of the respective roles of men and women within traditional Nigerian society was swiftly dealt with. The name Kabaisi is actually a title which means 'Your Highness'. It also means he whose authority cannot be questioned. 'I do what I want to do anyway so why do I need to make a fuss because women are here and men are here [she indicates two levels with her hands]. I don't have any problem', she laughed. 'I feel comfortable about my place in this life. Before I married Kabaisi I said to him, 'My only question to you is will I be able to practice my spiritual work?' And once he said 'Yes', why we can deal with other things as they come up. If he'd said 'No' we wouldn't have gotten married. So where's the problem?'

The problem could have been back home in his village in Nigeria. Kabaisi has four other wives. 'I have to admit to feeling a little apprehensive about going over there,' said Iyalu, 'because he and I had met here in the United States and I knew the other women had a say in who the new wife would be. I'd come prepared to be defensive and I didn't know whether I was going to have to fight or run or what so I put it in the hands of God. It was my dream to get to Nigeria – even if I died there. I didn't care. People could have taken me off into the bush and killed me. I really did not care. I was going to Nigeria at last. The Motherland. Anyway, we greeted one another and everyone was just so nice. One of the women came forward to embrace me and said, in Yoruba, 'I love you. Welcome to the sisterhood.' I was knocked out. I really felt at home. I remember one day sitting alone, feeling as if I could see my life like the pages in a book. There I was sitting in the very same spot as my ancestors, drawing water from the well, cooking, serving the Orisha and I *knew* I must have come from there, sometime way back in a past life, to feel such a powerful pull.

'This was my twenty-year dream come true at last. The hardest part was not being able to talk with the co-wives because there's so much they could have taught me. We were all sharing and laughing, knowing we felt the same way but unable to express it. The women were very independent, especially those over the age of menopause. They had a lot more power and freedom and were proud of getting older which is something *we've* lost and I found myself saying, 'OK.

Where's all this repression I've heard bout or is it just Western concepts? When it came time for me to leave, everyone was crying, even the children. Being a water child myself, tears came easy. It was horrible. I didn't want to go. Before I got married I have to say there was a part me that was thinking, 'What are you getting into, girl?' But now after three years with my husband I find him to be one of the most understanding people I have ever come across – very kind and compassionate. He's a priest himself on the Ifa level [higher than a Babalawo, one able to decode messages from Olodumare the Supreme Being made manifest to mankind by Orunmila, the god of Wisdom]. He's a traditionalist so he knows such a lot and can put up with things such as 50 chickens sitting in the hall when he comes home! He respects my role and we can help each other.'

Iyalu took us into her little shrine room. The deity Ogun, guardian and warrior stands by the door – his essence represented by pieces of iron, nails, horseshoes and stones in little cooking pots. The altar to Yemonja, the Supreme Goddess, Mother of all things, has offerings of shells, starfish, bowls of salt water and other things to do with the ocean. There is a 'spiritual table' to honour the diversity of other influences – European and Native American, Jewish and tarot cards – and a family altar of *Egungun* – ancestral spirits.

I asked Iyalu if Femi and I could request a blessing from Yemonja for our endeavours and our travels. Yes we could. She would be happy to do it. First she poured a libation (whisky), took a couple of swigs of it and spat it forcefully and dramatically all over the altar. Then she invoked Yemonja, talked to her, prayed, picked up a rattle and shook it. She chanted, she sang, she asked for many good things for us. As she invoked the Goddess, a change did indeed come over her. It was as though the force which inhabited her body was somehow bigger than her although not separate from her. To speak of possession somehow smacks of frenzy, of being out of control. This was anything but. Iyalu became possessed of those qualities and energies that Yemonja represents and they flowed from her like magical tides as she sprinkled the salt water on our heads. Then she knelt and touched her forehead to the ground, inviting us to do the same. We gave thanks for the blessing and that was that. We hugged warmly, all awkwardness long since evaporated, and set off into the darkening twilight with Iyalu, in motherly mode now, making us promise to phone when we reached home safely.

The next day, I arrived a little early at Grand Central Main Concourse – that huge cathedral of a station where a hundred thousand people a day pass through. A small, middle-aged woman with frizzy orange hair and a defiant straw hat with flowers on it was setting up an amplifier and speakers. She took a guitar out if its case tuned it slowly and carefully then began to play and sing, in a beautiful voice full of heart-break and longing, the theme from Black Orpheus. Many bustling commuters stopped in their tracks, beguiled by the melancholy music of the Brazilian *favelas* filling the vast, cavernous space. Instantly I was 13 again when I went to live in Brazil and first heard about the African faith which had crossed the ocean in the slave ships and survived, transformed into *candomble*. I was moved, even way back then, by the deep indestructible well-springs that cascaded forth in the music of carnival, in the drums, the dancing, the candlelit processions and the mysterious rites and ceremonies that were tantalizingly just out of reach. As I listened to her song, the 'saudade' (that untranslatable Brazilian word encompassing nostalgia, sadness, regret for time passing, and bittersweet memories) got to me, lost in reverie, and my eyes filled with tears for all those who are exiled and homesick. I thanked the woman in the remnants of my Portuguese and went on my way. What synchronicity to be transported back to the origins of my connection at this time.

There was Femi again underneath the clock and we rode the 'A' train back down to Brooklyn to keep our appointment this time with Omi Olayinka – another priestess of Yemonja. She welcomed us warmly and invited us into her study lined with an extensive library of books on Africa and on Black Studies. Omi is a professor at Brooklyn College where she teaches courses on The Black Family and The Black Woman in America. She is the co-ordinator of a project called 'AIDS in Afro-Americans – It's Time for Action' and another on education in the inner-city. She has published research papers on such topics as Marcus Garvey, the Bantustans of South Africa and Mythical Nations.

She and her husband Baba-Ade who is a Babalawo, have created a little temple and centre for Yoruba studies in their house.

Omi has strong views about how the cut-backs in the education system have forced some of the Black Studies courses to close. 'So much knowledge has come to light since the degree courses were established in the sixties,' she said. 'There's still a need to really re-write a lot of our history – to question what has generally been said about people of African descent and then of course the more informed and empowered we are, the less we can be pushed around. We need to know that we all have a cultural heritage we can be proud of. African-American culture is really rich. My grandfather, for example, was a ragtime jazz musician who played with Scott Joplin and Jelly-Roll Morton. He taught my father and my father taught the five of us brothers and sisters to play piano and we each had to play another instrument too (I play bassoon). We all entertained one another. My father was an artist and our house was always full of other artists and intellectuals from all over the world. Then came Civil Rights and my parents were active all the time. Everyone was. It was just a matter of time until exposure to an African-based religion would come our way.

'Being a musical household, we were well grounded in the gospels and the spirituals and there were always debates going on about which branch of Christianity was the most preferred. My parents made it clear that whichever one we chose was alright by them so long as we were upstanding citizens living righteously. Discovering the Yoruba religion was, for me, more of an Afro-centric link than a spiritual one. Like most people that discovery came when I went for a 'reading'. That reading was phenomenal. The person who did it was an African-American priest of Sango. He drew shells – sixteen shells – and was able to tell the whole experience of what I was going through at the time. How could he know all that? How could the cowrie shells tell so much? I had already been exposed to the I-Ching as a system of divination but seeing this other dimension with the sixteen cowrie shells was another step again.

'Orisha worship! Here was something more tangible to me than the Christian experience. I can understand thunder and lightning. I can see and feel the change in the seasons. I can sense the sacred in all these things, God in everything, everywhere – the physical manifestation of the Orisha in terms of what we see – the ocean, the mountains, the rivers, the trees and the rocks. The powers behind all these natural forces, in our Yoruba culture, are the deities – the Orisha. I can tell my children, when there is a storm; "Oh that's just Sango speaking. Don't be afraid," and we can sit in the window and watch the lightning. After getting a series of readings, the next step is receiving the *aleke* – the beads. This is like a baptism. A blessing. It is a beautiful symbolism. In actuality the *aleke* represent circles of light surrounding the person. I was initiated as a daughter of Yemonja. Wearing her beads around my neck means that Yemonja extends her reach around me and through Yemonja, all the other Orisha encircle me with bands of light. I now walk with protection. My responsibility is to listen to that guidance and try to lead my life in accordance with the correct way of acting.'

The reading of the cowrie shells has many parallels with our own ancient system of divination, the runes, or the Chinese way of the I-Ching. (In South Africa I saw the *Sangoma* in Soweto 'throw the bones' for me as guidance for a journey.) It's a way of trying to interpret what's going on in your life while at the same time inviting a deep connection to the natural cycles and energies of the earth and the cosmos. They are a tool for self-realisation and a way of revealing the truth of the present moment and of our lives within it. The Babalawo uses the cowries to offer wisdom and guidance. The teachings are in the form of stories and parables, chants, songs, rituals, dances, prayers, even drumbeats depicting various aspects of Yoruba life passed down by word of mouth, generation to generation by the Babalawo.

'What I love about this religion is that you learn to understand the power of the feminine,' said Omi. 'Women have always held a very highly respected role in Yoruba society. In my course at the university I teach that, yes, we came to the United States as slaves but we are the descendants of queens and queen mothers and priestesses of power. Prior to colonialism African women were the most socially organised in the world. We came to America with a deep memory of that link. In the forcibly broken families – torn apart and sold all over the place – where men were not able to protect their wives and children it was the women who had to hold things together as best they could. We were forbidden to speak our language or to practise our religion. Those of us who weren't driven crazy became numb. Our self-esteem was eaten away but now the rediscovery of the Yoruba rituals and ceremonies for the rites of passage through life is giving us a strong basis for rebuilding our communities.'

Femi and I were invited to attend a Festival of Obatala held on a river boat in the East River. There were scores of worshippers forming a procession, offering gifts of food and uttering prayers to the God of Creation. The Master Drummers of Brooklyn arrived and the singing began. Everyone seemed to know the Yoruba words. Many people had tears in their eyes. These descendants of African queens, priestesses, farmers, hunters, medicine people, builders, artists and chiefs are waking up after their long sleep to the sacred ways of their ancient ones and finding themselves anew. When people asked me why I was there at the Festival of Obatala I said, 'I am the mother of Ibeji.' When Tim and Femi left home as young adults we gave them each an Ibeji figure so that they would never be separated from their twin. And there I was with my Femi. In fact she was really my passport to be there at all. Even though the Yoruba religion itself doesn't particularly resonate with her (she has been a Buddhist for years), she said that for her to witness the passion and intensity with which her native culture is embraced by people who have taken several generations of sorrow and suffering just to get back to where she started, has been an eye opener. It was a profound experience to share it all with her. Both of us were feeling quite awed by the enormity of the strange destiny that brought us together as mother and daughter in this lifetime.

★

A few months later I was in The Gambia writing a chapter on the emerging resistance movement to the traditional practice of circumcising girls – or FGM, as it is known (female genital mutilation). I was also doing a piece for *Traveller Magazine* about sustainable tourism in the country. In Banjul I met up with my friend Geri who runs a small eco hotel. It was the quiet season so Geri could take a few days off and we took the opportunity to do a bit of travelling together. We hailed a bush taxi to Bakau and made our way through the maze of muddy, rain-flooded backstreets to the legendary Sacred Crocodile Pool – a heaving, seething green pond with dozens of menacing snouts barely protruding and mosquitoes jumping like raindrops all over the surface. The crocs are inert, fed daily with fish by the custodian, and just lie around the edge like logs patiently allowing people to approach them. Since ancestral times, washing or immersing yourself in their putrid water is supposed to bring fertility to barren women. The air was heavy with silence except for the monkeys calling and leaping through the trees and the disconcerting rustle of baby crocs, malevolent extras from Jurassic Park lurking in the undergrowth. As in the Florida Everglades I got the distinct feeling that the wild animals who live here are only biding their time. One false move and there would be nothing left of you but bleached bones.

As night fell we went down to a bar on the beach enticed by the electrifying sound of wild drumming. A group of young men with a variety of drums were playing up a storm – not a show, as such, just a bunch of talented musicians jamming. For the price of a beer we listened spellbound for two hours. It was wonderful to see such a concentration of potent male energy harnessed to a creative, peaceful purpose. As someone said, 'If you can bring that warrior energy into the heart of the community, its fire will warm the village. If it stays outside, it will burn the village down.'

Another day we went to an eating place built on stilts out in the creek in the middle of the mangroves. Pirogues glided silently by as we feasted on a plate of creek oysters with lime juice. The whole place looks like a fantasy from a Bacardi ad man's storyboard – old mamas with gold teeth sitting around shelling oysters, furniture made out of salvaged ship's timbers and rope, slippery children's bodies silhouetted against the sun splashing in the water and paddling hand-made dug-outs, an old man singing because he caught a fish. Some days are just perfect and this was one of them. The sacred can be right there in the simplicity of life being authentically lived.

I had brought with me the address of a Gambian traditional kora player whom I had met at a storytelling festival in Wales. 'If ever you are in my country come and visit', he had said – little suspecting that I would actually come. It turned out that he was from a famous family of hereditary Griots – the great troubadour/historians of this part of West Africa. Griots originated in the thirteenth century in the Mande empire of Mali. Storytellers, musicians, orators – they preserve and pass on down the generations the oral history of their people. It is exceptional skilled and beautiful music with many maestros becoming world famous such as Toumani Diabaté from Mali, Foday Musa Suso and Sona Jobarteh from The Gambia and Soriba Kouyate from Senegal. We arrived on the auspicious day a new baby had been born in his compound and were invited to stay and share the celebrations. A tremendous honour.

Next morning – a trip to the interior. We set off in a jeep for our up-country expedition heading east on the southern bank of the great Gambia River for five hours non-stop until we reached Georgetown. After the crush and squalor of urban shanty-town poverty, rural African life looks so much more tolerable, preferable. The immaculate villages with their swept compounds, neat fields of peanuts and corn, shady baobabs and round, straw-thatched huts of baked-earth bricks are pleasing to the eye and harmonious to the spirit.

At the ferry-crossing to Georgetown, a flight of achingly beautiful children scramble onto the tailgate of our vehicle each trying to thrust a scrap of paper with their name and address into our hands – begging for us to be their 'special friend'. Each one an SOS, a message in a bottle from a hopeful little individual marooned forever in anonymity and obscure rural poverty. It's no use taking one or ten or a thousand for out of the shadows come a thousand more. 'Send me a postcard. Give me pen, a dalassi, an empty plastic bottle, a banana. Choose *me*!'

The motorised ferry no longer runs so passengers have to haul the craft across the wide brown waters by a steel hawser. And there is the tiny town with its long and tragic history as the capture and holding place for slaves on their way down river to the waiting ships. A weighing scale, a streaked and filthy building full of bats is all that remains and an underground cell where trouble-makers, rebels and ring-leaders were shackled – their food thrown down through the one small ventilation shaft, their only drinking water a sink hole that filled with river water at high tide. At the far end of the dungeon are two airless punishment cells – one for men, one for women.

We asked the guide to leave us alone for a while and take the candle with him. He looked at us strangely but did as we asked. As the light receded and the suffocating blackness closed in, Geri and I sat in the dirt in the women's punishment cell and held hands; thinking about what happened here; meditating on the terrible suffering, the fear and the despair that is stored in these walls – suffering that is still borne to this day by their Caribbean and African-American descendants, people like Iyalu Opeado, priestess of Yemonja in New York whose roots were so cruelly pulled up and transplanted half a world away; the disproportionate amount of black men in American jails; the continuing harassment and murder of black citizens in America by the police …

The grief here is palpable and hangs in the fetid air like an ectoplasm. Nothing can ever undo the abominations that took place in this hell hole but we offered our witness and our sorrow. Those men, women and children are not forgotten. *(As I write this now in 2020, the Black Lives Matter movement is gaining strength everywhere following several recent police shootings of unarmed black men in America and the death of George Floyd who suffocated to death as a group of policemen restrained him and knelt on his neck while he begged 'Please! I can't breathe!')* Will it make a difference? We thought the assassination of Martin Luther King would be a turning point. Or the election of the first black American president but the inexplicable cruelty and stupidity of racism is still endemic.

Georgetown is actually on an island – Macarthy Island – in the middle of the mighty river. To get to Jangjangburreh Camp we have to cross on another ferry to the north bank. The camp, a popular tourist destination, looks like a film set. There is a poignant irony in Europeans spending hundreds of pounds to come to Africa to stay in a hotel cleverly disguised as an African village so they can enjoy the fantasy of not being tourists; of tasting the real thing; of returning to a once-upon-a-time communal society – whereas the reality is that most Africans would give their eye teeth to live anywhere else and the children beg you to take them away. We stay one luxurious night as guests of the owner.

About a hour from the camp is one of the most mysterious sites in the whole of sub-Saharan Africa – the Stone Circles of Wassu. I have wanted to visit them ever since I saw a photograph. This is one of the great unsolved archaeological riddles – as yet only partly excavated – of our time and, as yet, the only stone circles to be found in Africa. In the middle of a flat, arid plain far from any village is the place; several circles made from massive megaliths of laterite – some over six feet tall and probably once much taller. We have the place to ourselves and use the opportunity once again to sit in this sacred site and bear witness to what happened in these parts long ago.

The next days are a mixture of relentless jolting over rutted roads so dusty that our throats seize up and rare pleasures worth everything to experience in the company of two knowledgeable bird-watchers we meet along the way. They lend us their powerful binoculars and show us what to look out for. It is a revelation. We see kingfishers, Abyssinian Rollers, West African eagles, hornbills, herons, Senegal parrots, long-tailed glossy starlings, an exquisite yellow and brown swallow, hammerkops and many more.

Another night, this time at Tendaba River Camp where there is a cacophony of drumming and dancing galore in the firelight – the wonderful, bonkers Mandinka dancing where the women challenge each other as they leap one at a time into the circle, arms going like windmills, knees pumping up and down. You can so clearly see the origins of tap-dancing, street dancing, Brazilian carnival dancing – carried like windblown seeds from these shores during the sorrowful years of the great African Diaspora to spring alive again in the genes of their descendants as soon as they found their feet. We are dragged into the the arena and although I think I am too tired to dance, the music of Youssou N'dour and Jaliba soon fires my blood. I can't sit still. The delighted off-duty waitresses teach me some steps and there I am dancing with them. I can do it! I never feel overweight in Africa. I feel like a woman. In fact my bottom feels pitifully small by comparison. Under-endowed, by local standards, in the rear department I can only marvel at the rotating moons around me.

Riding home through the frangipani and jasmine-scented tropical night, Africa breathes its hot breath on us. Past street markets where a thousand little lanterns like a sprinkling of fireflies illuminate the family groups sitting around – selling little screws of peanuts, roasting a fish on a charcoal brazier, cradling a sleeping child, bedding down for the night where they live their lives on the roadside. We stop for a meal at a little stall – fried chicken, benachin, couscous, mangoes. The perfect end to a memorable adventure.

CHAPTER SEVENTEEN

My memories have flown backwards now to 1959. We've been married a year and Richard thinks it's too early to start a family as we have no money, only a single mattress on the floor of our little flat and orange boxes for furniture. I really want a baby so I decide I will give one a fighting chance by poking holes in my contraceptive diaphragm.

One little tadpole makes it through to dock with the mothership, showing a determination right from the beginning that has stood him in good stead all his life and nine months later becomes our beloved firstborn son Ben.

He was dismally failed by the rubbish comprehensive school we sent him to but an amusingly named 'cross-cultural exchange' – one term with Eton College – introduced him to a few of the friends he would have forever. 'Mum, they read books here and have actual conversations,' he said, amazed, on the phone. 'It's not just bragging about beer and football.' None the less there were many advantages to having had a non-elitist childhood. He has always felt totally at home in any social environment and, along the way, managed to educate himself.

His other lucky break came about earlier when he was about nine years old. I had taken Femi to a child modelling agency reasoning that being chosen for her distinctive beauty would give her more confidence and a pride in her looks. They signed her up straight away but as we were leaving the agent spotted Ben in the back of my car and said, 'Ooh lovely little blond boy, I can always get work for him.' I said I wasn't really interested – I didn't want to morph into one of those ambitious acting school mums, armed with a wet flannel and a comb in their handbag, hissing at their offspring, 'Don't forget to smile at the director!' Ben begged, 'Please, please,' so I said, 'Well, if something really interesting came along I might consider it.' Not long afterward – a call from Bonnie Kids, 'I've got the Royal Shakespeare Company on the phone looking for a child to play Mamillius in the *Winter's Tale* with Ian McKellan and Judi Dench at the Aldwych Theatre.' What could I say? Of course I agreed and that was the beginning of wonderful years for him learning the craft of acting with the best. More Shakespeare; A season in Stratford; television series'; films and theatre and working all over the world.

In his early twenties, a relationship with a lovely girl Marinka resulted in the birth of his son Jay and, subsequently, his marriage to Kate gave him two beautiful daughters Freya and Kalila. Everyone gets on and the siblings love one another. Jay married Ciara (I conducted their wedding on a hilltop in Tarifa, Spain looking out across the sea to North Africa.) They now have two daughters so Ben has become a doting grandfather.

For the past twenty-seven years he has devoted his life to creating GIVE!, an annual four-day festival of music, dance, art, cabaret, storytelling, and poetry. This has been the fulfilment of his passionate vision of a place where people of all ages from all walks of life can come together to delight in finding each other, to share, to trust, to be open and willing to be their authentic selves, to dance the cosmic dance, to rest in the eye of the radiant heart where the whole universe resides. As he puts it: 'GIVE! is our opportunity to celebrate that which unites us rather than divides us – whatever people's passionately held views about the burning matters of the day. It is an opportunity to go beyond division for a brief beautiful moment in time and rediscover our common humanity and to seek out and celebrate the best in each other. When we come together in a safe beautiful space with the intention of finding a common frequency we become greater than the sum of our parts – we think with an expanded mind and we feel with an expanded heart. These have been tough times but Love and Kindness and Tolerance are still available to all of us no matter how grim the world can sometimes seem.' A festival of love and friendship.

In my role as celebrant, I have been honoured to perform the introductory opening ceremony each year. More than just a festival, GIVE! has become a huge gathering; a loose community of like-minded souls who have found each other. Francesca (always known as Poonie), in the early days, became an essential part of GIVE! creating the 'Healing Area' – a large marquee where therapists could offer a range of treatments, yoga, meditation and massage.

One regular participant whose contribution is to build tree-houses recently wrote: "This is my chosen family and it chose me. Something in me deep, deep down felt like I had something to give but I had no idea what it was or how it might be … over the years we have grown very slowly … and having been together so long we have had families, our kids have become wonderful funky adults, amazing creatives, artists, musicians and have grown with our culture of kindness, generosity, honesty, care and love. The next chapter is theirs."

(As I write this, the Covid-19 pandemic has brought everything to a grinding halt leaving an uncertain future.)

Ben was a baby when we went to live in Nigeria. The twins joined the family the following year. Then in '63 Matt came along – born in Lagos – (the only child we actually *planned*, following a previous miscarriage) and, in '65, a daughter conceived the night Richard returned from shooting a documentary film about St Francis of Assisi. We named her Francesca. There was to be a ten-year gap before Fauzia arrived so those first five grew up together with young, inexperienced, skint but loving parents. It was a pretty wild childhood but they all seemed to avoid getting into any serious trouble and generally covered for each other. We had some great holidays and even managed, by buying the tumbled-down little village house in Tuscany, to take them to Italy once a year.

As we couldn't afford private education and didn't really approve of it anyway they all received appallingly inadequate schooling – sacrificed on the altar of our beliefs in the new comprehensives. We hated the old system of the 11-plus – an exam at the age of eleven whereby clever children went to grammar schools and the less bright were sent to secondary moderns for 'vocational training'. How harmful that would be for children in families with varying abilities.

Ben was rescued by the acting world; Femi got a grant to the London School of Contemporary Dance; Tim got a job as an apprentice goldsmith in Hatton Garden, became a boxing champion and marathon runner; Matt followed Ben into the acting world also got some interesting jobs with the RSC and some film and television work, then drifted for a while, had a short ill-starred marriage to Natalie, then had two wonderful children, Maddison and Harry, with his second wife Tracey who sadly died in her thirties and finally married lovely American Beth and became a very good driving instructor. He is a peace-loving, easy-going dreamer (often known as 'Hammock Man' or 'The Velvet Jedi') who enjoys making music and growing things in his garden.

By the time it came to Francesca, she begged us to take her out of her comprehensive saying the peer pressures made it impossible to succeed academically. As she was the last of the first five we found the money to send her to a private girls' school where she did manage to get her A levels and went on to achieve a university degree in psychology and a training in specialist sports massage. *(There are now many excellent comprehensive schools but in those days they were pretty awful.)* Poonie married Nello and had her first son Jake. Then with second husband Greg, Fin arrived – the last of my thirteen grandchildren.

Fauzia, ten years later, had a tough time at school having started so far behind and having had so many long periods in hospital but she showed a talent in art and design and managed to achieve enough of a basic groundwork in education to see her through. A brief relationship with Alberto gave her her son Raffi.

So now they are all grown up. Middle aged, in fact, with families of their own and all very close.

How can I write about the death of Francesca?

Our beloved, beautiful Poonie died on June 3rd, 2014. Throughout the last fifteen months of her illness and horrendous treatments she managed to hold onto her extraordinary vitality, her love of life, her sense of humour. She was the epitome of grace, compassion, acceptance and courage. Fifteen years earlier she had survived the first bout of cancer and gone on to raise lots of money on a sponsored horse ride in Patagonia for the Teenage Cancer Trust. Now the cancer had returned – very aggressive – stage 4. We were, of course always hoping for a miracle. What we couldn't know was what form the miracle would take. *She* was the miracle. She showed us how to live well right up to the very last moments of her life and when the time came, how to surrender into death.

While she was in hospital, Richard brought Jake over to Guernsey to visit but it seemed best for them to return to London before the end. Greg managed to arrange for her to come home from the hospital for her last few days and placed a bed downstairs where she could see the sea in the place she was the happiest she'd ever been. He and I kept vigil throughout the last forty-eight hours taking it turns to change her oxygen cylinder every two hours. One of us sat with her constantly, kissing her and holding her hand. Occasionally she woke from the arms of morpheus into full lucid consciousness. When Fin came in to see her on the last day before going off to school she opened her eyes and smiled. She said, 'Hello my handsome boy, shall we watch a film together tonight?' Fin kissed all her fingers and left and she sank back into her semi-conscious state. In another lucid moment she woke and stroked Greg's face as he was weeping softly and told him how very much she loved him – how much happiness he had given her. Over and over she said, 'I love you, my Gregor. I'm so lucky.' After that, her breathing became more erratic. Her pulse was weakening. I sang her all the old lullabies from when she was a baby: 'Lily of Laguna', 'The Skye Boat Song', ' Lula Lula Bye Bye'. I know that at some level of consciousness even though she appeared completely out if it, she heard us say, 'You can go now darling with our blessing'. Greg held her in his arms as she took her last breath in and I kissed her as she breathed her last breath out. I am so grateful I was given the privilege of being with her at the threshold. So grateful that I was chosen to be her mother in this lifetime, to have been with her at the beginning and at the end of her marvellous life. The nursing team let me wash her myself. A clean nightie, a spray of eau de cologne, a last service for my beautiful child. Child of my love. Child of my heart. Child of my body. Ben arrived from London and we sat by her body. Together we did a transcendence meditation – holding her in our hearts and visualising her becoming a column of light as her spirit flew free and she changed from a warm dead girl to a white alabaster chrysalis.

She loved this poem by Pearle Cleage. It could have been written about her:

And we danced too wild, and we sang too loud, and we hugged too hard and kissed too sweet, and threw back our heads and howled just as loud as we wanted to howl because now we were all old enough to know that what looks like crazy on an ordinary day looks a lot like love if you catch it in the moonlight.

These were Richard's words at her funeral:

Here in this beautiful church on this beautiful island we have come together, both family and friends, to mark the death and to celebrate the life of Francesca, our beloved Poonie. Except today we are all her family. We are all a part of that family she loved and who loved her – and we loved her to bits.

We loved her for so many things. We loved her for the way she danced the dance of life, so generously, holding back nothing, as if there was no tomorrow. We loved her sense of fun, her mischievousness …and her outrageously rude laugh. But we also loved her serious side – her sharp, perceptive intellect that would have no truck with anything phoney or dishonest, with injustice or cruelty, with the naysayers and despoilers of life.

From as far back as I can remember she was always wonderfully wilful, ploughing her own furrow, knowing her own mind, knowing always where she was going – a masterful woman, you didn't mess with Poonie!

But if that might make her sound a little harsh, no – as we know she was the most warm, the most giving, the most passionate of friends – as she was a daughter. But even as a child there was always a certain undercurrent of melancholy; an awareness of the poignancy and paradox of life. It went hand in hand with a powerful spiritual understanding.

In this last year when her beautiful strong body was hammered with the horrors of chemotherapy; and in the brief intervals between, when she extraordinarily bounced back, determined to live her last days to the full, she did pass through a dark night of the soul. But she emerged. She emerged as if transfigured into a place where she had found serenity and a quiet certainty that this, all this that we know, quite simply, was not all. Yes, she feared what the process of dying might entail – who wouldn't? – but now she no longer feared death itself. She was entering the great unknown. This feisty, heroic, and simply quite beautiful woman died as she had lived …courageously …radiantly …with great splendour. Before she died she asked me if I would read at her funeral a very brief fragment of prose I had sent her many years ago. From *Look Homeward Angel* by Thomas Wolfe: Today I dedicate it to Greg, to Jake and to Fin;

> *'They clung together in that bright moment of wonder, there on the magic island, where the world was quiet, believing all they said.*
>
> *And who shall say, whatever disenchantment follows, that we ever forget the magic, or that we can ever betray, on this leaden earth, the apple tree, the singing and the gold.'*

I am not the first mother to lose a child and I won't be the last but that is no consolation. There is no greater grief and it takes as long as it takes to find a way to laugh again and find reasons to get on with life. Both of us loved the poetry of Mary Oliver and I learned one of her poems, 'In Blackwater Woods', to say at Poonie's funeral. The last words are these: '… *to live in this world, you must be able to do three things: To love what is mortal; to hold it against your bones knowing your own life depends on it; and, when the time comes to let it go, to let it go.'*

Over time I have learned to bear the sorrow, to live without her physical presence. When she visits me now, she comes as shards of sunlight sparkling on the river that runs past my island home and I know she lives on transformed; that her light-filled energy can still arrive unexpectedly to create shimmering patterns on my sitting room ceiling. But even just writing these words today I have howled and howled like a mother wolf with a dead cub. 'You shouldn't have died! You shouldn't have died!'

And then nine months later, on February 24th 2015, my Richard died. How could I lose them both one after the other? He had developed a lung infection after the catastrophic floods on our island had caused mouldy patches to form on the walls; he had breathed in toxic spores which became dangerously airborne as they dried. At first it was thought to be pneumonia but it turned out to be a rarer form – Acute Interstitial Pneumonitis. I think he actually died of a broken heart. He didn't outwardly express his grief for Poonie like I did – remaining strong for me as I fell apart – but he never got over the death of his adored daughter and he never came out of hospital. Ben and I were with him at the end.

We had fifty-seven eventful years of marriage – a few clashes, some rocky rapids and many, many fabulous times when we basked in sunny uplands and had adventures travelling together or we would meet at the end of a film location: Nepal; Syria; Bali; Peru; Sicily; Hong Kong; India; Sri Lanka; New England …And through it all we loved each other.

When we went to Buenos Aires to learn the tango I wrote this in my journal:

A dream and a passion fulfilled.! To dance the tango in Buenos Aires with the love of my life. Finally, our six children and thirteen grandchildren safely launched, the time has come to learn the Argentine tango – a new way to be together, a new way to make love – beautiful, erotic, melancholy, exciting. B.A. is a vibrant city: Huge steaks, great wine, gorgeous music, terrific tango teachers who didn't mind that we were rubbish. A fantasy for years – made real at last.

Richard wrote this:

So I went to Buenos Aires. Would magic happen? In my seventieth year, rhythmically challenged, would ten days of tango classes mean I would metamorphose into the twinkle-toed tanguero of Twickenham.

Well, no such luck. Instead I was to know something else – what the tango is for the Porteños, the locals of Buenos Aires. No Valentino rose-between-the-teeth, no macho strutting, nothing like those splendid stage shows they send abroad. Simply a dance of intense sharing, Zen-like in its seeming simplicity, sexy, sad and celebratory, like a fierce and tender summation of life's experience.

A clue to how different we were in so many ways – me, the keen dancer, all optimistic, eager, throwing myself in wholeheartedly; him, melancholy, the non-dancer longing to be a part of it, always on the outside looking in; wanting to do it for me. The reality was mostly creeping round the outer ring of the 'milonga' dance halls desperate not to bump into another couple, me frustrated and disappointed trying not to show it because I knew how hard he was trying. Sometimes if I danced with a suave Porteño it felt like the real thing but that wasn't it – I only really wanted to dance with Richard because he was my man. Well, we kept on going to lessons back home and over the years we improved a bit. Eventually, with lots of f-ing and blinding, and hours of practice we learned one routine to Astor Piazzola's 'Oblivion' and we danced it in front of all our children and grandchildren at his eightieth birthday party. A triumph, bless his heart.

And we went to Havana – still in the Castro era – to learn the salsa. We had separate teachers so we could progress at our own pace. Whereas tango is all passion and brooding intensity – someone once called it 'a vertical representation of a horizontal act' – salsa is pure fun. We loved Cuba and stayed in a family's home. It is a joyous thing, watching the locals dance in shabby clothes and broken-down trainers with such ease and grace. Even little children – absolute naturals. How they embodied the complex rhythms as loose as bits of electric flex. And we loved listening to the fantastic musicians. Impossible to sit still. A total delight.

Richard and I met when I was sixteen and he was twenty-four and we married the following year. Both oddballs. How lucky we were, against all the odds, to have found each other. Fifty-seven years of loving, growing, raising a family together, great adventures, the blessing of six wonderful children and thirteen fabulous grandchildren.

Although born and bred on a farm in Berkshire, Richard was always striving to lift off, to escape from his quintessentially English self, to feel his boots leave the ground in magical flight, to be free, to enter the world of the exotic. His early experiences as a soldier in Korea introduced him to that wider world and becoming a film maker allowed him to enter those other cultures. He would have loved to be a fantastic linguist, an amazing dancer, a great bongo player – I think he fell in love as much with my cosmopolitan, Jewish, arty, Hampstead family as he did with me. He achieved the realisation of a dream when he bought and restored our little house in the Tuscan village of Santa Fiora. He was probably happier there than anywhere else on earth although, sadly, fluency in the Italian language eluded him even after forty years of trying! Perhaps in the last ten years or so he became reconciled to being who he was – an Englishman and a true gentleman.

Richard lived his life with great intensity and a fair amount of melancholy. The little child unable to protect his mother from his father's unpredictable rages became the passionate crusader against injustice and abuse of power – my valiant Richard the Lionheart. He was brave and unafraid to stand alone against the bullies and the tyrants. Even as a child he would fight for what he believed in – abolishing beating at his school when he became head boy; in the army – going up against senior officers about the general attitude of contempt for the local people and treatment of prisoners; at the BBC, getting fair remuneration for contributors to his programmes; winning a battle against the local town council to get a grant for Femi to go to the London School of Contemporary Dance. Whatever it was, he would never give up. He was that rare person who was courageous enough to make his own moral decisions even if it made him unpopular.

He was also the master of the mixed metaphor. He once famously said: 'If you sit on the fence and don't stand up to be counted, you wont have a leg to stand on.'

Dearest beloved man, my life's companion, though I weep your loss, you now dwell forever in that safe place in my heart where no pain can reach you. T. S. Eliot said, *'Love is most nearly itself when here or there does not matter,'* and now Richard belongs to the world of no place and no time – just eternal love where Poonie waits for him. Richard's alter-ego was The Little Prince. He loved all the writings of Antoine de St. Exupery. Here are some lines from 'Citadelle' that he once sent to Poonie:

The Old Coppersmith

He was full of years and the light of words had grown dim for him –
Yet he was becoming ever more luminous.
With trembling hands he continued perfecting his work, which had become for him an elixir, ever subtler and more potent.
Escaping by a miracle from his gnarled old flesh, he was growing happier,
More invulnerable.
And, dying, knew it not, his hands being full of stars.

On reflection, there are many reasons why his death probably came at the right time for him. He was eighty-one and although still vigorous and fired up about politics and injustice, his strength wasn't what it once was and I know he would not have become a serene old man. He would have been angry and frustrated with himself for his physical frailty and inability to carry on making films. Always a passionate European, he would have been distraught at the coming of Brexit; He would have been in despair over the rise of Donald Trump; he would have grieved dreadfully over the destruction of Syria where he had made three films – a country he loved and where we had travelled together…Palmyra, Aleppo, Damascus, Homs. I'm glad he never had to know those tragedies but I MISS HIM. I loved him with all my heart. I miss holding each other and talking in bed in the morning; making love on a deserted beach in Greece; waking up on a houseboat in Kashmir; or a log cabin in Maine; or a rice boat in Kerala; or a treehouse in the Wynad Hills; marvelling at the mosaics in

Ravenna; climbing Kinder Scout in the Peak District; lighting candles for Poonie in the Cathedral of Monreale in Palermo or Kataragama in SriLanka; the hot-air balloon at sunrise over Cappadoccia; the faded glamour of the old Bela Vista hotel in Macao; and more than forty years of exploring Italy from our dear old house in Santa Fiora.

It's hard to be alone after so many years together – no more holding hands on a walk in the country, no more a gentle foot massage in the evening, a kiss on the back of the neck while I'm cooking, a shared conspiratorial look at a boring party, the joys and the worries about the family, sitting together on the sofa with the dog, someone else to deal with the fucking taxes and crumbling paintwork and although I have managed to find a place of relative happiness and contentment as a widow, I can be ambushed by music. The other day, unexpectedly, Ravel's 'Mother Goose Suite' on the radio, or Kurt Weill's 'September Song' or Piazzola's 'Oblivion' and I am awash in tears and sobs: 'You shouldn't have died!' 'You shouldn't have died!'

I was able to conduct his funeral myself at the beautiful natural Greenacres burial park in the Chiltern Hills. I couldn't trust anyone else to do it and, by now, I was well practised. For years, ever since my parents' funerals I had hated the dreary, impersonal one-size-fits-all traditional Jewish or Church of England services I had attended and longed to find another way. My career as an Independent Celebrant came about by accident. A student on one of my writing courses asked me, out of the blue, if I would do a marriage ceremony for her and her boyfriend. I said it would be my first and we would have to make it up as we went along but my deep love of ceremony and ritual would help me remember what to do. I have often thought that one of the challenges of this life is to remember what we have forgotten. It was a beautiful day in springtime in a woodland clearing in the Oxfordshire countryside. Red Kites soared above as we stood with the guests in a circle surrounded by trees. We re-enacted an ancient pagan tradition of hand-fasting while the bride and groom said their vows with flower crowns on their heads. Not legal in the eyes of the law but remedied by a quick visit to a Register Office. It was lovely and felt so right. This is what I wanted. I couldn't have done it when I was younger but now I was seventy and asked the Universe to let me have ten years!

I tried to find a course to go on but didn't like the Humanist approach. Too limiting. Too fundamentalist atheist. No mention of spirituality. Then I found a company in Devon with similar ideas to mine who offered a residential funeral celebrant training. Green Fuse in Totnes. I would start there. Weddings I could learn on the job but funerals needed a lot of information and planning: how to be with grieving families; how to put together a unique, beautiful, appropriate service; a knowledge of poetry, of music, of florists; dealing with the unexpected; keeping to pre-ordained crematorium time-slots. It seemed as if all my previous life experiences had led me here – the writing, the grief counselling, the healing, my love of poetry and music … this would be a way to give something back to my local community. I was ready.

Well I've now had the ten years I asked for. I've done about 500 funerals, 50 weddings and several baby-namings, house blessings and even a divorce blessing ceremony and, somewhere in the middle, my own darling Richard's funeral.

Our children and grandchildren spoke beautifully. Colleagues said lovely things. We played his favourite Ravel and tango music and laid The Little Prince to rest in the woodland under the Scots Pines where, one day, I will join him.

CHAPTER EIGHTEEN

And now in my eightieth year having been granted those ten years, I've retired from my celebrancy work and travelled back – swept along on tides of my vivid childhood memories – to Brazil. São Paulo: the scalding cafezinhos with so much sugar you could stand your spoon up; the early morning bakeries where we bought delicious hot pãozinhos for breakfast with catupiri cheese and marmelata; the old colonial post office where stamps with no adhesive were purchased, then a queue at the vat of glue with a little glue brush to fix the stamps to your green and yellow airmail envelope. I wrote a lot of homesick letters to my old friend Sharon who still lived in Van Nuys until I started to love being here; the choking exhaust fumes from the old buses that made your snot and your petticoats black; being sent to the grocery store every day to buy 'uma douzia Coca Colas' and a bottle of gin for mum; another dog (named Puppy); finding dozens of baby mice in a nest of shredded newspaper in a suitcase on top of the wardrobe; and a black maid named Nadia. Nadia sang hymns all day and it was stressed to us that Brazil was the most egalitarian country in the world where it didn't matter what colour you were.

We couldn't help but notice, though, that all the maids and other lowly jobs were done by darker skinned people and all the bosses, politicians and bankers were white. The writer Gilberto Freyre was really the author of this national egalitarian myth in his books about the mixing of the races that began with the sexual shenanigans on the sugar plantations between masters and slaves; between Portuguese and Africans; between Portuguese and Indios until after a few generations all were blended into Brazilians. It's a nice fable but not really accurate. The poorest of the poor are the 'favela' dwellers – black – and the peasants from the NorthEast – 'caboclos' of mixed race who live in the one-room shacks along the Amazon Highway – miners, loggers, construction workers – duped into living here by promises of land (mostly poor quality).

The Trans Amazonica Highway was the big issue about which Richard made his film *The Claiming of the Amazon* in 1973. It clearly showed the tragedy of the destruction of the wildlife habitat, the disastrous ecological consequences of climate change from the ruthless logging, the increasing clearing of the forest for cattle ranching and mono crops of oil palms and soya beans, the conflicts between the road builders and the local indigenous tribes, the murders and the violence, the greed, the self interest. Today, with Bolsonaro's right wing government, the situation is even worse.

Ever since meeting David and Pia Maybury-Lewis back in the 1950s I had been drawn to the Amazon and curious about its indigenous inhabitants. Since childhood, exposures to different cultures and languages and people had taught me a different way of thinking and for that I have to thank my dear old Dad with his Wandering and Wondering. I have also become more aware of the depth of his love and understanding of the philosophy of Martin Buber: 'I and Thou' – the importance of really *seeing* and experiencing another human being as a person, a 'thou', not an 'it'. Essentially inseparable from oneself. How were we all connected? Where did I belong? What could I learn? This is the journey I've been on all along even though trying to read Buber has always felt a bit indigestible, I think that is the gist of it. We're all just people. So, where will this unfolding story take me?

This time it has taken me to Manaus in the centre of Amazonas State – 1,000 miles from the sea, accessed only by river voyage or flight.

I read this written on a wall:

'O Brasil não foi descoberto não
O Brasil foi invadido e tomado dos Indigenas do Brasil'

('Brazil was not discovered — no
Brazil was invaded and taken from Brazil's indigenous people')

Marcal Tupai

I have looked at many old illustrations and the city is not what it once was during the height of its prosperity — the short-lived rubber boom. Then, expanded and gilded by the wealthy rubber barons — it had extravagant churches, glorious architecture and the world-famous Opera House — now, the city is sad and decaying. The main industry is the manufacture of computer components. Fortunately, the Opera House where once great opera stars from Caruso to Callas sang and Margot Fonteyn danced has recently been restored. There are regular concerts now which are free so that local people can enjoy them too and queues form round the block an hour before opening. It's an extraordinary anomaly — a fancy Neo-Classical style confection in the heart of the jungle. I have always wanted to come here. Luckily the Orchestra Amazonas was playing on my first night and the Opera House was a short walk from my little hotel.

It would also have been my sixty-first wedding anniversary. And I thought all day, as I walked down to the port to catch my first glimpse of the mighty Amazon river, about my darling man and my great good fortune to have found him. What did I know at the age of sixteen? And yet somehow I did. I chose the right life's companion for me. I toasted him with a couple of Caipirinhas in a local eating place where the smell of grilled fish and manioc had enticed me in.

Richard would have come here to Manaus as a starting point for shooting *The Claiming of the Amazon*. He flew, with a translator, into the interior by helicopter to film with a remote tribe and was very conscious of the potential damage that such a contact could have but felt that the story needed their voices. He said they were the most intuitive and gentle people he had ever met — friendly and affectionate if they thought you looked lonely; respectful of your space if you seemed to want to be alone. He also mistakenly left his Malaprim behind in the hotel and got malaria very badly from which he nearly died.

Later he recalled his surprise that there were hardly any children in the village. Babies were not being born and it felt as if the tribe were gradually allowing themselves to become extinct. Like the remaining pockets of indigenous peoples in many parts of the world their spiritual life had always been extremely important to them and, with the guidance of their shaman, regularly used the hallucinogenic 'gifts of the plant kingdom' to communicate with the spirit world. Maybe they could see the writing on the wall.

When Europeans first arrived in South America, there were over six million indigenous people. But the colonists brought persecution, slavery and diseases to which local people were not immune. Some fled into more and more remote areas but after Brazil's capital moved to Brasilia and the military government began 'opening up' the interior in earnest, many tribes who had been protected by remoteness suffered.

Brazil's Amazon is home to more uncontacted tribes than anywhere in the world – maybe 100 isolated groups still reside in this rainforest. They have been living in the Amazon for thousands of years, in harmony with their surroundings, slowly accumulating a detailed knowledge of the rainforest flora and fauna and how to live here. But can they continue to survive in today's rapacious world? And can we survive without the Amazon? Can we afford to lose their knowledge of this vital and unique ecology? Probably not. Earth could lose twenty percent of its oxygen if the Amazon Rainforest were lost. Why do we continue to blunder in and think we are entitled? Conquer, consume, expand and damn the consequences.

Same story in Tasmania, Australia, America, Canada … a trail of tears. I don't expect to meet any native people on my Amazon journey but I am so aware that this is their land.

Down at the busy port I watched the departure of the big river boats that ferry passengers up and down to Belem at the mouth of the river. Hammocks are slung on deck and a notice advises padlocking your rucksack to the pole. I've travelled uncomfortably most of my life but I'm too old for hammocks this time for my journey up the Amazon and have booked a passage on a small boat with a cabin.

In the meantime I linked up with a nice old guy who took me for an explore around the city. Manaus doesn't have a lot to recommend it apart from being the jumping off point for a trip on the Amazon. We had a look at the old restored mansion of a nineteenth-century German rubber baron. Now a Palacio de Governo. Such lovely architecture. Pity the random hideous modern concrete apartment blocks have turned what once was a beautiful city in its heyday into the ugly sprawl it is today. The whole place feels neglected and rundown. The few beautiful houses painted in pastel shades – the last evidence of past glories – rain streaked with tropical mould. We took a taxi across a couple of bridges that connect different parts of the city to see the social housing that was built to re-house the slum-dwellers – mostly very poor immigrants from Venezuela over the border – sadly looking as shabby and filthy as the slums they were meant to replace and a hotbed of crime and drugs where you would be ill-advised to walk by night.

Then on to the banana market – MOUNTAINS of hands and stalks of every type of banana from the tastiest black ones to the fat red ones, the familiar yellow ones, sweet tiny ones, and plantains for frying. How do they sell them all? Also mountains of pineapples, watermelons, passion fruit, avocados, breadfruits, limes and all those amazonian fruits whose names I can't remember – little red ping pong balls you have to peel. The fruit market segues into the massive fish market. So many enormous fish like the one I tried the night before. Even a stall selling piranha fish. I never knew they were edible. One wonders how there could be any fish left in the Amazon with so many here on the marble slabs every day. How finite are the resources we take for granted.

My new old friend is there to wave me off on the bus to the port at 5 am the next day and there is my boat at anchor. The river still quite high after the rainy season which ended in June. There can be a six meter difference in the level. A landing craft is waiting to ferry us out. There are sixteen passengers on board. I am the only single and easily old enough to be everyone's mother. I love my little cabin in the stern. We will be travelling 300 miles upstream on the Rio Negro. The river was so named because it looks black from a distance.(below Manaus the river is called the Amazon; above are all the tributaries that feed into it (originating far away high in the snows of the Andes Mountains in Peru and Bolivia – two of the largest being the Solimões and the Rio Negro – but they're all the Amazon.) The colour of the water – like strong tea – comes, I'm told, from the humic acid, a phenol-containing vegetation from sandy clearings that doesn't fully break down.

Thunder and lightning and a ferocious rainstorm crash around us as we set sail but that's how it is – unpredictable. It can change in minutes. We're heading first into the Anavilhanas Archipelago. From the air as we flew in to Manaus it looked like a tangle of silver ribbons. On the map it looks like a nest of snakes and everywhere the dense green foliage. It seems impenetrable but it is actually teeming with life of every kind in every inch with nothing visible from above to the naked eye except flitting birds and green green green like an endless crop of broccoli.

On that first afternoon we get into a small launch and spend a few hours drifting close to the bank and going into the throat of the forest on flooded channels. Glad I bought those expensive binoculars but surprisingly few creatures allow us to see them; a three-toed sloth with a baby, a couple of lovely swallow-tailed kites, a white-fronted toucan, a red macaw, an olive oropendola and a tarantula on a tree. Huge cloudscapes pile up in the sky threatening rain, some dramatic zig zagging lightning strikes but then a glorious sunset of pillowy pink cumulus.

The cook on the boat makes all delicious local dishes and our guide introduces us to a variety of typical Amazonian fruits and shows us how to prepare them.

The pattern of the journey every day will be a dawn canoe paddle exploring the flooded edges of the forest where we slip silently in among the tangle of trees growing in the river; a mid-morning launch ride to a little sandy landing beach on the edge of some dense forest – all togged up with hiking boots, long trousers tucked into socks, wrap around protective gaiters and long-sleeved shirts – for a three-hour walk into really thick jungle. No path or trail but the boatman knows the area and hacks a way through with his machete.

In the afternoon another forest walk or, if a settlement is nearby on the bank and they invite us to come ashore, a visit. The final adventure of the day is the night time paddle out onto the black waters far from the boat in a canoe to lie back, look up and experience the trillions of stars in the immense sky with no light pollution – occasionally shining a powerful torch into the treetops to spot the eyes of night creatures. So magical.

In the rain-forest, our guide is passionate and knowledgeable about the trees, the seeds, the germination, the canopy, the forest floor, the symbiotic relationship of the whole seething, breathing, interdependent complex explosion of LIFE! The ingenious ways trees communicate with each other through systems of roots and fungi.

Looking up, my eyes follow the trunks of some enormous trees one hundred and more feet tall until they disappear into the canopy. They are supported, like medieval cathedrals, by huge buttresses twice as tall as me. Thousands of small opportunistic plants on the forest floor are just waiting for a patch of sunlight then the race is on! Things grow at an astonishing rate all trying to reach for the sky. A thin tree, a *marajá*, covered in vicious spikes was pointed out. Brazilians use the name to describe politicians 'because nothing can touch them'. Walking in the jungle is by no means straightforward. Or flat. For a start all the protective clothing makes you terribly hot and the humidity leaves you dripping with sweat and steaming up your glasses and camera lens. The forest floor is spongy and unpredictable with hidden holes; ants nests; termite mounds; fallen logs to climb over; spider webs; sticky or thorny plants you don't want to grab onto and hanging vines. Three hours is just about the limit of my endurance. Back at the boat the most wonderful cold shower of my life and a chance to wash my steaming clothes and hang them on the top deck where they dry in a trice.

After lunch, a wee siesta then back in the canoes for the first opportunity to visit a village. These sort of staged visits always make me feel uncomfortable but this was done with sensitivity and great respect. It was a pretty ramshackle place where the *caboclos* grow manioc and catch fish. There is a little school and some children and chickens running about. Fortunately my fellow passengers are not the kind to rudely point their cameras at everything. The village women have made some handicrafts to sell – necklaces of seeds etc. – and depend on the occasional arrivals from the outside world to make a little cash. We watched the local lads play a game of football – the Brazilian number one passion. Our guide told us a story of his own life – how he had grown up in just such a subsistence farming village on the banks of the river and dreamed of going off to school but his father had insisted that he stay and learn how to grow manioc – the absolute staple of every Brazilian meal.

Back on the boat for the most spectacular sunset that unfolded as we sailed into it and we almost saw a giant otter but he was gone in a splash. The final expedition, after dinner, was the best thing of all. The night paddle in the canoe. The powerful searchlight held by the guide picked out eyes showing in the blackness. A large bird, a Papu, like an owl sitting high up on a branch; lots of bats; an iguana; a huge tarantula; a night hawk; a nightjar and a skulking caiman in the shallows. The most exciting part was heading deep into small openings and silently moving through the flooded trees, huge strangler figs and hanging roots and vines. Like I imagine the Louisiana swamps. I thought of the runaway slaves who took off from the sugar plantations and fled into the jungle, trying to find their way in such inhospitable territory. Some did. Some blended into a life with the indigenous folk. Most died in the attempt or were recaptured. Peter Robb's book is very interesting on that time in the history of this country. Slavery here was even more widespread than in America and it went on for longer but somehow the racial mix has worked out better in the end. Less toxic, anyway.

With the searchlight turned off we just paddled silently in the pitch black. Overhead, out in the open was the glorious night sky – a velvet bowl of diamonds that we city dwellers almost never have the opportunity to see. Speechless with wonder. So rare to experience a completely dark night and be able to marvel at the infinity of the firmament. I felt as if I could breathe in and fill my lungs with stars. We could hear the eerie sound of howler monkeys grunting in the blackness.

On other days – so many new things to see and learn: an egg-eating whiplash of a snake swimming alongside my canoe; families of pink river dolphins surfacing and diving; a glimpse of a capuchin monkey and a tribe of spider monkeys; a woodpecker; kingfishers (my favourites); a mob of Black Ani's streaking across the sky and landing like Christmas decorations on a lone tree sticking up by itself in the middle of a channel. Also herons and beautiful Black-headed Blue-winged Terns. Unforgettable sunrises – first winking through the dense bush then bursting out, blindingly reflected in the river.

One day, feeling my eight decades, I was so tired and achey I almost skipped the expedition but then I gave myself a pep talk – 'How could you miss such a chance! You'll regret it if you don't go.' So on with the protective gear and the muddy boots and the insect repellent and the sun screen and back in the canoe. Of course I couldn't miss it. We came ashore and faced quite a steep uphill walk and a stream to ford. A tough challenge but every walk brought new experiences. This time I saw a few types of tree I hadn't seen before: Mahogany, a very tall hardwood tree used for boat building and furniture making; a 'finistrate' tree which constructs windows in its trunk as it grows to create oxygen and preserve energy. Everything is useful to something else. Howler monkey poo is tidied away in minutes by beetles and flies; roots and vines to make rope; a special sap secreted by a tree into which a certain beetle lays its eggs. Once they've hatched and gone the sap congeals into a flammable pitch used for boat caulking and fire lighting; orchids and philodendrons making their home on a host tree; fruits and nuts on the forest floor for the animals to eat. Lots of slippery rotted logs and twigs and creepers to navigate without tripping over and landing in an ant's nest.

Our guide, Edi, is very knowledgeable and able to spot things which would be hidden to most eyes – A huge Capuchin monkey swinging by his strong jointed tail as if it were a fifth limb way high up above and a Brown Bearded Saki monkey with a big furry tail which is only used for balance not grip. We saw a large, venomous jumping fishing spider; the smallest frog the size of a thumb-nail and a large, supremely well camouflaged tree frog; an almost invisible owl-like bird called a Greater Potoo which lays its eggs in a hollow and then just sits there looking like a bit of bark.

One night, out in the canoe – a million fireflies winking in the blackness like sparks from a windblown campfire; a massive tarantula on a tree trunk in the flooded forest and two large boas wound around a fat branch. Quite spooky seeing the eyes of a large caiman like two illuminated ping-pong balls just above the surface of the water. Suddenly, a spectacular lightning display that lasted an hour – frogs all rejoicing at the heralding of more rain and sure enough, huge black ominous skies appeared in a flash and down it came soaking us to the skin. Just managed to stuff my camera and binoculars into a plastic bag.

The expedition took us up the Cuieras River – a tributary – to visit a manioc plantation, a little farm carved out of the unforgiving sandy soil where the owner, Maria, and her family have laboured hard on the their few acres to plant enough manioc trees to sustain them. She showed us the complex process by which the deadly cyanide is extracted. Then the rinsing, boiling, sieving and drying of the resulting fine sandy grain which Brazilians like to put on everything. The family also have several tropical fruit trees and raise a pig and a few chickens. Edi said that if such a simple life would be to your liking you could set yourself up for about $2,000 US. The family, like many such small-holders along the banks of the river are descended from the hardy mix of rain-forest 'indios', Portuguese, Africans and peasants who migrated from the poverty stricken North-East having been promised jobs and land. A school boat collects the children in the morning, takes them to a village a couple of miles up-river and brings them home again at the end of the day. The village has a rudimentary medical facility and it's fifty miles by speedboat to Manaus in case of emergency.

I was not expecting to meet any indigenous tribal people and I really hope they manage to stay out of reach in the remotest parts of the Amazon but I guess that as with any indigenous people left anywhere in the world, while our greed encroaches on their territory, the great tragedy is that their days are probably numbered and an entire way of knowing will be lost.

★

We were on the return journey back towards Manaus and along the way came to a place where a family of pink river dolphins were sleekly cresting and disappearing near the flooded edge of the forest. 'Good place for piranhas', said Ed. The legendary terrors of the Amazon – a shoal of which can attack a stray cow and devour it right down to its poor little hooves in minutes. Instead of speedily heading in the opposite direction we were given a bucket of bait and a simple fishing rod! Greedy little blighters chomped eagerly on the hooks and were hoiked aboard the canoe and into a basket. They are fearsome looking creatures – two rows of needle-sharp teeth surrounded by a small, round, brown and red body. 'Dinner tonight', said Ed.

About a mile further down stream was a lovely sandy beach and a reasonably safe place, I was assured, for a swim in the tea-coloured water. In the rainy season the little beach would be completely covered but the waters had receded enough for us to come ashore. There were a few vultures loitering hopefully on top of the bare, flooded tree skeletons. Good visibility and the boat crew larking about in the water gave me confidence. We were advised to shuffle our feet a bit in the shallows to warn the stingrays and give them a chance to swim away. What a wonderful experience and the deep fried piranhas with rice and sliced plantains sprinkled with manioc made a great end to the day. Eat them before they eat you.

As we got close to Manaus there is the strange sight of the Meeting of the Waters where the Rio Negro slips under the silt-laden muddier waters of the Amazon itself. Difference in temperature and composition means the two don't instantly mix but form a distinct line where they meet and eventually blend. At its widest point the Amazon is 3,000 kms wide with an island the size of Switzerland in the middle. So powerful is the river, it pushes the ocean for 2,000 kms as it pours into the delta. Tour boats with 100 people on board and launches with rows of tourists zoom up and down. Loads of trash in the river. So glad I had the opportunity to experience the silence and solitude of the quiet upper reaches. No other boat but ours, peaceful dawns, enchanted starry nights …

One final night walking up and down amidst the frenzied activity of the night streets of Manaus. People selling everything under the sun from bottled water to Jehovah's Witness pamphlets, to single strips of viagra pills. Sex is definitely alive and well in Brazil. Girls with long tanned legs and big bottoms in micro shorts and platform heels hang on the arms of tattooed boys as sleek as otters. It's times like this when the melancholy sometimes overtakes me. The homesickness. Missing my Richard.

I found myself thinking of that old Andy Williams song:

> 'Hello Young Lovers whoever you are
> I hope your troubles are few.
> All my good wishes go with you tonight
> I've been in love like you.
>
> Don't cry young lovers whatever you do
> Don't cry because I'm alone
> All of my memories are happy tonight
> I've had a love of my own.
>
> I've had a love of my own like yours
> I've had a love of my own.'

That song came into my mind again next morning at the breakfast bar on the roof of my little hotel in Salvador de Bahia as a dreamy-eyed, post coital couple sitting at one of the tables couldn't keep their hands off each other. He kept reaching over to stroke her face and she had a hand on his knee under the table. They leaned in to kiss lingeringly as their coffee got cold. A couple of tears pricked my eyes. 'I've had a love of my own like yours' … and a quick flash-back to all the places we loved each other from Iona to Bali passed before my mind. 'I've had a love of my own'. And now I'm an unwilling refugee in the land of widowhood. But I'm alright really. No use being sad. On with the day … Salvador awaits.

★

Salvador de Bahia – the place of my dreams. The most African city in Brazil. The place where the best music, dance and capoeira (a unique mixture of acrobatic dance and martial arts) comes from.

I am not staying in the Pelourada which is the prettiest, most restored and most touristy area but a more bohemian, seedier area which feels more genuine. I have engaged a guide, Bruno, who seems like just the right person (although I don't agree with his pro-Bolsanaro politics.) I told him that I'm not really interested in all the gilded rococo churches etc but would really like to see more of the Candomble – the Yoruba influenced religion which has miraculously survived the great slave diaspora and kept the flame alive.

This, of all places, along with Puerto Rico and Cuba, was the principal guardian of the Orishas – hiding in plain sight in the guise of Christian saints. Here the religion never really died. It maintained a low profile for over 300 years and resisted the enormous power of the Catholic church to rope everyone in. But it's not easy for an outsider to establish contact with Candomble and the 'sisterhoods'. They are of necessity quite secretive and not open to visitors – even one as qualified as I believe I am, being the mother of Yoruba twins but we'll see. Bruno will try his best.

I wandered around the cobbled night streets on my own looking for some dinner and found a perfect small fish place for a typical moqueca (the signature dish of Bahia) a delicious fish and prawn stew made with coconut milk and palm oil. The streets here fill up late on a Saturday night with couples out for a good time and families sitting around in groups having a few beers. Music pouring out from every doorway and I came upon some guys showing off their capoeira moves to the beat of the berimbao – an evocative percussive one-stringed instrument. The dancers whirl and kick and flip and somersault at lightning speed never quite touching. Electrifying to watch and then – oh joy! – the samba music started and onlookers jumped up to dance. Someone beckoned to me to join them and thus did my dream come true – to dance the samba one last time in Bahia. Now I can die happy. Afterwards, this old granny toddled back to the hotel slightly the worse for wear after a couple of caipirinhas. Interesting fact: no other woman that I have seen in Brazil has white hair. Old ladies here dye theirs an unforgiving black which only seems to accentuate their lined faces. God knows how old they must think I am. But, credit to the gorgeous capoeira boys, it didn't stop them inviting me to dance.

★

Bruno is scathing about the education system in Brazil and the fact that most people know nothing about their history and are unable to reach higher standards in university hence a kind of fatalism and lassitude about any changes, an acceptance of the corruption, no desire to be proud of their country, no heroes other than footballers.

In the Pelourinho – the square in the heart of the UNESCO heritage area here (a horrible history: Pelourinho means pillory or whipping post where slaves were publicly punished and executed) there is a statue to a black man named Zumi. He is revered as a leader of the slave revolt. But although, yes he existed, Bruno says he wasn't at all what he's made out to be. He has been made a convenient figurehead but in reality he was no hero. He just wanted to be a chief himself. He became a leader of his community but purely for his own ambition. He never fought for abolition and he had slaves himself. Another statue commemorates the first bishop to be sent here by the Catholic church. The poor unfortunate man was captured by a tribe of cannibals as soon as he came ashore and ceremonially eaten.

★

The town of Cachoeira about an hour and half drive away is a sleepy place full of crumbling old colonial buildings. The town was famous for sugar plantations and on the other side of the Paraguaçu River – across the British built bridge – is São Felix, famous for its tobacco plantations. I've come here because Bruno thinks this might be the place for me to learn a bit more about Candomblé. This is where you find the purest and strongest centre for Orisha worship in the whole of Brazil. Here is The Sisterhood of the Good Death. This is an organisation that was founded in the 1700s by freed black women slaves. The purpose was to try and raise money to purchase the freedom of other slaves. If you had the money you could buy yourself

276

out. The sisters were also primarily concerned that everyone should have a proper funeral and burial and that slaves who died should not just be unceremoniously dumped in a hole in the ground. Nowadays, a decent funeral for all is still part of their mission. They continue to raise money by cooking and selling food on the streets and asking for donations. The money they collect also goes toward paying for the elaborate festival and feast they hold in mid August. Although nominally Catholic, they use the statue of the Virgin Mary (as 'Our Lady of the Good Death') to parade around the streets, most of the women – who must all be over forty to be members – are senior mothers in the Candomblé houses. These Candomblé houses are all over the town, dedicated to one or other of the deities: Yemonja (Yemayá), Oshun, Ogun, Oludamare, Oxalá, Xango (Shango) and are a direct connection to the spiritual practices of the black slaves brought over from Nigeria. The Catholic church leaves them pretty much alone although recent elements within Candomblé would like to be separated from 'the conqueror's religion'.

We asked around for where we might find the most senior Big Mama – Mãe Preta or Black Mother. Everyone knew where to direct us; down some winding streets, turn right, turn left, up a steep hill, near to a little church, at the end of the lane … . We drove there on spec not knowing if we would be welcomed and luckily, just as we arrived a large group of white-clad (and blood-spattered) followers were gathering for a special ceremony about to take place and we were invited in. As a participant you can ask the Orisha for anything regardless of its effect on anyone else but you must speak your request out loud. It is not a silent prayer. And then you must deal with the consequences. If you have wished harm on someone for your own gain it's your responsibility to face your karma, as it were.

This was a house of Oshun, the deity of the river and the ceremony involved a lot of ritual animal sacrifice. On the upper level of the house the higher initiates were being initiated into the top level of seniority. The seventh level. Downstairs on the veranda next to where we were seated were seven novices standing and swaying with their eyes closed. Furious drumming by young boys accompanied all this. Everyone else was chanting the prayers in Yoruba. Another mother – the very welcoming and friendly Donna Lucia explained to us in Portuguese that they only use the Yoruba language for their ceremonial work. After some time a man in very blood-stained trousers came down the stairs with a pail of liquid. The novices kneeled on the ground touching their foreheads to the ground. He sprinkled the contents of the pail over everyone including me. A blessing, I was told. Perfumed water. It smelled like piss. More unsuspecting chickens were seized and carted upstairs followed by a great deal of squawking.

Then all of a sudden five headless goats were carried downstairs and taken outside to the yard to be dismembered and cooked. Then one after another, huge enamel bowls piled high with headless chickens, ducks and tortoises we're brought down and carried into the house followed by the novices who then danced and whirled in a frenzied trance – shrieking as if possessed – accompanied by more wild drumming by the young lads. We were invited to sit inside to watch but asked not to take any photographs. This is the point where they are taking the spirit of Oshun into themselves and pledging to serve her. The animal sacrifice is all for her and the resulting food then shared with the needy.

The house itself was all white inside with hundreds of fluttering white ribbons and white flower arrangements. Blood and feathers soaked the doorstep sprinkled with manioc. Apparently, the sacrifice of that many goats and other animals indicated a very important occasion and one by one after a final flourish, the initiates – led by Mãe Baratinha a very large older woman wearing long white skirts, embroidered top and head tie exited backwards through the door to the yard to assist with the food preparation. I found all the sacrifices a bit grisly but the ceremony fascinating and I was happy to know the poor animals' deaths would not be in vain.

Dona Lucia explained everything and was intrigued to hear, in my half-remembered halting Portuguese, about my Yoruba twins and my experiences of spending time with Orisha followers in Lagos and New York. Portuguese words sleeping for over sixty-five years in the deepest recesses of my brain were beginning to rise to the surface and I found I could still communicate.

Well, I did what I had come to do. I had returned to Brazil, I had unspooled a thread of memories and connected up the dots. I had walked in the forest and swam in the Amazon and danced the samba in Bahia where the delicious, irresistible music still managed to evoke some echo of response in my creaky old body. I had been allowed to witness a candomblé ceremony. As always, walking alone in faraway places has been a trade off between solitude and loneliness. I like travelling solo but the heartache now is ever present as there is no one waiting at home for me. In past times I'd know he'd be standing there at the arrivals barrier reading a newspaper and we'd hug each other and I'd feel the touch of his hand on my face. Every so often now my heart will be suddenly pierced by a memory, so poignant I struggle to hold back the tears, of us just strolling along together, his arm around my shoulder, my hand in the back pocket of his jeans … talking, laughing, sharing stories.

Now it was time to go home alone to my little island in the Thames. Just in time, it turned out, for the forced end of all foreign travel as the great Covid 19 global pandemic took hold of the world and shut everything down. As I write this one year on, hundreds of thousands of people have died in every country and many more are being treated in hospitals struggling to cope. We are awaiting the vaccine but it will be a long time before anything like the old normal will return. My timing was more fortunate than I could ever have known. Being in 'lockdown' I know I am luckier than most. I live in a beautiful place looking out on the river, I have a little dog for company, marvellous books to read and enough food in my fridge. I set my radio alarm to come on at 6.45 so I can wake up to the BBC Breakfast programme's daily 'Bach before 7' and charge my body with a stream of joy before I do anything else. Gratitude for all this gets me past the bumps in the road – the pain of encroaching arthritis; the moments of sorrow and grief; the losses; the knowledge that the lurking cancer in remission may very well get me in the end … . But for the moment I'm still here.

★

I want to leave these thoughts and memories for my children and grandchildren. Certainly I'm no academic and my passionate longing has only ever been to slip lightly into other worlds, to experience other cultures wholeheartedly and to be accepted as a fellow human being; a traveller, a seeker. I thank my unusual childhood for giving me my first glimpse of different realties. I thank my lovely dad for trying so hard to navigate an incomprehensible post holocaust world; for his curiosity, his innocence, his gentleness and his sweetness. I thank my amazing mum for her practicality, her fierce loyalty, her ability, against all the odds, to cope with whatever was thrown at her and for knowing how to keep her family together. They taught me all I ever really needed to know. I thank my beloved children for their support and I thank my darling Richard for loving me for the fifty-seven years we had together.

The End